ISBN 978-1-331-27856-6
PIBN 10168155

1 MONTH OF
FREE
READING

at
www.ForgottenBooks.com

By purchasing this book you are eligible for one month membership to ForgottenBooks.com, giving you unlimited access to our entire collection of over 1,000,000 titles via our web site and mobile apps.

To claim your free month visit:

www.forgottenbooks.com/free168155

English
Français
Deutsche
Italiano
Español
Português

www.forgottenbooks.com

Mythology Photography **Fiction**
Fishing Christianity **Art** Cooking
Essays Buddhism Freemasonry
Medicine **Biology** Music **Ancient
Egypt** Evolution Carpentry Physics
Dance Geology **Mathematics** Fitness
Shakespeare **Folklore** Yoga Marketing
Confidence Immortality Biographies
Poetry **Psychology** Witchcraft
Electronics Chemistry History **Law**
Accounting **Philosophy** Anthropology
Alchemy Drama Quantum Mechanics
Atheism Sexual Health **Ancient History**
Entrepreneurship Languages Sport
Paleontology Needlework Islam
Metaphysics Investment Archaeology
Parenting Statistics Criminology
Motivational

CHICAGO'S

CENTENNIAL CELEBRATION

OF

WASHINGTON'S INAUGURATION

APRIL 30, 1889

CHICAGO

MDCCCLXXXIX

CHICAGO:
SLASON THOMPSON & CO., PRINTERS.
1890.

PREFACE.

The committee intrusted with the publication of a volume as a souvenir of Chicago's celebration of the centennial anniversary of the inauguration of George Washington as President of the United States, and the beginning of constitutional government in America, have completed their task. They now have the honor to offer it, through the General Executive Committee, to the public. They claim for it no literary merit save that which it owes to the distinguished citizens of the republic who lent their assistance to the celebration. It is a compilation. Out of the hundreds of earnest, thoughtful sermons that were preached on the occasion, out of the hundreds of eloquent orations that were delivered, they have chosen such as in their judgment would best inculcate the lessons which it was the purpose of the celebration to convey. They have been compelled by the limitations of a single volume to omit many addresses that were in every way worthy of preservation, equally worthy, perhaps, with some that are to be found in its pages. With such an embarrassment of riches the work of selection was a difficult one, and it will be remarkable if they have made no mistakes.

It is the hope of the committee that this souvenir volume may obtain wide circulation. They believe that its pages contain patriotic germs which should sink deep into the minds and hearts of the young, and hereafter bear fruit that will be for the glory of the republic. If it shall do no more than impress the truth that a Nation, not a mere aggregation of states, was inaugurated a century ago, it will have accomplished much. If it shall create a desire for a closer knowledge of Washington, Jefferson, Madison, Franklin, Hamilton and all those grand patriots who were present at the birth of the Nation, the study of American history —a study too much neglected in our public schools—will do the rest.

In conclusion, the committee have only to express the thanks due to those who have kindly aided in the preparation of the volume, and to record the pleasant nature of the associations which this labor brought about. It is peculiarly gratifying that from the inception of the plan of the celebration to the completion of the book, there was a unanimity of sentiment and a cordiality of relations that have made the recollection of the work like a sweet savor to those who participated in it.

CONTENTS.

Exercises in the Schools—

VI.

VII.

I

THE PREPARATORY WORK

Chicago's Centennial Celebration

OF

Washington's Inauguration

April 30, 1889

THE PREPARATORY WORK

At the annual meeting of the Union League Club of Chicago, Jan. 22, 1889, the following resolutions were unanimously adopted:

RESOLVED, That this club should celebrate, in a manner befitting so great an occasion, the 100th Anniversary of the inaugural year of the United States of America, as established under and by virtue of our existing Constitution, an event second in importance to no other of a political nature in the history of the world.

RESOLVED, That a committee be appointed by the President, consisting of the Committee of Political Action and ten other members of the club, to consider the propriety of a public observance of the event under the auspices of this club or otherwise, and that this joint committee be empowered to make all needed arrangements in case such public observance be deemed expedient.

This was the first step in the work which culminated in the celebration of the Washington Centennial throughout the West and South—almost throughout the nation.

The committee of seventeen was appointed. It held two meetings, at the second of which, Feb. 2, it adopted the following resolution:

RESOLVED, That we celebrate the 100th Anniversary of the Inauguration of the United States of America, as established under and by virtue of our existing constitution, by organizing as many gatherings as can be arranged for satisfactorily, of Americans, whether native or foreign born, who are devoted to the Constitution of the United States and to Republican institutions—to liberty regulated by law.

At this meeting the committee organized by the appointment of Mr. S. W. Allerton, chairman, and Mr. E. F. Cragin, secretary. For a month the subject of a suitable demonstration on April 30 was quietly but earnestly discussed. It seemed advisable to the committee that the matter should be brought more prominently before the people, and in a measure divested of the semblance of a private enterprise of the Union League Club. Something in the nature of a public proclamation was deemed the best means of accomplishing this, and on Feb. 5 the following address was issued:

The 30th of April, A. D., 1789, in Federal Hall, in the city of New York, the inauguration of the government of the United States of America under the Constitution formed in convention and adopted in that body at Philadelphia, Sept. 17, 1787, took place. Both houses of Congress there assembled and entered upon their duties. George Washington took the oath of office as the first President, and this nation was born and entered upon its constitutional existence.

The event is to be celebrated in the city of New York the 30th day of April next, the Centennial Anniversary of the birth of the Nation. The independence of the colonies had been proclaimed in Philadelphia, July 4, 1776. The confederate union of the States had been agreed to in Philadelphia, July 9, 1778, but the country was acephalous in its government until the adoption of the Constitution and the occurrence of the great event which it is now proposed to celebrate.

It has been customary to celebrate the Declaration of Independence as the central idea of our early manhood, and it has been good for us to be reminded that we are free and independent of foreign control; that when we attained our majority we threw off the paternal yoke and assumed individual responsibility.

But this was not enough. It required only four years' experience to show us that the country needed a National Constitution, with an efficient executive head, if we would be a united body, securing order and good government at home and protection from abroad. The accomplishment of this greatly needed end was

reached on the memorial day of this nation which we now propose
to celebrate. As great an event as the Declaration of Independence,
it was surpassed by the affirmative act which made us a constitutional government and united people.

It is to be hoped that the celebration of this momentous and
far-reaching event, the most important in the history of modern
times, will be as generally observed as was formerly the day of the
Declaration of Independence. It is an event which made the whole
American people a united body by virtue of that great charter of
the United States, whose opening words are:

"We, the people of the United States, in order to have a more
perfect union, establish justice, secure domestic tranquility, provide for the common defense, promote the general welfare, and
secure the blessings of liberty to ourselves and our posterity, do
ordain and establish this Constitution for the United States of
America."

To many citizens it has seemed peculiarly appropriate and desirable that the citizens of Chicago, who are mostly immigrants
from the older states or foreign countries, should avail themselves
of this occasion to unitedly reiterate their declarations of attachment to the principles of our National Constitution and devotion
to the maintenance of our Republican institutions.

The undersigned have been requested to act as a committee
and take the initiative in calling attention to this subject. They
have accepted this duty, and though assuming no authority beyond
that of all other citizens, they deferentially suggest that it would be an
appropriate and perhaps the most feasible way of celebrating the
constitutional birth of this great nation for all our citizens, whatever may have been the land of their birth, or their religious beliefs,
or the societies or associations to which they belong or organizations with which they may be connected, to meet in their respective places of association the 30th of April next, and testify in such
manner as shall seem to them appropriate, their appreciation of
American national liberty, regulated by written law, and their
thankfulness for the national unity and protection which have been
secured and maintained under the Constitution of the United
States.

It is not the intention of the committee to make any suggestions as to the peculiar action of such assemblies beyond inviting
general coöperation and unity in rendering thanks to our Heavenly
Father for the blessings of our constitutional free government and
national unity.

The wisdom vouchsafed to the framers of our Constitution has been exemplified in the growth and prosperity of the nation and the permanence of the provisions of our organic law. Few changes have been made in the essential features of the Constitution, and under it, from a handful of people, the population of the United States has so expanded that we now count 60,000,000, a larger number of civilized inhabitants than ever existed in any other united, self-governing nation.

Having assumed the initiative, we invite the coöperation of all our fellow citizens, whether of native or foreign birth, that there may be in this city the day of the celebration of the hundredth year of our existence as a nation, a unanimous expression of patriotic union and devotion to constitutional government, free institutions, and liberty regulated by law.

The press of Chicago, daily and weekly, secular and religious, and of all languages, are requested to give this address a place in their columns, and call public attention to the same.

A. C. BARTLETT,	ROBERT E. JENKINS,
H. N. HIGGINBOTHAM,	C. L. HUTCHINSON,
JAMES W. ELLSWORTH,	HENRY S. BOUTELL,
SAMUEL W. ALLERTON,	FRANKLIN H. HEAD,
RICHARD S. TUTHILL,	JOHN A. ROCHE,
GEORGE SCHNEIDER,	MAX A. MEYER,
J. McGREGOR ADAMS,	JULIUS S. GRINNELL,
EDWARD F. CRAGIN,	J. Y. SCAMMON,
EDSON G. KEITH,	

COMMITTEE OF UNION LEAGUE ON CENTENNIAL CELEBRATION,
APRIL 30, 1889.

The address thus issued had an immediate effect. A public demonstration became not only the popular wish but the popular demand. And out of the suggestions and advice which were volunteered to the committee there gradually developed the grand conception that the Chicago celebration should be not a merely local affair, but the nucleus of a patriotic and fitting commemoration of the day throughout the land. With this idea uppermost, the committee of seventeen proceeded with its work.

To extend the interest in the movement and enlist the coöperation of representative citizens of foreign birth or extraction, the membership of the committee was increased to fifty. The first meeting of the full committee—subsequently known as the General Executive Committee—was held on the evening of

Feb. 11, on which occasion a banquet was tendered to the members by the Union League Club. After supper the Chairman, Mr. S. W. Allerton, delivered the following address:

GENTLEMEN: You have been invited here this evening that we might ask you to join us in celebrating the birth of a nation, the beginning of constitutional government on the American continent, one hundred years ago. We wish particularly to secure the coöperation of citizens of foreign birth. We wish you to share our enthusiasm upon that occasion, that there may be awakened in you, if it be not already awake, that patriotic sentiment which will move you to go to your own people and say to them: "It is time for us to become Americans;" which will inspire you to teach your children the American patriot's love for the Stars and Stripes, the emblem of liberty.

Inspired by the immortal words of Patrick Henry, "Give me liberty or give me death," our fathers went to battle, and in the ensuing ordeal of bloodshed and hardship and privation, men were developed with ability to form a government that gives to all men, under a written Constitution, equal rights with reciprocal duties.

Can an independent, free-thinking, liberty-loving people do less than honor the names of Washington, Hamilton, Franklin, Jefferson, and all the great and patriotic men of that time who did so much for humanity? Their love of liberty has made America the home of the down-trodden and oppressed of the whole world. Their wisdom has given every man whose foot touches the soil of the American republic a chance to develop and use God's greatest gift—his brain. In the history of civilization no people have advanced so rapidly in life's great work as the American people. In the last hundred years, no people have made the progress that we have made. We surpass all other nations in the invention of labor-saving machines, which lighten the burdens of men and help them to advance in all the conditions of life. In America, any man with industry, economy, morality, temperance, and a love of justice, can gain a home, an independence, and become such a man as God intended him to be.

Yet, under this great and wise Constitution the century has not been one of uninterrupted prosperity and harmony. Thirty years ago there were men who, in the vain hope of maintaining property rights in their fellow-men, sought to divide the Union. They failed, and to-day the most enlightened among them thank God for their failure. They are to-day as loyal to the Constitution and the nation as their brothers who frustrated their mad design.

Let us extend our hearts and hands to our brothers in every state in the Union for eternal peace and good will, that we may stand as one man to sustain and perpetuate the Constitution bequeathed to us by our fathers. So long as time shall last, may the Stars and Stripes wave over a united, free and independent people.

Mr. Allerton was followed by Mr. H. S. Boutell. Then the meeting lost all trace of formality. One after another the guests made short, patriotic speeches. The enthusiasm was unbounded, and when the meeting closed, all felt that the 30th of April offered, perhaps, a grander opportunity than ever before for imparting to the people, and especially to the young, a lesson in patriotism that would live long in memory. The report of the committee of seventeen was gladly accepted, and the initiatory steps that had been taken were heartily approved. The meeting adjourned until Feb. 20.

From this time on the work was carried on persistently and systematically, and, it may be added, absolutely without friction. It is really remarkable that in a body where every shade of political opinion, every religious denomination, and almost every nationality was represented, the harmony should have been so perfect, so uninterrupted, from first to last; but where all were filled to overflowing with the spirit of patriotism, there was no room for discord. The general outlines of the plan of celebration were agreed upon at one of the earliest meetings. The aim was to secure the participation of all, old and young, native and foreign-born, in commemorative exercises which would tend to develop interest in national life and quicken patriotic impulses. The programme, therefore, was to be substantially as follows:

9 a. m.—Service of praise and thanksgiving in all the churches.

11 a. m.—Commemorative exercises in all the public, private, and parochial schools.

3 p. m.—Mass-meetings and patriotic addresses in the large halls in the central portions of the city.

9 p. m.—Fire-works.

On the subject of the mass-meetings there was a very interesting debate. It was by some thought desirable that halls be secured in the outlying portions of the city and meetings held for the benefit of foreign-born citizens, at which they might be addressed in their native tongues. But this idea met with little favor and was by none more strenuously opposed than by foreign-born members of the committee. " What we want," said one of these, "is to gather together under one roof all patriotic Americans, whether they be of native growth or of foreign importation. We want the Germans and Poles, French and Scandinavians, Italians, Spaniards and Russians to rub shoulders with the descendants of the pilgrim fathers, to listen with them to addresses in the language of their adopted country, and to sing with them in that language the national anthems of America," and under the influence of this sentiment it was forthwith resolved that there should be one public meeting in the Exposition Building, and that if it should become necessary for the accommodation of the multitude to hold other meetings, they should be in halls located as near as possible to that building so that the crowds might mingle. This resolution was carried out to the letter.

The character of the celebration having been determined, the General Executive Committee appointed a number of sub-committees and assigned them their work. Each chairman was authorized to add to his committee as many members outside of the General Executive Committee as seemed necessary or desirable for the accomplishment of the purpose in view, so that shortly after the work was begun there were several hundred laborers in the field. It is not possible, in the narrow limits of a single volume, to set forth in detail the work that was done, nor to fully explain the method of its accomplishment, but some conception of its scope may be conveyed by the titles of the sub-committees. These were:

Finance.	School Celebration.
Religious Services.	Centennial Souvenir for Children.
Speakers.	Pyrotechnic Display.
Halls.	Loan Exhibition.
Organization.	Programme and Arrangements.
Decorations, Mottoes, Etc.	Outside Decorations.
Music.	Charitable Institutions.
Messages and Resolutions.	Reception of Invited Guests.
Audience.	Press.
Suspension of Business.	Souvenir Volume.

General Observance of the Day in the Northwest.

The duty of the Finance Committee was, first, to collect

money for the expenses of the celebration, and, second, to super-
vise its expenditure.   It was estimated that about $25,000 would
be needed to carry out the plans of the General Executive Committee, and the original intention was to secure the money from
a few wealthy and generous men.   After one or two large subscriptions had been solicited and obtained, however, the plan
was abandoned for the wiser one of securing small contributions
from the body of the people, and thereby cementing their interest in the celebration.   The labor thus necessitated was enormous, but it was accomplished by the appointment of sub-committees, representing almost every trade and industry in the city.
The efforts were eminently successful.   More money was sub-
scribed than was needed for the celebration.   Much of the
money came in sums of $1.   Clerks, laborers, book-keepers, even
school children, contributed their mites.   Over $1,500 came
in small sums from the retail grocery trade alone.   These small
subscriptions counted up slowly and multiplied the work of
collection, but long before the day of celebration the grand
total of $25,667.09 was in the hands of the treasurer.   The
effect was just what it was intended to produce.   Every man
who gave a dollar felt a personal interest in the celebration.   He became a part of it, a shareholder in it.   The
amount contributed did not signify.   The donor of a dollar bill
was placed on precisely the same footing with the giver of
$100.   There was no class of citizens who could, by virtue of
their large subscriptions, claim privileges from which their poorer
fellow-citizens were excluded.   There was nothing to arouse
jealousy, nothing to suggest social distinctions.   Chicago feels
that in the demonstration April 30, 1889, she set an example
worthy, both on principle and in results, of being followed on all
subsequent occasions of a similar nature.

One of the most important sub-committees, though it appears
last upon the list, was that on "General Observance of the Day
in the Northwest."   To this sub-committee was confided the
duty of arousing the whole country, save that portion which was
assumed to be tributary to New York, to a realizing sense of the
national and patriotic significance of the Centennial.   As a
preliminary step, the following address was prepared and circulated throughout the Western States and Territories:

1789—LET ALL CELEBRATE—1889.

The Centennial of Our

NATION'S BIRTH-DAY!

APRIL 30, 1889.

DECLARED BY CONGRESS A NATIONAL HOLIDAY.

At the instance of the General Executive Committee, the following brief addresses have been prepared and published for circulation through the Northwest.

TO THE PEOPLE OF THE NORTHWEST:

The purpose of this forthcoming celebration is to commemorate the first inauguration of George Washington as President on the adoption of our National Constitution, of which the 30th day of April, 1889, will be the 100th anniversary.

Notwithstanding the previous Declaration of Independence, the real birth of the United States, AS A NATION, dates from April 30, 1789, when the inauguration of the first President under the newly ratified and matchless Constitution, formally ushered the United States into the family of nations.

New York and Chicago—the one the commercial metropolis of the East, the other of the West—have adopted measures for the proper observance of the memorable day.

In Chicago it is proposed that there shall be a suspension of business, and an assembling of citizens in all the churches at as early an hour as 9 o'clock, for religious services of thanksgiving and praise to God, after the manner of our forefathers, to be followed by the gathering together in all of the public schools of their hundred thousand, or more, scholars for appropriate exercises, addresses, and national music, and for the presentation to all the pupils of medals as souvenirs of the patriotic occasion. Later in the day the adult citizens to assemble in the largest halls to listen to distinguished orators; and, finally, the exhibition in the evening of fire-works to conclude the patriotic programme.

The title of the "Committee on General Observance of the Day" throughout the Northwest indicates its purpose, and this committee is charged with the duty of publishing a brief outline of the proposed celebration, not to dictate to other communities any special form or order of celebration, but to propose an interchange of views—to receive as well as to give suggestions if desired. It were needless to multiply words in extending a cordial and fraternal invitation to our fellow-countrymen to appropriately celebrate this red-letter day in our national history; to join, not in boastfulness, but in devout thankfulness to the Ruler of Nations for the prescience of our forefathers in devising that Constitution which for one hundred years has challenged the ever-increasing admiration of mankind, and also for blessing the new-born nation with its first President in the person of Washington, now the world's accepted type of the loftiest manhood and most exalted patriotism.

Not alone in cities, but also in the hamlet and on the farm, let us raise our flags and our voices in honor of the priceless heritage of our Constitution and our Washington. And, above all, let our children—the young to whose charge the destiny of the nation is soon to be confided, be imbued with the intensest love of country, and their loyalty to its proud memories and beloved institutions be so enshrined in their hearts as to insure the perpetuity of the republic.   THOMAS B. BRYAN, *Chairman*.

CHICAGO, March 13, 1889.

An address, prepared by the Clergymen's Committee, was also scattered broadcast. It was as follows:

Address of Chicago Clergy to their Brother Ministers in the Northwest.

Within an hour of high noon, on the thirtieth day of April, in the year of our Lord 1789, General George Washington was inaugurated President of the United States of America. Seven years of war had ended in the independence of the Colonies. The Constitution had been adopted by the national convention assembled in Philadelphia, and had been duly ratified. Congress had convened in New York to induct into office the first President. With the inauguration of George Washington began that wonderful national life, that drama of civil liberty and organized power which is soon to reach the end of its first hundred years. History makes no record of a greater century. It is, therefore, fitting that every citizen should mark this approaching Centennial and for the moment stand with head uncovered as though on ground made holy by sacred memories and inspiring hopes.

It is expected that over each state house and schoolhouse in the republic the nation's flag will wave. Patriotic orators will recall the trials and victories of the commonwealth.

We, the ministers of religion, must not permit the temples of God to be silent when all else is eloquent. Sanctuaries, the largest and the lowliest, in city or country, should offer worship to the King of Kings.

When General Washington was approaching his inauguration he requested all reverent citizens to assemble in their churches, and, with praise and prayer, to intercede for the nation and himself, as he was assuming his great trust. At the hour of 9 o'clock in the morning the people complied with the devout request, and the various churches in the city of New York were filled with intensely earnest worshipers.

The Inaugural Address, pronounced on that impressive occasion, contained these words:

"It would be peculiarly improper to omit in this first official act my fervent supplication to that Almighty Being who rules over the universe, who presides in the councils of nations, and whose providential aids can supply every human defect, that His benediction may consecrate to the liberties and happiness of the people of the United States a government instituted by themselves for these essential purposes, and may enable every instrument employed in its administration to execute with success the functions allotted to his charge. In tendering this homage to the Great Author of every public and private good, I assure myself that it expresses your sentiments not less than my own, nor those of my fellow-citizens at large less than either. No people can be bound to acknowledge and adore the invisible hand which conducts the affairs of men more than the people of the United States. Every step by which they have advanced to the character of an independent nation seems to have been distinguished by some token of providential agency."

From the ceremony of the inauguration the first President, attended by the national Congress and high officials, proceeded to a house of worship and invoked for the young nation the presence and blessing of God.

Have we fallen away from the religion of our fathers? Has not the God they worshiped been with this country in all the long journey since that inauguration day? Has He not been a light in darkness, a power in weakness?

We, a committee appointed in the name of the churches of Chicago to send forth a word of greeting and of request, do hereby invite all congregations and their pastors, wheresoever these fraternal words may go, to assemble at 9 o'clock in the morning of April 30th next, each congregation in its own place of worship, and according to its own form, and emulating their example, express the gratitude to God and the trust in Him which filled the hearts of our fathers on that great morning one hundred years ago. May it thus be made most manifest that religious faith and gratitude have grown with the growth of the Union.

CHICAGO, March 14, 1889.   SIMON J. McPHERSON, *Chairman.*

A month later the following was issued:

THE CENTENNIAL CELEBRATION.

IT BEING impossible to answer separately all the letters from the towns and villages of the West, the Committee on General Centennial Day Observance issue herewith the patriotic songs called for, and this circular reply to the request for "further hints, suggestions, and interchange of views as to the object of the celebration."

In the circulars already issued there will be found an outline of the Chicago programme, which, doubtless, will commend itself in some features, according to the available means and resources of different localities. As in those circulars stated, the observance need not be expensive, but it should be universal and hearty. The committee return thanks for the suggestions and information furnished by numerous correspondents, and are gratified at the lively interest manifested by the villages in farming communities. The great object of the commemoration is not display, but to awaken the people to a realizing sense of the blessings they enjoy under free institutions, resulting so largely from the adoption of our matchless Constitution. The nation which at its birth numbered fewer souls than constitute the present population of Illinois, now enters with far more millions than states upon a second cycle of a hundred years. At the threshold let us pause, neither boastful in the retrospect nor presuming, except in prayer and hope, to measure that destiny which is present only to the eye and ken of Omniscience.

The Centennial day's observance should serve to kindle anew the fires of patriotism in the hearts of the people.

That the result may be practically beneficial, it is important that speakers should not only unfold the Constitution before their hearers, but that *patriotism* itself be defined, as a comprehensive term embracing most of the duties incident to our relation to society as well as to government; for the love of our country is inseparable from the love of our countrymen, and both impose upon us the duty of so ordering our lives and conducting our affairs as will best conduce to the general welfare.

All the inhabitants of this rich and heaven-favored region should unite in regarding this Centennial year as an era of their lives as well as of their country, and invoking patriotism for their guidance, should ask what are her requirements, not only for great and heroic actions, but also for consistent and exemplary citizenship.

In that behalf it behooves us to place the highest estimate upon the right of suffrage, and to cast our votes uniformly in favor of honest government and reputable candidates, with our best judgment, in the light that is vouchsafed to us. In a republic, individual ballots are the warp and woof of liberty. Let us see to it that we conscientiously weave that fabric as a priceless heritage for our children.

Are not these among the behests of good citizenship: That we should strive to throttle corruption whenever and wherever it presents itself—that in gratitude for God's bounty to us, we should vie with each other in good work—that we should bestow due care upon our farms and our dwellings, introducing into the former the most approved culture, and into the latter fireside amenities, home affections and sunshine, into both neatness, order, and economy; that we should be considerate and humane toward all in our service; that we should promote the diffusion of knowledge; that we should practice and inculcate in others industry, sobriety, and godliness; that we should gain and maintain the mastery over ourselves, in times of political excitement as in common life, permitting no cyclone of passion to lay waste our friendships; that we chase away all shadows of discontent, and inscribing anew on our hearts the Golden Rule, stifle within us the spirit of detraction, conscientiously heeding the injunction: "Be just, and fear not; let all the ends thou aimest at be thy Country's, thy God's, and Truth's."   THOMAS B. BRYAN, *Chairman.*

CHICAGO, April 22, 1889.

The programme for the Chicago mass meetings was made a part of the above address, with the hope that it might be adopted, wholly or in part, wherever the day was to be celebrated.

The responses from every direction, and especially from the West and South, through which the addresses were circulated by the tens of thousands, were most satisfactory. The very general observance of the day was highly gratifying, and in conducing to the patriotic purposes desired, compensated the Committee on General Observance for their arduous labors, and for the time and effort expended. It is a source of unfeigned regret that, notwithstanding the copious and highly entertaining reports received from a vast number of places, of their appropriate and most commendable observance of the day, the production of them in this volume seems impossible, as the matter would exceed all practicable bounds, and any preference shown to some, with the suppression of others, perhaps equally meritorious, would appear, and in fact would be, an unjustifiable and invidious discrimination.

At the suggestion of the General Executive Committee, the Governor of the State and the Mayor of the city issued proclamations requesting that all places of business be closed on April 30, and that the people assemble in their several places of worship, as did the forefathers one hundred years ago, to hold such religious services of thanksgiving, praise, and prayer as might seem appropriate in view of what God had done for our nation in the past century, and to implore that He would continue to lead and guide us. This request was generally complied with.

The sub-committee on outside decoration performed its part so well that almost every building in the city, the humblest dwellings included, displayed flags and other appropriate devices.

The members of the General Executive Committee, and indeed all who were engaged in the preliminary work of the celebration, were deeply impressed with the importance of conveying to the minds and hearts of the children of the republic the significance of the Centennial, and various plans were suggested with this object in view. Upon the recommendation of the City and County Boards of Education, and several heads of private and parochial schools, whose advice had been solicited, it was arranged to hold commemorative exercises in every schoolhouse in Cook County. As an additional means to the same end, it was decided to present a souvenir medal to every pupil. The sub-committee appointed to take charge of this branch of the work was authorized to procure 190,000 medals, but almost before the design was completed the order was increased to 250,000. This was done for the purpose of supplying the smaller towns that had adopted the Chicago plan of celebration and could obtain the medals in no other way. From the eagerness with which the little ones sought the medals, and the jealous care with which they have guarded them since the Centennial day, it is believed that no better plan could have been devised to fix in their memories the lessons contained in the school exercises. It is also worthy of note that the children of larger growth—the men and women who contributed to defray the expenses of the celebration—were as eager as the little ones to obtain the souvenirs, and they still cherish them as sacredly. However, the supply was more than equal to the demand, and at the last meeting of the General Executive Committee the sub-committee was directed to divide the remaining medals among the orphan asylums of the Northwestern States.

The experience of the various sub-committees that had charge of the arrangements for the mass-meetings was peculiarly illustrative of the rapid growth of the interest in the celebration. The Committee on Halls was appointed in February and directed to provide seats for 15,000 people. The Exposition Building, Battery D Armory, and the Cavalry Armory were secured, whereupon the Committee on Speakers was directed to find orators, the Committee on Music to find bands and choruses, and the Committee on Decorations to obtain flags and mottoes for three meetings. The applications for admission tickets were so numerous, however, that by March 1 the Hall Committee was ordered to provide for 35,000 people, and the plans of the other committees had to be modified accordingly. Later the estimate was raised to 50,000 and finally to 100,000. In the end, although every available hall in the neighborhood of the Exposition Building was secured, two large tents erected on the Lake Front Park, and rostrums erected in Dearborn Park and Lake Front Park for open-air meetings, there were thousands who, after making a tour of all the meetings, found themselves unable to get within hearing distance of any of the orators.

The musical feature of these mass meetings was characteristic of the entire celebration. It was determined at the outset that the bands and choruses should not be provided for the entertainment of the audience, but rather as a stimulant to vocal endeavor. It was designed to raise from the people themselves a sort of patriotic hozanna to harmonize with the tenor of the speeches. To accomplish this purpose, it was necessary that the selections should be popular and patriotic. Such time-honored national

anthems as "Hail Columbia," "Red, White and Blue," "The
Star Spangled Banner," and "America," suggested themselves as
the most appropriate, and they were sung with a spirit and
enthusiasm that scarcely knew bounds.   The choruses and bands
merely led.   The former, it should be recorded, were volunteers.
Singing societies and church choirs were invited to assist in the
exercises, and in most cases they readily complied with the re-
quests made of them.   Three thousand men and women of
musical ability were thus gathered together, who, with earnestness and good nature, sought to carry out the wishes of the committee.   The chorus once formed, its members were assigned to
the various halls and leaders, and tickets stamped with the place
where they were to sing were issued to them.   At the suggestion
of the committee, the 3,000 singers gathered together on the
evening of April 27, through a drenching rain, and rehearsed till
the musical directors were satisfied that there would be no hitch
or break on the day of the celebration, and, it should be added,
every division on that day acquitted itself to the satisfaction of
the thousands who assembled.   The growing demands of the
Executive Committee, owing to the constantly increasing dimensions of the celebration, made the engagement of sufficient
bands a matter of considerable difficulty, but these were eventu-
ally secured, and every hall and place of meeting was adequately
supplied.

Little remains to be said of the preparatory work for the Centennial celebration.   The accounts given elsewhere in this volume of the special features of the celebration speak for themselves.

It was deemed proper by the General Executive Committee
to tender resolutions of thanks to many who had generously
given their time and attention to the undertaking, and the Hon.
J. Young Scammon was made chairman of a committee to make
acknowledgment to the press of Chicago -for its enthusiastic
coöperation.   His report, which is herewith reproduced, was
broad enough to cover the entire ground of organized gratitude,
and was adopted as a sufficient acknowledgment to all.   It was as
follows:

To the Executive Committee formed to institute and have charge of the celebration of the 100th Anniversary of the organization of the Government of the United States of America under the Constitution:

The undersigned was appointed a member of the committee raised to consider the propriety of adopting resolutions of thanks to the public press of Chicago for the efficient, patriotic services rendered by this great instrument of public opinion in promoting this most important event in our national existence.

The members of the committee have not found it convenient to meet together, and, as I promised to prepare a report on my individual responsibility, I submit the following:

I considered the propriety of singling out the press for the special recipient of our thanks, and in determining the form for the expression of our grateful emotions I was led to look over the whole movement, and in doing so I have been unable to see why the press should receive our thanks beyond the various other agencies which have contributed as one man to render effective our wonderfully successful celebration.

The press is acknowledged as the general mouthpiece of the public, yet it is mainly an auxiliary rather than a former of public opinion. It catches the popular breeze and gives it wings, and woe to the man or association that fights against the wind of it. Perhaps it may be proper to quote Judge Storey's lines: "Here shall the press the people's rights maintain, unharmed by influence, unbribed by gain;" and certainly in relation to our great celebration nothing but that which is commendable ought to be said of the press. But in comparison with the various other agencies and committees it ought to be remembered that in this matter the press followed its legitimate and proper rôle in its regular business, while the other parties were not veterans but volunteers in the patriotic army.

While we give the veterans of the press all due honor, let us not forget the volunteers, nor by comparison take from the latter the guerdon to which they are entitled.

I. To the directors of the Union League Club is due the existence of the committee, and the powers with which it was clothed, the use of the club house, the preliminary entertainment of the voluntary committee, and the grand entertainment at the banquet on the evening of April 30.

II. To the Executive Committee, and especially its president and secretary, all the general arrangements and manner of the celebration, and the careful superintendence of its management and the general success of the whole affair.

III.   To the Committee on Religious Services, for the most per-fect and complete union of all religious bodies in Chicago, with-out any one surrendering individual or sectarian or distinct faith or peculiar claims, an almost universal service of grateful acknowl-edgment to our Heavenly Father for the blessings of civil and religious liberty which we all enjoy, and which are secured to us by the National Constitution, thus demonstrating that there is an American religion in which all can join in patriotic devotion.

IV.   To the Committee on Finance and its sub-committees for the necessary funds to render the celebration effective, satisfactory and an honor to us, the city and the country.

V.   To the Committee on General Observance of the Day throughout the Northwest, for the most efficient and successful efforts to cause the day to be duly honored in our new, greatest quarter of the republic.

VI.   To the Committee on Celebration by the Young People of our Schools, for the most patriotically instructive celebration the world ever knew.

And to all the other committees, which are too numerous to name in this paper, the greatest credit for zeal, labor, good judg-ment and efficient work, without which some links would have been wanting in the bright chain which binds in one bundle the most successful efforts for a universally patriotic celebration our country has ever witnessed.

With all these facts before us, it seems unwise to make any invidious comparisons, but that we should let the acts of the vari-ous participants in this gratefully patriotic labor speak for them-selves.   As Mr. Webster said of Massachusetts, " Look at her. Here she is.   She speaks for herself."   So does our celebration, and so should it in history.   I therefore submit the following resolution:

RESOLVED, That a committee be appointed to receive from the various committees detailed statements of the labors and services rendered by them, including copies of all circulars or other papers issued by them in furtherance of the celebration of the 100th Anni-versary of the organization of the government of the United States under the Constitution, and that such committee prepare a prepara-tory statement (to be printed in the volume to be issued by the Committee on Publication) of the proceedings of the various com-mittees, and the means employed by them to render the celebration a success.

J. YOUNG SCAMMON.

All which is respectfully submitted.

Union League Club of Chicago, May 8, 1889.

The reports were duly made, and it is from them that the account of the work given above has been compiled.   One suggestion by the secretary of the Executive Committee needs special emphasis. It was urged by this officer that April 30 be set apart as a commemoration day in every decade, the next celebration to be held on April 30, 1899. Ten years, it is commonly said, covers the school life of a child. Ten years prior to the Centennial Celebration the men and women who were prominent in bringing it about were, many of them, high school boys and girls, and ten years hence the children who received souvenir medals will be in the active walks of life and happy to carry on a similar work. There seemed, therefore, to the committee a distinct need of such an observance.

" Perhaps oftener would not be wise "—these are the words of the secretary's report—"but as often as this is requisite in order to reach the young people of the schools. If this plan is carried out each decade, all school children will have such an opportunity as the school children of Chicago, Cook County and the Northwest have had this year. Fourth of July is a day calculated to arouse enthusiasm for independence—independence of thought and action, independence in the breaking down of old things—a day for the removing of barriers, a day that is understood too much by the children (I speak from memory as well as observation) as a day of license, freedom from law and restriction. Things are allowed on this day which are allowed on no other. This is well, but we need such a day as April 30 to give emphasis to our Constitution, to creation rather than destruction, to the distinct national idea, to rejoice not that we have thrown off the yoke of England, but that we are a nation with national ideas and a history. Could this day have been observed in the decades of the last century throughout the land, perhaps love for the nation might have so far modified love for the state as to prevent a grievous civil conflict."

It is with the purpose of furthering such a scheme, of keeping fresh in the minds of those who participated in the celebration of April 30, 1889, the deep significance of the day, and of transmitting to future generations a record of the glad outpouring of the people to mark the first Centennial Anniversary of genuine national life, that this souvenir volume is issued. The design of the committee having its publication in charge is to publish new editions from time to time and give the volume the greatest possible circulation. In this way it is hoped that the national idea will be emphasized and strengthened.

II

SERVICES IN THE CHURCHES

SERVICES IN THE CHURCHES

At the Cathedral of the Holy Name, corner State and Superior streets, a solemn high military mass was celebrated at 9 o'clock. The beautiful church was crowded with worshipers, who came to return thanks that religious persecution was forever a thing of the past, and that the adoption of the Constitution of the United States heralded for all time freedom to worship as the heart dictated. The celebrants were the Rev. M. J. Fitzsimmons, the Rev. F. N. Perry as deacon, and the Rev. J. M. Scanlan as subdeacon. The mass was the usual mass for the day, with a collect of thanksgiving. The church was devoid of any unusual decoration, save a large American flag, placed in front of the altar of St. Joseph by the Holy Name cadets, who formed the military element of the congregation. Dressed in zouave uniforms, they marched into the church in a column of fours. The acolytes serving mass also wore the uniform. Archbishop Feehan, wearing a purple cassock, cope and beretta, with white surplice, occupied a seat in the arch-episcopal throne. The choir gave Hayden's third mass, "The Imperial;" "Veni Creator," Cerillo; offertory, Cello Solo, Browne; overture, "Jubel," Von Weber. The Rev. J. P. Muldoon ascended the pulpit, being escorted thither by a platoon of cadets. His text was Romans xiii.: 1: "Let every soul be subject to the higher powers, for there is no power but from God and those that are ordained are of God." After an eloquent sermon he closed with a brilliant portrayal of the advantages which Catholics enjoyed as American citizens, and a reference to the services of France and Lafayette when the young republic was struggling for existence. After mass,

Archbishop Feehan pronounced the benediction. Services were held in many of the other Catholic churches, but in many instances the exercises consisted of the usual mass for the day and impromptu addresses.

From the spire of the First Presbyterian Church, 260 feet above the sidewalk, floated in graceful folds the Stars and Stripes. The interior of the church presented a bewildering array of flags, flowers, bunting, and banners tastefully and picturesquely combined. It was an unusually gorgeous sight for a church scene, witnessed by 2,000 persons crowded within its walls. The First Regiment, under the command of Lieut. Col. Charles R. E. Koch, with gold-trimmed gray suits, white helmets, relieved by the sober-garbed veteran corps at its head, occupied a double row of seats reserved for it. The men were headed by the Elgin Military Band, under the direction of J. Hecker. Stuart's famous portrait of Washington hung in the centre of the great wall of flags. The Sunday-school children occupied the right and left galleries, while the superintendent, Mr. Henry W. Dudley, sat with the pastor and others on the platform. The notes of Buck's "Triumphal March" rolled up from the organ, under the touch of the organist, Mr. Clarence Eddy. The singing of the Doxology followed, and the Rev. John D. McCord offered prayer. "The Star Spangled Banner," solo by the double quartette, chorus by the congregation, organ and Elgin band, wrought the people up to a degree of enthusiasm which was intense. Reading of the Scriptures, and a fantasie on American airs by the band, were followed by prayer by the pastor of the church. Then "Hail Columbia" sounded forth triumphantly, Mr. W. T. Carver singing the solo and the children of the Sunday-school the chorus. The Rev. John Henry Barrows, D. D., pastor of the church, delivered an oration on "A Hundred Years," after which "America" by the congregation, choir, organ, and band rang out, the benediction was pronounced, and the exercises of a day that will ever be remembered by those participating in them, were ended. The programmes of the services of the First Church embodied the programmes for Centennial Day and the preceding Sunday, which had been observed as a day of thanksgiving and patriotic devotion. They were printed on rich white paper, in red and blue—the national colors—with a portrait of Washington in blue on the frontispiece, and were models of neatness and beauty for a souvenir programme.

At the Second Presbyterian Church, the Rev. Simon J. McPherson, D. D., delivered an earnest and thoughtful address on "The Character of Washington." He dwelt at length on the great care Washington gave to everything claiming his attention, and believed it was, in part, this faithfulness to minor details that saved the American Republic. He held up his disinterestedness and freedom from office-seeking as an example to the politicians of our day. The office seeking the man, not the man the office, such was the picture drawn by the distinguished speaker of the great Washington. Such a civil service was what we of the present day needed, but, according to the speaker, were not likely soon to have. The organ loft and space in rear of the pulpit were beautifully draped with flags, and the floral decorations were in admirable taste.

More than a thousand people were gathered at the Third Presbyterian Church, on the corner of Ogden and Ashland avenues. The Rev. Dr. J. L. Withrow, the pastor, offered a thanksgiving invocation. The national hymns, "America," "The Star Spangled Banner," and "Hail Columbia," were enthusiastically sung, and over twenty short addresses, all breathing the spirit of thanksgiving and patriotism that characterized the day everywhere, were made. Among the thoughts expressed were these, that such great gatherings prove that the people do believe that God lives and hears prayer; that an increasing and intelligent sentiment for Sabbath observance is rising over the land, and that there are always enough good men to overcome the forces of evil, and that the awful crime of intemperance is becoming more and more hated by the people.

The Fourth Presbyterian Church, on the North Side, witnessed a repetition of the scenes of thanksgiving, flowers and decorations shown in other churches. A large American flag, gracefully folded, formed a fitting background for a handsomely-framed portrait of "The Father of his Country." The singing of national airs opened the exercises of the day. The Rev. Dr. M. Woolsey Stryker remarked, as he opened the Scriptures to read the lesson,

that "he was a man of dull spiritual imagination who could not
apply to our country the promises to Israel." Dr. Stryker made
a short address, abounding in patriotism and religious fervor, and
the services closed with the singing of "America."

The Eighth Presbyterian Church was handsomely decorated,
both within and without, with the national colors. A large congregation was present at 9 o'clock to participate in the exercises.
The pastor, the Rev. Thomas D. Wallace, D. D., and the ruling
elders, occupied seats on the platform. Piety and patriotism
blended in hymn and prayer, and a reverent, grateful spirit
marked all the services of the hour. After several of our country's anthems had been sung, and the hymn,

> Great God of Nations now to Thee
> Our hymn of gratitude we raise,

the Invocation and Lord's Prayer followed. and Dr. Wallace made
these introductory remarks:

To-day we celebrate the completion of a century of constitutional life. We may well thank God and take courage. We are
here with common consent as Christian citizens to recall and record the goodness of God in our national history. He hath not
dealt so with any nation. We have heard with our ears, O God,
our fathers have told us what work Thou didst in their day; for
they got not the land in possession by their own sword, neither did
their own arm save them, but Thy right hand and Thine arm, and
the light of Thy countenance, because Thou didst have favor unto
them. From a small seed has grown a giant tree of liberty; from
a few states, more than forty; from 3,000,000 of people, 63,000,000;
from a handful of corn, a great harvest. What was then untamed
territory is now the well-ordered domain of majestic commonwealths. Founded in faith and freedom, our institutions are the
fruits of God's providence and man's fidelity.

Every step has been a struggle, every day has closed with a
song, and we have finished one hundred years with peace in all our
borders, prosperity in our coasts, and quiet confidence and gratitude
in our hearts. This flag, thank God! has no star erased, and is
to-day, in fact as in name, the symbol of a free nation. Let it float
forever over the peaceful homes of a pious and patriotic people.
Truth shall spring out of the earth and righteousness shall look
down from heaven.

I welcome you to this sanctuary, and under the shelter of the
Almighty wings, let us trust that the red of this flag shall symbolize

the blood which was shed to pay the price of freedom, and the living current which to-day would flow for its defense. The white shall stand for God, the Light in which we would live, in which our victories were achieved, and by which our liberties and peace have been conserved. The blue shall stand for the celestial canopy over us—yet touching us all around the horizon; it shall stand for God and man linked together—for the accomplishment of the loftiest purposes touching human life upon this planet.

All hail the day! Let us reverently pay our tribute of praise to Him who crowns this century of our national life with abundance of peace and grace.

The congregation then sung Dr. Leonard Bacon's hymn:

> O God, beneath thy guiding hand
> Our exiled fathers crossed the sea,

which was followed by reading of selections from Psalms xliv. and cvii., by pastor and people. The following national hymn, written for the occasion by Mr. J. P. Bates, was sung by the choir:

> As pilgrims halt at heat of noon
> Beneath some friendly wayside shade,
> And celebrate the priceless boon
> Of guiding hand in progress made;
> So this great Nation stops to-day
> In onward march to larger things,
> And seeks by voice and act to pay
> Its tribute to the King of Kings.
>
> One hundred years ago, our land,
> Still weak and bruised from lengthened strife,
> Made Washington, with patriot band,
> The Leader of its legal life.
> A Constitution's binding force
> Cemented many into one,
> And shaped the infant Nation's course
> Through toils and dangers just begun.
>
> Among the Powers of the world,
> We won the name of brave and free,
> And made our flag in air unfurled,
> Emblem of might from sea to sea.
> And now, behold! what God hath wrought
> In us and for us by His power!
> To Him be lifted every thought
> In gratitude this favored hour.

As vestal virgins at their shrine
Rekindled sacred fires when low,
So let our homes and altars shine
With true devotion's warming glow.
The founders of our Nation's weal,
Wise men and strong, deserve our love;
Recount their deeds with ardent zeal,
And breathe a song of praise above.

Mr. Ephraim Banning, a ruling elder in the Eighth Presbyterian Church, then delivered an able address, and Mrs. Hemans's hymn, "The Pilgrim Fathers," was sung as a solo by Mrs. Wallace. Mr. Thomas Hood, another of the ruling elders, offered prayer, and "America" was joyfully sung, and the benediction offered by Dr. Wallace.

The Church of the Covenant (Presbyterian), the Rev. D. R. Breed, D. D., pastor, held union services, which were participated in by the pastors of the Baptist, Wesley Methodist, Grace English Lutheran, Fullerton Avenue Presbyterian, Belden Avenue Presbyterian and St. Matthew's Reformed Episcopal Churches. More than a thousand people were present. A delegation of Grand Army veterans occupied seats in the body of the church. National flags were displayed on the walls. A large chorus choir representing the several churches, and under the leadership of Mr. S. P. McDivitt of the Church of the Covenant, led the singing. Mr. McDivitt opened the services with a few well-chosen words of welcome and of congratulation on the occasion which had called the people together. After the singing of "The Red, White and Blue," prayer was offered by the Rev. W. H. Burns of the Wesley Methodist Church, and selections from the Scriptures were read by the Rev. H. H. Barbour, pastor of the Belden Avenue Church. The exercises were continued in the following order: Hymn, "God Bless our Native Land;" addresses by the Revs. L. M. Heilman and R. F. Coyle, the Grace Lutheran and Fullerton avenue pastors; hymn, "The Star Spangled Banner;" addresses by the Rev. R. D. Scott of the Belden Avenue Presbyterian Church, and the Rev. Herrick Johnson, D. D., of the McCormick Theological Seminary; hymn, "My Country, 'tis of Thee;" benediction, pronounced by the Rev. W. H. Burns.

The services at the First United Presbyterian Church, corner of West Monroe and Paulina streets, were conducted by the pastor, the Rev. W. T. Meloy, D. D. The church choir rendered special anthems and the people united in singing Psalms c. and lxvii. I. G. Brown, M. D., and Mr. D. H. Henderson, veterans of the Civil War, led the people in prayer. Addresses were delivered by Mr. T. H. Gault, the Hon. James F. Claflin, and Charles G. Davis, M. D. The services were solemn, impressive and patriotic. The addresses abounded in expressions of loyalty to the country, while acknowledging that security and peace were to be found alone in the blessing of Him by whose power we had been exalted among the nations of the earth. The Union flag decorated the pulpit, but the praises sung were not to our country but to our country's God. The speakers rejoiced that gratitude to God had been awakened, while devotion to the old flag with its white of purity, its red of glory, and its blue of heavenly beneficence, had been intensified.

The services in the various Episcopal churches usually consisted of an abbreviated form of morning prayer, with appropriate psalms and hymns, that being the order set forth by the Bishop of Iowa and recommended by the Bishop of Chicago for use in this diocese. The service, which was specially appropriate, was compiled by the Dean of Davenport, from the offices contained in the Proposed Book, in the preparation of which Bishop Provoost, who officiated at St. Paul's Chapel on the occasion of the religious observance of Washington's Inauguration, April 30, 1789, was concerned.

At Grace Episcopal Church, Wabash avenue, the services were conducted by the Rev. Clinton Locke, D. D., with special prayers, and selections from Washington's first Inaugural Address.

St. James's Church was well filled with devout worshipers. The rector, the Rev. William H. Vibbert, S. T. D., officiated. A full surpliced choir sang the responses and the choral parts of the service. The regular service already mentioned followed the morning prayer. The anthem was the "Misericordias Domini," followed by the 118th Psalm: "O, give thanks unto the Lord, for He is gracious; because His mercy endureth forever." It comprised the Te Deum arranged by Smart in F, the Apostles' Creed, Collects for the day, for peace and grace; a prayer for our civil rulers; a special thanksgiving, general thanksgiving and a prayer of St. Chrysostom. Dr. Vibbert addressed the people briefly, speaking of the connection of the church and religion with the efforts of the people of 1776, for liberty and constitutional government.

At St. Andrew's Protestant Episcopal Church the regular services observed in the other churches were held, after which the rector, the Rev. William C. DeWitt, delivered a sermon. The musical portion of the service was rendered by the surpliced choir, the congregation assisting in the hymns: "God Bless our Native Land;" "Before the Lord we Bow;" and "Come Thou Almighty King." The only decorations were the national colors worn by members of the assembly.

At Christ Reformed Episcopal Church the Second Regiment of Infantry, Battery D of the Artillery, and Bunker Post 373, G. A. R., gave a military aspect to the gathering. The Rt. Rev. Bishop Charles Edward Cheney gave a noble address, and welcomed the veterans and militia in a speech of thanks for their attendance, which, he thought, linked the past and the present. The ladies of the church, assisted by Mr. Edward H. Turner, had spared neither time nor effort in making the edifice one of the most elaborately decorated churches of the day. The people commenced gathering early, and many were obliged to go away on account of difficulty in obtaining even standing room.

St. Paul's Reformed Episcopal Church varied the usual exercises of the day by having forty-two young ladies of the High School, dressed in white, represent the states of the Union, while Miss Edith Foster personated the Goddess of Liberty. Bishop Fallows delivered a scholarly address on the subject: "A Review of the Century."

The services of the Wabash Avenue Methodist Episcopal Church were held in the Sunday-school room. The national hymns were sung, and brief addresses made by the pastor, the Rev. R. H. Pooley, and Dr. D. S. Smith, Mr. Charles Busby, and Dr. A. Burr.

At the Centenary Methodist Church the observances of the day were brief, but none the less patriotic. The Rev. H. E. Jackson took charge of the exercises, and the Hon. L. L. Bond gave a short address.

The Trinity Methodist Church, Indiana avenue and Twenty-fourth street, was handsomely decorated, and potted plants, flowers and bunting added their attractions to the music and the bright and interesting speeches. The musical exercises consisted of an organ voluntary; the hymn, "O Worship the King, All Glorious Above;" a solo, "The Red, White and Blue," by Mrs. L. Hasbrouck; the hymn, "Mighty God, While Angels Bless Thee," selections from Washington's first Inaugural, and remarks by the pastor, Rev. F. M. Bristol, D. D., which were followed by an address delivered by the Rev. Arthur Edwards, D. D., editor of the *Northwestern Christian Advocate.*

The Centennial exercises at the Ada Street Methodist Episcopal Church were made peculiarly interesting, because under the auspices of a Washington Historical Society, which had been organized several months previously to study American history with special reference to the Constitution. The society consisted of young people, and two prizes were offered for the best essays upon "Washington as a Patriot." The essays were read, and the gifts awarded as a feature of the Centennial service. Inquiries came from other portions of the city as to whether persons not members of the Historical Society could compete for these prizes. As a result of the question, Congressman William E. Mason offered a third prize for the best essay upon the subject already assigned, to be competed for by any one outside of the church. The competitors forwarded their productions from all parts of the city. They were read by the appointed judges, with the following results: Miss Lena Caldwell received the first prize of the society, Miss Alice McClurg the second prize, and Miss Nellie McKay special honorable mention. To J. Wilbur Reed was awarded the Mason prize. Presentation speeches, appropriate and eloquent, were made by Congressman Mason, Samuel Polkey, and R. W. Vasey. The prizes were two gold medals and a work upon "American History." Congratulatory remarks were made by Mr. C. O. Boring. Miss Fleming recited "Washington's Drummer Boy" very effectively. The congregation, which completely filled the house, sang "Guide me, O Thou Great Jehovah," and "America," with joyous enthusiasm. The church was most elaborately trimmed with bunting and flags; bunting was on the gallery railings, and flags were nailed to the pillars, attached to the organ pipes, and around the beneficent face of Washington, as it beamed from the wall. A flag was also given to each person in the audience. A beautiful souvenir programme was prepared and presented to all present by Mr. I. A. Fleming. American colors were also given to the children. The Rev. J. P. Brushingham, the pastor, delivered the address and presided over the devotional exercises.

At the First M. E. Church more than ordinary interest was manifested, owing, in part, to the presence of the Grand Army soldiers, who marched in line to the church, and whose presence acted as an inspiration to Centennial enthusiasm. The "Sons of America" were also present, every camp in the city turning out in full numbers. Eight hundred marched in step to the music of Maj. Nevans's Band. The auditorium was crowded to its utmost capacity. When all the seating and standing room in the building was taken, the surging multitude crowded the halls, where, while they could not see the orator, they could hear his sonorous voice and join in the frequent applause. The Rev. A. W. Bolton, D. D., commander of the U. S. Grant Post 28, G. A. R., pronounced the oration.

The people of the New England Congregational and the La Salle Avenue Baptist Churches united with the members of Grace Methodist Church, and together they celebrated the day. The choirs of the three churches were under the guidance of Mr. E. S. Fogg. The church was adorned with small flags, and bunting draped the rails, organ and pulpit, while potted plants added their loveliness and fragrance to the architectural beauty of the church. The principal oration was by the Rev. Mr. Thames, on "Character," after which the pastor of the church, the Rev. Robert McIntyre, made a patriotic and brilliant address.

Plymouth Congregational Church was honored by the presence of Gov. Fifer and his staff, as guests of the day. All except the Governor were in full uniform. The Governor entered, followed by Gen. J. W. Vance, adjutant-general; Col. W. S. Brockett, inspector-general; Col. Theodore Ewert, assistant adjutant-general, and Col. Frank Clendenin, Col. H. Kohler, Col. Charles Bogardus, Col. Louis Krughoff, and Capt. R. B. Kennedy, aides-de-camp. Miss Josephine Lester, as the Goddess of Liberty, sat at the right of the Governor, and behind sat 500 Sunday-school children, all carrying flags. The Rev. F. W. Gunsaulus, D. D., gave the oration, which, though brief, abounded in patriotic thoughts and brilliant sayings.

At the Union Park Congregational Church, Prof. G. S. F. Savage offered a prayer full of touching sentiments and devout thanks for the blessings of the past century. The Rev. Dr. F. A. Noble, the pastor, read the Inaugural of President Washington, and Prof. G. B. Wilcox of the Congregational Seminary, gave a thrilling address. The platform was decorated chiefly with flowers, and an oil portrait of the man whose memory was the principal theme of nearly every address.

The Imperial Quartette and a full choir gave a patriotic and beautiful song service at the First Congregational Church, the Rev. E. P. Goodwin, D. D., pastor. The Hon. C. C. Bonney gave the oration of the day, speaking earnestly and ably on "The Centennial of Constitutional Liberty." Prof. H. M. Scott, D. D., of the Congregational Theological Seminary, also spoke, and mingled with the enthusiasm of the day was an undercurrent of religious thanksgiving for the boon of a secure and unmolested liberty.

Music, happy faces, flowers, patriotic enthusiasm, bunting, and flags greeted the attendants at the First Baptist Church. Instead of a painting of the beloved Washington, a marble bust found a resting place amid the flowers just over the pulpit. The Rev. Dr. P. S. Henson, the pastor, spoke of the country in its infancy and followed its growth to the present time. The Civil War, he said, removed a cancer that soothing syrup could not help, and so the knife had to be resorted to. Yet the Southern people were to-day lovers of the flag. He expected to see the flag of our country floating over Canada and Mexico ere long, and in time he believed it would advance across the isthmus and rule South America, being an emblem of freedom to far-away Patagonia. The second century would bring great poets and great statesmen, but never would the man be found who would eclipse the fame of Washington. The greatest among others would be far behind him. Washington was our noblest patriot and statesman; he was our sovereign, our king.

The Fourth Baptist Church celebrated the day in the lecture-room.   The red, white and blue were visible in profusion, and here, as nearly everywhere else, was to be seen the face of him whom all revered.   Simplicity marked the programme, and a short but heart-felt speech by the pastor, the Rev. J. Wolfenden, and music by the choir, expressed the earnest feelings of the people.

The Immanuel Baptist Church was handsomely trimmed.   The service was long and varied.   The Orkney and Shetland Benevolent Societies, and George H. Thomas Post 5, turned out in full force.   Essays on patriotism were read and money prizes awarded to C. A. Smith, A. H. Morris, Miss Mattie Coleman of the Moseley School, and the Misses Lorimer, Strawbridge, and Stoffer.   The Rev. Geo. C. Lorimer, D. D., preached the sermon, which glowed with patriotism.

At the Second Baptist Church, the decorations were on a magnificent scale.   The church was canopied and draped with the national colors.   The quartette choir was assisted by an auxiliary choir and quartette.   The Rev. Dr. William M. Lawrence, the pastor, spoke briefly but eloquently to a large audience.

The beautiful St. Paul's Universalist Church, corner of Thirtieth street and Prairie avenue, was finely decorated with flags. There was a full attendance and the exercises began with devotional sentences and the following exhortation: "Dearly Beloved —We are met together with the memories and mercies of a century of national life to gladden and to solemnize our hearts.   Let us acknowledge the Source of all our country's good and greatness.   Let us confess ourselves servants of God.   Let us seek to renew in the light of the Gospel, the virtues and the aspirations which alone can make us a happy people."   A psalm read responsively, an anthem, the Scripture lesson, and prayer, followed.   "The Star Spangled Banner" was sung before, and "America" after an admirable address given by the pastor, the Rev. John Coleman Adams, D. D.   He held the closest attention as he offered "A Friendly Word to Patriots," speaking from the text, "Other men labored, and ye are entered into their labors." He said in substance: "I suppose that the best uses to which we can put this Centennial occasion are by no means those of self-gratulation. Merely to rehearse great deeds done is not a performance which greatly edifies. Two things are needed to make that exercise profitable:

"First, a lively sympathy with the spirit and the purposes of these men of old. We must be able to feel something of Washington's high-mindedness, something of Henry's ardor, something of Sam Adams's love of country; else how can we read with intelligence the Farewell Address of Washington; what meaning will there be for us in Henry's words, 'I am no longer a Virginian but an American;' how shall we feel the solemn devotion and love in Adams's words, 'This is a glorious morning for America.'

"Second, a right reading of the lessons of the past to our own age. We are to remember in every such an hour as this how what is now history was once a living present, and seeing the beneficent influence of the events which were, we are to remember the import of those which are."

Dr. Adams spoke of what we owed to our institutions, and said that the Constitution was an embodiment of Christian principles. He dwelt at length on how much our institutions owed to the character of our citizens, and spoke of the personal character of the Constitution-makers, and closed by declaring that "We celebrate a victory of peace."

"Old Hundred," sung by over two hundred voices, ushered in, and "America" closed the ceremonies commemorative of the day, celebrated at the Church of the Redeemer. "The Life of Washington" was the theme on which the Rev. Charles Conklin, the pastor, discoursed. He spoke at length of the character of the first President and his influence in the formation of the Constitution, dwelling on his patience, faithfulness, and patriotism. The congregation sang "Hail Columbia," after which one of the church officers addressed the people and another offered prayer. After singing another of the national songs the gathering dispersed, carrying in their hearts lessons and sentiments not soon to be forgotten.

The Third Unitarian Church employed in observance of the day the regular choral service for national occasions. The Rev. Vila Blake spoke to the people at length, his discourse being divided into three themes, and between each part solos were sung. The first theme dwelt upon was Washington and the Rev-olutionary War, after which the organ sounded forth a triumphal march, and Mr. Morgan of the choir sang "The Sword of Bunker Hill." Mr. Blake next spoke of Washington's victories in times of peace, when Mr. Phillips sang "Land of Peace and Concord," which had been set to an old Welsh melody. The third division of the sermon related to Washington's lesson and example, teach-ing us that true freedom is obedience and justice, and Miss Holmes sang "Freedom, fair Freedom," arranged to an air from Handel. The pulpit platform was very tastefully decorated with the national colors.

The Church of the Messiah made a special service for the day. The edifice was decorated elaborately. The chil-dren from the Home for the Friendless attended, and the Rev. David Utter spoke briefly on the events which called together the people to worship and rejoice. He argued that a nation's prosperity was not assured alone by its limitless territory, its commercial resources, its inventions, or its agri-culture. The basis of its perpetuity lay in its government, in its Constitution, and so long as its Constitution found an echo in the people's hearts so long would the nation continue and prosper.

The English Evangelical Lutheran Church celebrated the day in truly patriotic spirit. For an half-hour before the services the bell rang out its joyous invitation. The audience chamber was crowded. The services began with the "Regular Order for Morn-ing Worship," as set forth in the Church Book of the General Council of the Evangelical Lutheran Church in North America, the Thanksgiving Introit, with prayers for magistrates, being used. The Scripture lessons were from Deut. viii., and Ps. cvii. The Rev. H. W. Roth, D. D., pastor, spoke as follows:

It is befitting that we hold such a service. When a man reaches one hundred years his friends joyously greet him. God made it the duty of Israel to celebrate their jubilees. Iceland and Russia have celebrated their one thousandth anniversaries. China, the oldest nation, has celebrated many others still more ancient. As a nation we are very young. We were first dependent colonists, then colonies in the Revolution, then a Confederation, with all its attendant conflicts and dangers. Through the guidance and great wisdom of Washington, peace ensued, the Constitution was adopted, and from this day one hundred years ago, as Washington took the oath of inauguration as first President, our national life distinctly dates. Loyal is the Lutheran Church to every flag whose protection she enjoys; and for ourselves, many of us born in other lands, and for our children, born in this fair land, we most heartily engage in the fit and patriotic observance of this most happy day.

Men die, but the nation lives. The fathers, where are they? Xerxes wept that of his million soldiers about to invade Europe, in one hundred years not one would be left. Of those who took an intelligent part in the occurrences of one hundred years ago, not one is with us to-day. When this Centennial Anniversary occurs again, our sixty millions of present population will have been gathered to the dust. Our nation, despite the doings of death, still lives. How rich and vigorous the life which the United States of America has lived, both for the nation and for humanity! Her statesmen, soldiers, jurists, theologians, preachers, philanthropists, physicians, teachers, poets, authors, inventors and multitudes of good men and noble women, have made the nation rich, great, prosperous, powerful and a blessing to the world. All thanks to God for His great goodness!

Will the nation continue? What is the future of the republic? That rests with ourselves. The past has taught us much. Our coins say "In God We Trust." Is this the inmost faith of our hearts? As a nation, do we fear God and reverence sacred things? Is the blessed religion of our Lord Jesus Christ abidingly present in our homes and lives, and does it rightly influence us in all the varied relations of our multiplied activities? If so, and we so continue, the future is no less sure for us than has been the past. But if not, so surely as we turn away from God, so surely will He turn away from us. May He mercifully grant to us all His gracious spirit, that we may "do justly, love mercy and walk humbly before God."

Prayer followed and the choir sang anthems appropriate to the day, and the services closed with the Doxology. On the preceding Lord's day, the Sunday-school, numbering 400, had a special commemorative meeting, with Scripture lessons, hymns, and an address from Pastor Roth on "Some Lessons for Young Americans from the Life of Washington."

SERVICES AND ADDRESSES.

THE REV. FREDERICK A. NOBLE, D. D.

AT UNION PARK CONGREGATIONAL CHURCH.

The God of . . . Israel chose our fathers, and exalted the people.
—ACTS XIII.:17.

To some men it is given to be wise beyond their time. On the 22d of November, according to the present mode of reckoning, in the year of our Lord 1620, in the cabin of the little ship which had brought the Pilgrim fathers to these shores, as she lay at rest, after her long and perilous voyage, within the shelter of Cape Cod, what has come to be known in history as the "Mayflower Compact," was read, and signed by the forty-one men who stood for all the families and represented all the common interests of the entire company.

It is a brief document, covering not more than a half page of an ordinary book, but it is long enough to hold this remarkable statement: "We whose names are underwritten . . . do by these presents solemnly and mutually, in the presence of God, and of one another, covenant and combine ourselves together into a civil body politic, for our better ordering and preservation, and furtherance of the ends aforesaid, and by virtue hereof, to enact, constitute and form such just and equal laws, ordinances, acts, constitutions and offices, from time to time, as shall be thought most meet and convenient for the general good of the colony, unto which we promise all due submission and obedience."

In speaking of this transaction, Bancroft says: "This was the birth of popular constitutional liberty. The middle age had been familiar with charters and constitutions, but they had been merely compacts for immunities, partial enfranchisements, patents of nobility, concessions of municipal privileges, or limitations of sovereign power, in favor of feudal institutions. In the cabin of the Mayflower humanity recovered its rights, and instituted government on the basis of 'equal laws' for the 'general good.' "

The characterization is not too strong, nor is the tribute too hearty. This was the organization of Democracy. Man, leaving behind him all the impertinent suggestions of class distinction, and advancing in the imperial majesty of his simple manhood, came to the front.

The germ of all this lay far back in an old and precious document. But not in Magna Charta, which was wrested by the Archbishop

of Canterbury and the angry barons from King John at Runnymede; and not in the Bill of Rights even, which Parliament, representing a long-suffering realm, forced from Charles I. twenty
years before this arbitrary sovereign lost his head, but not until
almost ten years after the Mayflower compact had been signed is
there to be found any such pronounced recognition of the equal
rights of man as is contained in this instrument which Carver,
and Bradford, and Winslow, and Brewster, and Allerton, and
Standish, and Alden, and the rest of that far-seeing and consecrated band, drew up and gave to the world.

Announced and set in motion in the administration of affairs at
Plymouth, this doctrine of equal rights, not yet carried to the
point to which it was sure to come, of the independent sovereignty
of the people, reappeared in the town meetings of the Massachusetts
Bay Colony, and compelled recognition in spite of the fears of Winthrop even and of Cotton; and in Rhode Island, under the broad
banner of Roger Williams, who had the foresight and the courage
to avow this large principle and to stand on it: "The sovereign
power of all civil authority is founded in the consent of the people;" and in Connecticut, where the influence of Thomas Hooker
—the most in-looking and out-looking man of the early colonial
times—and John Haynes, and the younger Winthrop, was so potential in securing what has been claimed to be "the first written
Constitution, in the modern sense of the term, as a permanent limi-
tation on power, known in history;" and in Virginia in the protests and rebellions of the every-day folk, often so pronounced,
against the usurpations of aristocratic burgesses and the arbitrary
rule of royal governors like Berkeley; and in Pennsylvania, where
the immortal Penn began his "holy experiment" by saying to the
settlers who had been induced to come over and occupy the state
it was in his heart to found: "You shall be governed by the laws
of your own making, and live a free and, if you will, a sober and
industrious people."

It reappeared—this doctrine of equal rights—all along the coast,
whose surging seas, whose deep and majestic forests, whose tonic
airs, whose largess life seemed to have something in them to breed
the spirit of freedom, from Maine to Georgia, wherever there were
isolated homes, or hamlets, or towns, or villages, or cities popu-
lated by souls intent on better opportunities for themselves and
their posterity; and any attempt to deny it or suppress it only
made the existence of it more evident.

It reappeared, still more radiant, and broadened out into what
alone can give solidity and perennial fruitfulness to equal rights—

the absolute sovereignty of the people—a little more than a century and a half after it had had voicing in the cabin of the Mayflower, in the sublimest and most influential form ever given to it in words, in the Declaration of Independence. In this the doctrine culminated.

How clear the statements of this great instrument! How lofty the sentiment! How abiding the energy! "We hold these truths to be self-evident: That all men are created equal; that they are endowed by their Creator with certain inalienable rights; that among these are life, liberty and the pursuit of happiness. That, to secure these rights, governments are instituted among men, deriving their just powers from the consent of the governed, and that, when any form of government becomes destructive of these ends, it is the right of the people to alter or abolish it, and to institute new governments, laying its foundations on such principles and organizing its powers in such form as to them shall seem most likely to effect their safety and happiness."

The Revolution, led by Washington, with its thunders of guns rolling on from Lexington and Concord to Yorktown, made that august declaration good. The Constitution, formed by a body of men over whom Washington presided, and whose superiors in political sagacity the world has never seen—John Langdon, Rufus King, Roger Sherman, Alexander Hamilton, William Livingston, Benjamin Franklin, Gouverneur Morris, James Madison, John Rutledge, Charles Pinckney—along with others, who, in addition to their uncalculating patriotism, are justly illustrious for the shining qualities of their minds, or their robust common sense, set their seal to that august document and made it operative.

Now one hundred years of national life, which have moved along the lines of ideas which were announced in the Mayflower compact, and reasserted in Rhode Island and Connecticut and Massachusetts, and kindled into flame in the Declaration of Independence, and for which the Revolution was fought and the Constitution was framed, with a great-grandson of one of the signers of the Declaration of Independence sitting in the executive chair to send back greeting to the Father of his Country, come in to demonstrate that government "of the people, and by the people, and for the people," is the best government ever devised and administered by men.

The love of liberty is indigenous to the human heart. Through these ages men have dreamed of liberty, and have felt that they were made for liberty, as they were made for immortality. One discovers everywhere tokens of a sense of the right to liberty, and of the value and joy of liberty. Appreciation of liberty is seen in the breast of the savage, and it moves on apace with the progress of civilization. Yonder in Central Asia, where the Indo-Europeans had their early home, and from whence they set out in their great Western migrations, the love of liberty was conspicuous. On the banks of the Indus, in the fertile valleys of the Euphrates, under the shadow of the mighty pyramids and along the borders of the Nile, in frigid Russia and in sunny Greece, under the soft skies of Italy and Spain, among the mountain fastnesses of Switzerland, along the slopes where the grapes are gathered and the herds are pastured in beautiful France, behind the dikes of Holland, over the plains and amid the forests of Germany, far north in the Scandinavian retreats, where muscle is trained by hardship and storms nurture the courage to do and dare; within the sea-girt Isle, whose scepter of authority has been wielded by an Alfred, by a William the Conqueror, by an Elizabeth, and by a Victoria; up in the Highlands, where the Bruces and Wallaces led their clans, and Burns sung songs as enduring as Homer's, and Scott waved his wizard's wand; in Ireland, where the echoes of the voice of O'Connell still linger in the air, persuasive, potential, and the name of Robert Emmet stirs like a bugle call; here in this broad land of America, everywhere, of what race or clime, man feels himself to be hindered, cramped, thwarted, cruelly wronged, without liberty, and the aspirations and cries of his soul and the struggles of his hands have been for liberty. It has been so whether under tyrannies ancient or modern.

Patrick Henry formulated it in fiery speech, but the brave sentiment had been domiciled in millions of hearts before: "Give me liberty or give me death." He was but joining hands with Demosthenes and Pym, and anticipating Warren, and Ellsworth, and Winthrop, and McPherson. What conspiracies there have been, what revolts, what revolutions, what long and bloody wars, what overturnings of dynasties and rendings of empires, simply because this instinctive love of liberty with which man comes into the world refuses to be overlooked or relegated into the background at the dictates of tyrants and usurpers and privileged classes, but will assert itself on every opportunity. What an element of pathos it lends to the picture which confronts us wherever we turn our eyes in the past—this patience with which the multitudes who make up the lower sections of the nations go through their tasks, bearing their heavy burdens, doing their enforced work, and consenting in a kind of dumb, despairing way, because they cannot help it, to be trampled into the dust by their pitiless oppressors, while there is all the time a consciousness in their souls—

very vague, no doubt, in many of them—that they were made for a better destiny, that they are not receiving their fair share of rights, and that it would be a blessed thing to break the chains of their heartless bondage and go forth with limbs and minds emancipated. How we sympathize with the fierce Maccabees in their heroic protests and their thunderous blows against unrighteous dominion, and with those Roman Gracchi in their desperate attempts to secure some larger measure of equity to the people, and with those German peasants, in their uprisings and wars, and with Netherland revolts, and English rebellions—with all, indeed, in every land and age who have been found ready to forget position and to risk property and life for the precious boon of freedom. It is because there is a feeling inborn in our hearts to interpret the feeling inborn in their hearts, and we are sure that this native instinct which takes us forward in the assertion of equal rights, and in the claim for self-government, is both a common one and God-given. It is not an accident, it is not an incident, that men love and long for liberty.

But what have the leaders of the world's civil politics been saying about this? Why, that it was simply a pleasant hallucination. The old Pharaohs, the Cæsars, the Tamerlanes, the Louises, the Charleses, have had no other thought. Despots, kings asserting their divine right of kingship, oligarchs, aristocracies, feudal lords, rulers in general, have wrapped the robes of royal complacency about them, and smiled and said: "This aspiration for freedom is only a vision of the imagination, an unsubstantial castle in the air."

Nevertheless, here in this land of America, this fond dream has been realized. For a full round century—in many respects the most fertile century since Christ was born—the people of the United States have been living under a Constitution of their own creation, under laws of their own enacting, under policies of their own shaping. Within this century, too, the people have grown in numbers, in wealth, and in power as no other nation on the globe. Freedom an empty chimera! Equal rights a fine theory impossible to be reduced to practice! Self-government a glittering speculation of fanaticism! Liberty under law, and law conceived and executed in the spirit of liberty, the unsolved problem of statesmanship! But here they are. Here is freedom. Here is equal rights. Here is self-government. Here is liberty under law, and law moving forward to the execution of its functions in the spirit of liberty; and 60,000,000 of people have shared in the joy and triumph of it!

It used to be said, and the charges have been repeated over and over again, that the people are incapable of managing their own affairs. A hundred years of such success that the record can be matched by no government under the sun, refutes the charge. Have the statesmen whom England has called into her service— her Peels, and Palmerstons, and Russells, and Disraelis, and Gladstones, and Salisburys—during the century just closed, gone straighter to the mark than those whom the suffrages of a democracy here in America have clothed with authority during the same time—her Washingtons, her Hamiltons, her Jeffersons, her Adamses, her Jacksons, her Marshalls, her Marcys, her Clays, her Websters, her Lincolns, her Grants, her Sumners? Did Italy know better what she wanted, even when she had for leaders such illustrious names as Victor Immanuel, and Garibaldi, and Cavour? Did Germany, back in the best days of the old Kaiser and of Bismarck, put our Western democracy to shame? Nay, verily.

It used to be charged, and the charge was the stock in trade of all who hated republics, that a government of the people and by the people, even though it might be honestly for the people, could not be made strong. A hundred years of unbroken self-government, in which every assault on the nation has been repelled, and every contest in which the nation has been engaged has been crowned with victory, meets this charge.

This survival of our government is not because our institutions and our policy have not been subjected to severe tests. On the contrary, we have been under terrific strains. Since the Constitution was set up, and Washington was inaugurated, we have had a war with England—God grant we may never have another—and a war with Mexico—in its spirit and purpose altogether to our shame, but overruled in the Divine Providence to the enlargement of the bounds of liberty—and a rebellion to suppress so gigantic that it shook the continent, and threw the trade and commerce of the world out of gear; but the people pressed their way through each war with foreign powers, and through the War of the Rebellion, from opening gun to the last echo of triumphant salute, with the directness and energy of a divine decree.

If democracy is so inherently weak, if the people are incapable of making a strong government, why did not England whip the United States in the War of 1812? Why did not Mexico send Scott and Taylor scampering back over the border and invade our capital, instead of having her own capital invaded and subdued? Why did not the great Rebellion succeed? Here were mighty sovereign states banded together and thoroughly organized—why did not these Confederate commonwealths break away from their allegiance to the republic, as the thirteen colonies broke away from their allegiance to the mother country? Simply because they could not do it. The people would not let them. The Constitution, which was thought to be only a "rope of sand," was found on trial to be a band of steel which disloyalty could not twist asunder. The grip of the people's hand, which it was thought would relax on the slightest touch, was found to be the grip of a vise. The answer the people gave to the gun which was fired on Fort Sumter was Appomattox, and when Grant, and Sherman, and Sheridan marched their victorious armies back to Washington, all the world knew that self-government is not the necessary synonym for weak government.

The simple fact is that self-government, from the nature of the case, is the strongest government it is possible to institute. Self-government has its basis in the common intelligence and in the common conviction of what is right. The people have ownership in self-government. It is a part of themselves. Its public buildings, its mints, its forts, its arsenals, its ships, its properties of whatever kind are their own. What other authorities on the globe would dare to trust everything to the good judgment and fidelity of the people, as the authorities of this nation do? Here we are, 60,000,000 of us, filling up the vast space which stretches away from the Atlantic to the Pacific, and from the lakes to the gulf, possessing an area, including Alaska, of more than three and one-half millions of square miles, with our local pride and prejudice, and with our varied and often diverse interests, yet we have only about twenty-five thousand soldiers all told, or one soldier to 2,400 citizens. In Italy, almost hopelessly burdened with debt, they think they must have one soldier to each group of eighty citizens. Think how much this one fact means in the way of lessened restraints on individual movements, of lessened drain on industry in the way of taxes, and of increase in the energy which goes into the development of material resources and the promotion of the general welfare. It is because the government is ours, and we administer it.

At the same time, under our Constitution, and with the spirit of loyalty which is in all hearts, that little army of 25,000 men symbolizes all the force resident in 60,000,000 of people. In an emergency calling for it, all the force there is resident in 60,000,000 of people would be available for defense. It is because the people are intelligently self-respecting. It is because the people cherish free institutions and are bound they shall be maintained. It is because the flag of the republic is their flag, and they will not permit it to be trailed in the dust nor dishonored.

What would the Sultan of Turkey, the Czar of Russia, the Emperor of Austria, the Kaiser of Germany give, or rather what would each of these sovereigns not give, for a loyalty and a strength like this? How long would some of the provinces and states over which these rulers wield their sceptres, which are literally rods of iron, abide in their allegiance if the grip of autocratic power were to be relaxed? But why does not California break away from the Union? Why does not Louisiana? Or Florida? Or New York? Or Minnesota? Neither of them wants to do it. Neither of them could do so, even if she wished it; but neither of them wants to do it. This government rests upon a firm foundation, for it rests on the confidence and affection of the people. It is impossible to organize a government on a firmer basis. The great republic takes its place beside the great monarchies in the consciousness of a strength, to say nothing of the general thrift and happiness, of which not one of them all can boast.

Not mere dreamers then are those who dream of self-government, and who love and fondly cherish the idea of liberty regulated by law. Their aspirations are of God, and they have immortal basis in the constitution of men. Everywhere, the wide world over, be it in the heart of Africa, or far-away Japan, or China, or India, or in the European States, or in the Canadas, or Mexico, or South America, wherever men toil unrequited, or bow to injustice, or feel the irksome limitations of tradition and caste and custom, let them dream on and hope on; for though their vision tarry it shall come by and by, and man shall enter into his heritage and be a man, one exercising his rights with due regard to the rights of others—be the master of his own activities. One by one the kings shall lay aside their robes of purple, and throw down their sceptres, and retreat into the insignificance and obscurity the most of them deserve. One by one the old thrones, whose shadows have smitten the state like a curse of vengeance, shall topple to their fall, and be gathered up and exhibited as curious ancient relics in the museums. One by one the puny princes, and the princelings, and the aristocracies, save as they are aristocracies of culture and character and moral force, shall come to be reckoned in any other way than as co-partners with the people in the administration of government. Royal houses have had their uses in times past; there may be royal houses which have their uses still; but to one schooled under a regulated democracy, schooled in liberty, sovereigns who rule by no right but the right of birth, seem only so much rubbish to be gently removed. They will be. Man is coming. It is not alone for ourselves, but for all the world, our republic exists.

This, perhaps, is one of the largest services rendered to mankind by the success of our "holy experiment" in self-government. There is not a throne anywhere on the globe to-day which stands so secure as it would have done had it not been for the great republic. There is not an aristocracy in existence whose assumptions are so arrogant, and whose prescriptive rights exercised with such a high hand, and whose treatment of the masses whose blood they suck for their own fattening, is so defiant as would have been the case had the United States never come into existence, had they gone to pieces under mismanagement, or jealousy, or mob-outbreak. There is not a group or class of honest toilers among any of the nations of Europe whose members do not front life with more possibilities and better prospects, in virtue of what the people of America have done to vindicate the manhood of man in this high business of self-government.

Our authorities have not been in the habit of intermeddling in the affairs of other people. We follow our own citizens and throw over them the protecting ægis of the government wherever they go, be it to Naples, or Vienna, or Constantinople, or Dublin, or the prison cells of Siberia, or the island of Samoa. Our merchants and our missionaries always feel that in case of emergency they have the tremendous force of their great nation behind them. But the influence of the republic on foreign powers and peoples does not come from the exercise of force, nor from the intervention of sharpness and cunning. England, France, Germany, Russia, Austria, Italy, Turkey, never quite dare to trust each other out of sight, and it is an unaccustomed state of affairs when they do not have some delicate question of diplomacy on hand, or when some of these powers do not think they have occasion to file protests against what some or all of the others are doing or propose to do. What an everlasting torment to them is the question of the balance of power. How they have to watch Constantinople, and Egypt, and India! What a simple thing in the way of a misstep might precipitate France and Germany, or England and Russia, or Austria and Turkey into war!

The influence on the world of this nation, with its free institutions and its equal laws and its independent life, has other explanations. It comes from what the nation is. This is the secret of the uplifting might and of the encouragement which those who are not fortunate enough to share the privileges of a free form of government find when they turn their eyes upon the great republic. It is a city set on a hill. It is a light whose beams penetrate wherever there is sufficient intelligence to discriminate between just and unjust laws. There is no corner of civilization so remote that it is not reached and influenced by the splendor of this example of self-government. It is an argument for the equal rights and sovereignty of the people which cannot be overturned by any sophistries of selfish rulers, nor by any sneers of aristocracy. Brought into contrast with what is here experienced, the limitations of arbitrary power, and the burdens imposed by hereditary authority seem more hateful and unendurable. As Turkey is a great object lesson to the world in tyranny and indifference to the welfare of the people at large, so this republic of ours is a great object lesson to the world of what men can do in a state when left to the unobstructed management of their own affairs. The great republic is pioneering the world into self-government.

In view of all this, two grounds out of many for devout gratitude to Almighty God deserve special mention. One is the character of the men raised up to organize this nation and set the machinery of our government in motion. What men they were! How manifestly they were chosen of God to discharge this high and sacred function. Who that believes Abraham was called of God to fulfill a particular mission, or that Moses was singled out to discharge one of the highest duties ever devolved on a human being, or that Columbus was fitted and trained by a higher power for his work of discovery, or that Martin Luther was an agent of Providence for bringing about the Reformation, or that the Pilgrim Fathers were guided by a light borne in on them from behind the stones of Plymouth Rock, can question for a moment that George Washington was selected of God, and anointed with wisdom from on high, to lead this American people out into independence, and then to cement the bonds of unity, and give the nation, organized under a Constitution which Mr. Gladstone has called "the most remarkable work known to modern times to have been produced by human intellect, at a single stroke, so to speak, in its application to political affairs," its magnificent projection along the lines of liberty regulated by law. He had splendid co-laborers— Adams, Jefferson, Hamilton, Madison, Franklin, Sherman, Morris— but to this man, whom we justly call the Father of his Country, it was given to be the master-soul of them all; and the more we study him and gather up the details of his life and character, his trust in God, his integrity, his fidelity, his unselfishness, his patience, his courage, his quick vision of what the exigency called for, his unfailing wisdom, his sublime patriotism—the more we feel we have cause to recognize the goodness of God in the gift of him to the people in that supreme hour, when what he was and did would tell on the nation and on the world for all time to come.

The other special ground of gratitude to Almighty God, which it would be little short of a crime not to mention, is the inestimable privilege of life under our free institutions. Not till one goes abroad, and by actual experience and observation of the way things go in other countries, is it possible to appreciate to the full the advantages afforded under a republic. There is an openness, an outlook, a liberty to go and come at will, a wealth of opportunity, in the land of free institutions to be found nowhere else. There are not the disabilities one encounters in a system of society which is organized on the basis of caste; and one is not all the time running up against thrusting traditions. They only are masters who are made masters by the free suffrage of the people, and in the administration of law they must keep within the limits prescribed by law. Nowhere else on the face of the globe can men say with so much fitness and truth: "The lines are fallen unto me in pleasant places, and we have a goodly heritage." Under God it has all come to us through the foresight and the trials and the sacrifices of a long line of illustrious men, reaching down from the hour when the foot of the first brave settlers touched these American shores to this present moment, of whom the most radiant and commanding figure is— GEORGE WASHINGTON.

PROF. DAVID SWING.

AT CENTRAL MUSIC HALL.

Our fathers trusted in Thee.—Ps. XXII.: 4.

Our fathers must often have said to each other: "Those who shall be alive a hundred years from this time will see here a great nation." When the inauguration of Washington had taken place, and friends had scattered to their homes, many a white-haired man must have said: "I should love to see this republic a hundred years from now." It is our privilege at last to look down upon a hundred-year pageant. The past century makes a noble mountain whose summit is near the clouds, but from which height we can look down and take in a delightful or a thrilling landscape. We cannot, in an hour, note all the details of the picture. There are upon earth some hill-summits which overlook a city; heights upon which standing one can point out the sea, the harbor, the ships of war, the spires of cathedrals, the parliament houses, the parks of trees and flowers, the bridges over the canals or rivers, the monuments reared in memory of genius or of the heroes, but there is no eye that would not weary with work and tears before it could from this hundred-year mountain see and perceive fully all that lies in the great vale below. There is a limit to the eye and the ear. However great be the scene or the music, the senses at last sink and sigh out the complaint that infinity is too great for man. Thus to-day memory sinks before its task, and laments that it cannot hold infinity in its arms. Not in one glance can the mind see the riches of many generations.

The men who assembled to worship for an hour before they should proceed to inaugurate the first American President were great men, not for that time, but for any time. One cannot think of those signers of the Declaration, cannot name the Franklins, the Hamiltons, Jeffersons, Adamses, and Madisons, without feeling that there was something in the last half of the eighteenth century that was able to turn great minds along paths of great political usefulness.

After great minds are born into the world it is yet a question what paths they will select and pursue. Angelo was as great as Shakespeare or Lord Bacon, but he differed from them by living in a period which made him choose art as a calling. Thus Shakespeare was led into the drama. Literature in its many forms took possession of many Drydens, Goldsmiths, and Addisons, and made the seventeenth century restore and enlarge all the splendor of the classic states. France, England and Spain ruled the world in that period, and when to the English literary names one adds Cervantes, Fénelon, Bossuet, Molière, and Racine, one will see that that triple empire was literature and magnificence. The classic literature and arts had indeed returned, but they had come back only to prove over again that nations cannot live upon beauty alone. The millions must have better food than the books of Louis XIV. and Queen Elizabeth. All the Shakespeares and Racines and Addisons had failed to benefit mankind. The eighteenth century opened with its sky all clouded. When the next procession of great minds came they were not carrying in their hands only the dramas and poems of the ancients and the moderns, not the brush of Raffaelle and the chisel of Angelo, but the sublime emblems of the liberties of the people.

Those who have time to trace in the past the causes of final results can easily find what power had risen to make statesmen arise instead of artists and essayists. We have time only to look at results. We cannot go to find who put the seeds into the ground in the cold spring; we can only go in midsummer and look upon the wide open blossoms. Behold in the last half of the eighteenth century the plants of freedom in full bloom! Men and women by the thousands had set sail from the Netherlands, from France, from Germany, from England, to find in the New World the arena of a reasonable life.

The laws of poetry and art, the greatness of royal descent and of court etiquette, had declined rapidly under an uprising study of the laws of human welfare. The same pressure which was turning tens of thousands toward America was exerting its power upon literature and oratory, and as if by magic, Addison had disappeared to make room for Pitt and Burke; Goldsmith and Dryden had been quietly superseded by Benjamin Franklin and Alexander Hamilton. Even the Christian religion became a higher law of earthly life, and the clergyman had a musket, and often was the Bible draped with the flag of democracy.

Many royalists had indeed migrated thither, but by the law of natural selection the majority of those who came to America came to get what they had the least of at home. Royalty has never been a good traveler. Its home has been, for the most part, too adequate to make a new world either a necessity or a pleasure. The spirit of liberty passed over Europe and selected those who were kindred to itself, and thus the three millions who lived on the Atlantic coast one hundred years ago were either liberty-lovers out and out, or they were loyalists, who were willing to have homes 3,000 miles away from their king. The Puritans, the Dutch, the Virginians, the Quakers and the Huguenots had been away from Europe for one hundred years, and the new exiles that were landing each month soon learned liberty from those who had been born and reared in the New World.

Not many of the three millions had ever thought of forming an independent nation, but they had learned to think of relations of a fraternal kind. All were willing to think of England as the mother country; but when it became evident that England was not so much a mother as a heartless collector of taxes, the idea of independence grew rapidly. The thought went from a whisper to an open word, from an open word to a shout, from a shout to a battle, from the battle to the republic.

We can now see that there was in the last half of the eighteenth century a power that was making new forms of greatness, the greatness of political ideas and of political leaders. This new spirit of freedom touched France, but it came too suddenly, and found that that country had not been slowly fashioning any Franklins and Washingtons. The Americans had come chiefly from the land of Baconian reason, the French from the times of romance, gayety and ardent passions. When the fever of liberty touched America, her sons sat down and drew up a declaration as calm as the Sermon on the Mount and almost as truthful; but when the fever of freedom touched Paris, the men called wise were found to have no wisdom, philosophers were found to be madmen, and while our colonies had a slow and sure revolution, France had only a gigantic massacre. Paris had indeed no religion, but had she a religion, it, too, would have been one of passion and insanity like that of the Turks under Mahomet IV. It will not do to ascribe all of the bloodshed of Paris to the atheism of the leaders, for the memory does not forget that Paris was the city in which 50,000 citizens were murdered in one night in the name of the Christian religion. Two reigns of terror blacken the memory of France: One was in the name of atheism, but the more dreadful was in the name of a Christian creed. What our nation should bless God for to-day is that our one hundred years came up from minds calm and thoughtful, and not from the fanatics who murder first, and thus exhaust the only force they possess—that of passion. The French could not do in one summer what our colonists had been meditating over and experimenting upon for more than a hundred and fifty years.

The founding of our nation was not merely a religious act: it was also the most intellectual movement of any epoch. Many forms of Christianity came, and each was intolerant toward the other; but this hostility was satisfied if only some geographical line was drawn between the sects. Those lines were like our state or county lines—not harmful to national business. The Pilgrim Fathers sailed for Virginia, but were compelled to land and settle at Plymouth. The Quakers, who came afterward, were expelled, and thus came the founding of Pennsylvania and Philadelphia. As soon as Roger Williams began to teach the equality of all honest Christian beliefs, he and his followers were expelled from the Massachusetts district, and thus came Rhode Island. All of the odds and ends of religious belief drifted to Rhode Island, and led Cotton Mather to say that Rhode Island possessed everything except " Roman Catholics and Christians." Meanwhile the Dutch were concentrating in New York Bay, and were buying land of all the early settlements; this was the least religious and the most purely commercial effort. Henry Hudson taught the Indians to drink rum. The first master of the Dutch settlement bought of the Indian chief the whole district of Manhattan for $24. The name Manhattan means " the place of drunkenness," but so vague is a word that this term does not tell us who was most frequently drunk—the white man or the Indian. In those long and slow years the Carolinas contained many exiles from France, and Virginia belonged rather to the aristocracy of England. So broken up were power and opinion that little New Haven and Plymouth were independent republics as to each other.

Thus religions and political ideas lay along the Atlantic like the patches of grains, trees, and grass on the English hillsides. But the wars with the Indians compelled these patches of white opinion to become one against the tomahawks and arrows of Indian opinion, and for 150 years the early lines continued fading, and New England and New York, Pennsylvania, Virginia, and the Carolinas were imperceptibly blending into one nation.

From whatever point of Europe the colonists had come, they had come in the name of a few ideas, which led the Swedes, the Germans, the French, the English, along one general highway of thought. The document which the Pilgrims drew up and signed in the Mayflower were the words which all the heterogeneous crowd would have signed at any time in the seventeenth or eighteenth centuries. These words: "We do by these presents solemnly and mutually, in the presence of God and of each other, covenant and combine ourselves into a civil body politic for our better ordering and preservation, and furtherance of the ends aforesaid; and by virtue hereof to enact, constitute, and frame such just and equal laws, acts, constitutions, and offices, from time to time, as shall be thought most meet and convenient for the general good of the colony, unto which we promise all due submission and obedience," would have formed the written basis of all those ship loads, but those forty-one men who signed that document signed for the whole of two centuries before Washington, and for the vast nation and multitude of to-day.

What a picture would that be could our times replace that ship upon the Atlantic and permit us all to look into that cabin and see those exiles sitting in conference over the kind of paper which should guide their conduct when they reached the land of their noble dreams. The Mayflower needed no steam-engine, for a vessel carrying men who were meditating on the founding of a free state should not hurry over the waves—the sails were rapid enough. Men having upon their minds so great a problem need nothing so much as the solitude and leisure of the ocean. The ship sailed for sixty-five days, but the speed was not too slow; the little ship was carrying a continent and a republic. It contained the destiny of sixty millions. In that wonderful patchwork of ideas a religious patch was always visible in the fabric. Reliance was divided equally between the militia and Divine Providence, and when war had begun at Boston, and Washington had only a ton of powder, and when his recruits were deserting by hundreds, his heart had to rest for months in Divine Providence alone. In one instance the General had to endure the heart-breaking picture of eight militia regiments flying before seventy British soldiers. This was Sept. 13, 1776, in the opening days of the long war.

Benjamin Franklin had, in his early life, made great sport of the clergy, and to avoid trouble for his opinions he went to New York and then to Philadelphia, where speech was more free; but Franklin remained quite true to the common faith in a divine hand as the chief reliance. When the Continental Congress was called in the Quaker town the opening service was read from the Episcopal Book of Common Prayer, thus revealing the fact that, as many colonies had combined for one liberty, so many creeds had met together in one God of men and of nations. That which bound Pennsylvania to Massachusetts in politics bound them also in religion, and thus the year which inaugurated Washington was the year which saw Puritan and Episcopalian and Quaker blend into one. Then came not only a union of states, but a union of sanctuaries. Christians were made brothers at the altar by being made brothers in the battle-field. On the day in which thirteen colonies became one country, thirteen creeds became one religion. Our Christian brotherhood began in the union of colonies. All that power of all forms which now comes up before our minds at the mention of the word "America," is here to-day simply because thought or knowledge is power. The new thought and new wisdom which in the seventeenth and eighteenth centuries were rapidly springing up in a new and vast continent were the hope of England, but to secure that hope all this western power must be laid at the feet of England. America must be nothing but England's great farm. For more than one hundred years the colonies were forbidden to manufacture anything. Premiums were paid to colonists, but they must manufacture nothing. England offered to supply slaves that the farm work might be done by a cheap proxy. Queen Elizabeth was a partner in a company for supplying the colonies with slaves. The succeeding rulers of England took up the dreadful business where death made Elizabeth let it fall. Charles II. renewed all slave charters; the Duke of York was president of a vast slave-stealing company, and in 1713 England secured from the other empires the monopoly of this trade, and at the time of Washington's inauguration England had stolen from Africa 1,500,000 of negroes, 200,000 of whom had died of suffocation in the holds of the ships that were tossing about between Africa and the American coast.

Thus England was preparing America to be her agricultural continent. It must secure all its manufactured articles from England, and must export its cotton and products only to her. It must buy its imports of only English ships. The colonies were forbidden to buy tea of a Dutch or Spanish ship. The women of the colonies were so aroused that they quit the drinking of tea. At last the long and unlimited despotism ended when fifty Boston-made Indians ran down with a gay war-whoop, and boarding a British vessel emptied its cargo of tea into the Atlantic in the sight of five or six thousand spectators. In each of these crises some colony would appoint a day of prayer. Sometimes it was Virginia, sometimes it was Carolina, sometimes it was New England that hurried to God's house. Two years before the war began the Virginia House of Burgesses resolved that the wrongs done any one colony must be considered as a wrong done to all. Thus were the seeds of union sown.

Thus for five generations did power of mind, of soul, of wealth, of a broad and free religion, accumulate on this side of the sea. England demanded that every ship that sailed should transfer to the foreign throne all the proceeds of this New World. The slow reaction against this process of beggaring a continent to enrich a foreign island was what was called at last the War of the Revolution. That event came slowly out of the reflection and wrongs of the entire colonial past.

A few of the greatest Englishmen declared in Parliament that the English despotism must end in war and in separation of the colonies from the mother country. William Pitt left his sick room to raise his voice once more in Parliament, and among his eloquent words came this sentence: "I have read Thucydides, and have studied and admired the master states of the world, and I must declare that for solidity, force of sagacity, and wisdom of conclusion, under such a complication of different circumstances, no nation or body of men stand in advance of the General Congress at Philadelphia. All attempts to impose despotism upon such men will be vain. We shall be forced ultimately to retract. Let us retract while we can, not when we must." His words were unheeded, for the English kings and aristocrats had been so long accustomed to ruling what they called a rabble that no new difficulty was to be feared in the weak colonists over the deep. Burke said: "England has so long sheared sheep that she thinks now to shear a wolf ·is the same task." King George, instead of doubling his wisdom, only doubled his wrath, and thus came those battles which raged along the Atlantic coast a hundred years ago. The sins of

England were mountain high, and therefore the colonial armies marched and toiled in the name of snow-white justice.

Wonderful scene! The hurrying home of Americans in London, the final call of Franklin upon Edmund Burke, the words of Franklin to Burke, that now England would lose her thirteen colonies; the journey of Washington to take charge of the volunteers around Boston; the daily practice of the militia; the raising of the new flag, the stripes without any stars; the councils held in France to plan some outcome for the New World; the secret councils in Spain for opposing England and aiding America; the efforts of the Dutch to retain their New Amsterdam for traffic; the inflamed zeal of American religion; the gigantic spirit of the whole world's new era, combine to make a page in history which has not often come in the checkered life of our race.

The impressiveness of the far-off scene lies as much in its material desolation as in its spiritual beauty. Our liberties were like a beautiful flower struggling to live in a desert or among rude trampling brutes.

Our recent Generals—Grant, Sherman, and even the Confederate Gen. Lee, suffered no such long drawn-out adversity as attended Washington for seven long years. His army often melted away by desertion more rapidly than it grew by enlistment. In a little skirmish in which he lost four men, two of them had frozen to death on the way to battle. Some regiments were shoeless and almost foodless. In one regiment of six or seven hundred, only ninety men had guns, and only seven guns had bayonets. Washington on one occasion cried over the dead on his battle-field. Every detail pointed toward tears. The ragged clothing, the bare feet, the poor weapons, the poor food, the long-delayed pay, the long absence from home, and then death; these formed a composition that made Washington weep.

So poor were the colonies, so hidden the outcome, that the money paid the soldiers was only printed slips of paper, and so worthless that a pair of shoes could not be bought for less than one hundred dollars. When we remember that Washington was about forty-four years old, in life's prime, fond of the pleasures of the world, an athlete, fond of the hunt and the chase, that he led that forlorn army for seven years, for six years never took time to make a visit to his estate at Mount Vernon, worked without pay, endured the constant distrust of many and the abuse of many, the memory winds up by bringing us into the presence of a moral hero who had escaped from fiction to live in a blessed reality. Three great objects gave us our liberties: France, Washington, and God.

France poured new troops and money around the American hero, the hero re-inspired his faithful soldiers, God held Washington and his army, America and France in the hollow of His hand. Ireland, France, Spain, and India all combined to draw from England's resources and mock her pride. Reading the signs of the times Washington hurried by day and night in his investment of New York, and in one month after this final marching of our little army began the British army surrendered, and England was conquered and our country was free.

Thus out of that poverty, those rags, the ashes which King George derided, came this Cinderella of Liberty, more beautiful in the reality than she was in the old classic legend, or in the modern story. What changes have come! Our state alone is greater than were all the colonies in those far off years. Our state could fight out in three months that battle of the Revolution; not only because of our material resources, but also because the ideas which lay in those early soldiers as only a vague hope lie in the minds of the present as propositions all wrought out. Washington had to fight in dark clouds, we live in the open sunlight of truth.

Our botanists can show us a little black seed out of which a marvelous cluster of flowers will come in a brief summer-time, a cobaca-seed whose vines and blossoms will decorate a whole wall; history can surpass the botanist, for it can point to a little germ of freedom, which, planted by loving hands, has spread over a continent, covering many states and territories with its lace-work of leaves and flowers.

In that olden time, at each crisis, in each hour of success and calamity, some one ran to each church-bell and rang it with energy by day or night. In trouble men sought God in their weakness; in success they went to Him with their joy. Shall our magnificent age do less? No! Let the Union of the States be perpetual—perpetual also the Union of the States and the merciful God!

THE REV. J. P. BRUSHINGHAM.

AT THE ADA ST. M. E. CHURCH.

I will read two scriptural passages, more as mottoes for an address than as a text for a sermon, viz: Joshua iv.: 21, "What mean these stones?" 1 Samuel vii.: 12, "Hitherto hath the Lord helped us."

The highest monument in the world except the Eiffel Tower, erected for the Paris Exposition, is the Washington Monument, a marble obelisk 555 feet high, in memory of the first President of the United States. Upon this 30th day of April, 1889, the American people lay the foundation of another monument to the memory of their Washington which shall be more enduring than bronze or marble, for it will be the expression of heartfelt thanksgiving and appreciation upon the part of a truly grateful people. There has been a wish expressed in several directions that the date of our presidential inauguration be changed from March 4 to April 30, in order that we might thus be reminded every four years of that great day in the beginning of our constitutional life as a nation. The most lasting memorial to Washington and the Centennial will be built up in the hearts of a grateful people who have learned to love constitutional freedom.

The name of Washington has grown with our growth, and strengthened with our years. History is the power that makes or destroys human fame. Washington has stood the test of history and the flight of years. When the rosy-cheeked children of generations to come shall say to the gray-haired fathers, as they did in ancient Israel, What mean these stones this memorial day? the answer shall come like the sweet sound of distant waters, "Hitherto hath the Lord helped us."

1. We learn from this Centennial of Washington's inauguration a lesson of patience. When we think of a struggle for freedom, protracted through eight weary years against overwhelming odds, and brought to ultimate victory, although Washington was often urged to give up the contest, we indeed marvel. Gen. Grant —he had all things in his favor; almost unlimited resources. It was with him only a question of time and courage and well-directed force. In the Revolutionary struggle it was a question of faith and patience. Washington had literally to weary Great Britain from sending troops to America.

Think of that convention in Philadelphia over which Washington presided, which framed our Constitution, sitting for five long months with closed doors and producing one of the most notable written documents the world has ever seen. Our nation lives in the sunlight of a glorious century of constitutional self-government and Anglican liberty because Almighty God has worked through the painstaking brains of Alexander Hamilton, Thomas Jefferson, James Madison and the other men of those times who were determined at any cost to draft a Constitution that would stand the test of time. I hope the American people will learn the lesson of patient thoroughness.

If the Old World has taunted us with anything justly in our own day, it is with superficiality in our work. Young friends, let us lay the foundation of mental and moral progress broad and deep and strong. Be patient and persistent with yourselves and with your life work. Be patient with your reforms. All great reformation is of slow growth. If our country is not what we would like it to be, let us say by the grace of God it shall be what it ought to be. Every foe shall be subdued. The slave power has fallen before the uplifted hand of retributive justice; the doom of alcoholism is sealed. Washington suppressed the whisky rebellion in Pennsylvania. An aroused public conscience will suppress another and more wide-spread liquor conspiracy, whose lines of power run through the entire web and woof of our social, economic and governmental fabric.

2. Another lesson from Washington and the Centennial is the lesson of self-sacrificing patriotism. He loved his country not in word simply, but in deed; he not only served as Commander-in-Chief of the Army without salary, but was ready to sacrifice his private fortune to the great cause of freedom. He refused to be crowned king, as did Cæsar at the Lupercal, but Washington refused with unfeigned sincerity. He stepped down from a greater than a kingly throne, the free ruler of a free people, in order to form a noble precedent for his native land. No greater magnanimity has been known in the history of the world. He sacrificed his personal preferences and personal friendships to the public good. Personally, his heart was melted toward Maj. André, the spy, who begged, not for his life, but for honorable execution; but loyalty to law, loyalty to the land he loved, triumphed over every other consideration.

At the close of the Revolutionary War, when difficulty arose between England and France, Washington was urged to take sides with the land of Lafayette; but however grateful he may have felt toward those who had helped us in a struggle for independence, he announced the great policy of America, no interference with foreign disputes and European warfare. As a soldier and statesman he felt that the interests of his own land must be guarded zealously first and always. Just as a father watches over his children, the eye of Washington was ever upon the thirteen original states. Napoleon's star of destiny was just rising when Washington's passed the horizon; but what a contrast! Napoleon had no equal as a military genius, but his hopes and ambitions all centered in self. Had he followed the example of Washington, he might have been loved at home and honored abroad as patriot, soldier and statesman.

Let the mammon-seeking, self-seeking, office-hunting tendency of our age, learn a lesson from that man who never sought an office, either civil or political. Said Daniel Webster at Bunker Hill Monument: "If our American institutions had done nothing more than furnish to the world the character of Washington, it would have entitled them to the respect of the world."

3. Another lesson suggested by this hour of patriotism is a lesson in religion, a lesson in Providence. Who doubts but that Washington was the child of Providence, that this entire nation has been divinely guided? It is said that this nation was born in the cabin of the Mayflower when the Pilgrim Fathers signed their memorable compact. But liberty does not spring full armed, like Minerva from the brow of Jupiter; liberty is a growth, its roots go back to the rise of the Italian free cities, to the Crusades which carried freedom to France and thence to England and thence to America. We must look back to the Magna Charta wrested from the hands of King John at Runnymede, to the translation of the Scriptures by John Wycliffe, to the invention of the printing press, and the Reformation of Luther. Liberty in church and state is a very long chain with many links forged in heaven.

The roots of American nationality go back to Leyden and Amsterdam, where the exiled Pilgrims prayed for liberty of conscience and freedom to worship God. Puritanism, notwithstanding early extravagances, is the back-bone of Republicanism. The great Virginian had an unfaltering trust in Providence throughout the long and painful struggle with England. He knew how to kneel in prayer at the birth-throes of a nation. In the hours of darkness and well-nigh of despair he knew the way to God. In the day of his triumph he did not forget to look thankfully to the God of all battles and of all victories.

As you hear the bells ringing this glad morning, remember that one hundred years ago the churches of the new nation were thronged with devout worshipers; remember that after President Washington was inaugurated in Federal Hall, the company immediately retired to church at high noon for divine worship; remember that about the first act of the new Congress was to appropriate money to print 20,000 copies of the King James version of the Bible. The roots of our liberties, therefore, reach down deep into the soil of faith in God. With the revival of patriotism may there come to us as a nation a deeper devotion and a holier, heart-felt faith.

It was commonly believed that Washington had a charmed life. An aged Indian chieftain came once to look upon the man whom he believed the Great Spirit shielded. He himself was detailed, together with other braves, for the specific work of taking Washton's life. Many carefully armed rifle shots failed to do the work at Monongahela. The aged Indian wished to fix his eyes upon the man whom he believed the Great Spirit shielded from well-aimed bullets. Superstition! No, *Providence.* So God will shield any nation who puts an unfaltering trust in Him. Said Garfield when Lincoln was assassinated: "God reigns and the government at Washington still lives." Yes, and it will live so long as we are true to our trust.

Under God we have crossed the threshold of the most magnificent century in the world's history. When Chancellor Livingstone opened the Bible at old Federal Hall, one hundred years ago, George Washington, having pressed the sacred page, threw back his august head and lifted up his eyes to heaven and said: "So help me God." Let that be our prayer for a century to come. The great man laid himself down to die at Mount Vernon and said: "I am not afraid to go."

> "His life was gentle, and the elements
> So mixed in him that nature might stand up
> And say to all the world, 'This was a man.'"

THE REV. H. W. THOMAS, D. D.

AT M'VICKER'S THEATRE.

Blessed is the nation whose God is the Lord.—Psalms xxxiii.: 12.

In the natural order of the affections, the love of self appears first. Then comes the larger love of home and friends, of language and literature, of laws and institutions. Over all these is lifted up the flag of a country, and hence, among the higher sentiments, patriotism must be regarded as the most noble. It is a part of religion.

In no other land should this sentiment be more soundly cherished than in this New World between the great oceans. We have just reached the close of the first hundred years of our national life. Many of the governments across the sea had perished, and the others were old and battle-worn long before this continent was discovered. Here, one hundred years ago, our fathers fought for freedom, and in prayers and tears and blood they laid the foundations for the first and best government on earth; a home to which the poor and the oppressed millions of the over-crowded countries of the Old World might come and enjoy the priceless blessings of civil and religious liberty; and here upon these foundations we and the coming generations should proudly go on and complete the noble structure, the ideal democracy in which all these many peoples and languages and religions shall in the ages to come be one great free nation, with one flag, the "Stars and Stripes," and one religion, the love of God and man.

And hence no apology is needed for bringing such a subject into the pulpit on this Sabbath, so near our National Centennial. The people in this land are wise in emphasizing such an event as an occasion for thanksgiving and patriotic enthusiasm. There is little danger of going too far, or of transcending the grandeur and the importance of our country's possibilities and welfare; but we may easily fail to appreciate our privileges and responsibilities.

Each to-day is the child of some yesterday. We can understand the present of any time only by knowing the past out of which it has come, and hence history is the great teacher in human affairs. But the events of the world are so closely related that history cannot well be studied in isolated periods, and hence the history of our country must be studied as the continuation under new conditions or as the outgrowth of the history of the countries of Europe.

One of the strange facts of our world is that this great continent should have remained so long unknown; that the civilization of Egypt, and Babylon, and Greece, and Rome should have come and gone, and Christ should have lived and died nearly fifteen centuries before this Western world was discovered. It is true that traces of an extinct race, higher than the savage tribes, still exist; but the continent was not discovered until the ships of Columbus reached the West Indies, only 400 years ago.

That we may have a clear outline view of our country, let us first trace some of the progressive steps by which we have come to be the owners of so large a part of this New World. Taking the discoverers in their order, the Spanish were the first: Columbus discovered the island of San Salvador in 1492, and took possession in the name of Spain. Ponce de Leon discovered Florida upon an Easter Day in 1512, and, finding the land covered with flowers, he called it Florida. De Soto discovered the Mississippi River, 1541. Cortez, with a little army, landed upon the coast of Mexico in 1521, and, pressing his way inland, conquered the country and annexed it to Spain.

Five years after the discovery of the West Indies by Columbus, or in 1497, the Cabots discovered the eastern coast of North America, and took possession in the name of England.

The French were a little later, but succeeded in acquiring vast possessions. Verrazzano explored the coast of Nova Scotia. Then came others along the St. Lawrence River and the region now occupied by Canada. La Salle followed the great lakes, crossed over the region now known as Michigan and Wisconsin to the shores of the upper Mississippi, and sailed down that river to the Gulf of Mexico. This was in the year 1682, and he took all this vast region over which he had passed in the name of France, calling it the Province of Louisiana. Of course Spain had a prior right of possession to part of it, but this was not known to La Salle.

And thus we see that what is now our country was at first held by three great nations of Europe. England claimed the eastern coast from Maine to Florida, and, English-like, claimed and wanted the whole continent; but Spain had a right to Mexico and Florida and all the great Southwest territory reaching on to the Pacific Ocean. And the French had the two great rivers, the St. Lawrence and the Mississippi, from their source to their outlets, including the great chain of lakes lying between; and under the name of the Province of Louisiana claimed what is now Louisiana, Arkansas, Missouri, Ohio, Indiana, Illinois, Michigan, Wisconsin, Iowa, Minnesota, Nebraska, Colorado, Oregon, and the Territories of Dakota, Wyoming, Montana, Idaho, Washington and the Indian Territory.

These different countries made settlements. The Spanish were the first, settling the town of St. Augustine, Fla., 1565, the oldest town in America. Sir Walter Raleigh attempted settlements in Virginia in 1587, but failed; and the first permanent English settlement was that of Jamestown in the year 1607. The Dutch settled New York in 1614, calling it New Amsterdam. The Pilgrims landed at Plymouth in 1620, and the same year the Swedes settled in New Jersey. The French settled Detroit in 1670, and a few years later established towns and settlements in Arkansas, Alabama and Mississippi.

And now comes the later history of the contests for the final possession of all these great regions.

At the close of the long French and Indian War in 1763, France ceded to Spain all of the Province of Louisiana west of the Mississippi River; and then ceded to England the territory east of the Mississippi, Ohio, Indiana, Illinois, Michigan and Wisconsin. In the year 1800, the Province of Louisiana on the west of the Mississippi River was receded by the Spanish to the French. In 1803, Napoleon I. sold all this vast region to the United States.

We have seen that Cortez conquered Mexico in 1521; but after being under Spanish rule for just 300 years, or in 1821, Mexico revolted and gained her liberty, and became known as the United States of Mexico. In 1836, Texas revolted against the United States of Mexico, and formed the Republic of Texas, and was admitted to the United States of America in 1845. Out of a question of boundary grew the Mexican War; and in the treaty of peace Mexico ceded to this country the old Spanish possessions, or California, Utah, Arizona and New Mexico. In 1867, we bought Alaska from Russia—a country one-sixth as large as the whole United States—for over $7,000,000.

These were the great changes by which the vast territory of this country has passed from the possession of different governments to that of one. How different our history might have been had France and Spain held their vast possessions here! We should have then, as East and West, North and South, been the subjects of different nations; and instead of the American Revolution that gave us independence, we should have been part of the French Revolution. And upon this continent, as in Europe, England and France and Spain would have lain side by side with their great armies to protect their borders.

It was only fifteen years after the nine years of the French and Indian War that settled the division of the territory of the continent, that the War of the Revolution began. This was a war of the colonies against the mother country; first, by Massachusetts to resist oppression, and then joined by all the colonies in the heroic struggle for independence. There never was a cause more just than that of the colonies. There never was a more unequal contest. The whole population of the thirteen colonies was not over three millions; they were poor; they had no ships of war, while England was mistress of the seas; they had imperfect arms and but little ammunition, and what was worse, they had no government. Only a number of colonies with a Congress that had no power to levy troops or raise money; and with all this there was a divided sentiment; a large number of the population were opposed to the Revolution and others were half-hearted in its support.

Washington, who led the forces, could not risk an aggressive policy; he could not let his own people know how poorly his army was supplied; he could only harass the enemy and wait for favorable opportunities to gain quick victories. Never was there better generalship; never a more patient and suffering army. But with all this, the independence of America could never have been won without the help of France. If American independence be a blessing to the world, then the world owes a just debt to Lafayette and the French people. France sent ship loads of muskets and cannon and men and ammunition; and France acknowledged our independence when the chances of success seemed so doubtful. Alas! soon poor France herself was in the dreadful agonies of revolution, and soon in deadly conflict with England.

Our independence gained, the next step was the formation of a national government. No one saw the need of this more than Washington, for he had felt the weakness of the colonial administration in the time of the Revolution. The feeble colonies were poor and burdened with debt; the divided sentiment was not yet united; the ideas of state sovereignty were even then present and strong. The convention called to prepare a Constitution labored long and hard; slavery and state sovereignty were the difficulties to be met and overcome: the one by compromise, the other by the nearest approach to an ideal government ever devised by man—the autonomy of the states and the union of all in one nation. We copied our flag from the blue sky and the bright stars, and we modeled our Constitution after the order of the solar system; the sun in the center and the planets in their orbits; the Constitution supreme in its national sovereignty, and the states free in their separate spheres, but all united in the indissoluble bonds and the eternal strength of the Union.

Another question to be met was that of religious liberty, and upon this point the framers of the Constitution ventured upon new ground, and showed a courage and a far-sighted wisdom and statesmanship that must forever challenge the gratitude of freemen. For 1,400 years, or since the days of Constantine, the church, through all its vicissitudes, had been in some way related to and dependent upon the state. In Catholic countries the Popes had often dictated to the kings; in Protestant Germany and England the church and state were united. The doctrine of the divine sovereignty of kings carried with it the associate thought of the sovereignty of the church. If the state could not be trusted to the people neither could the church. But here in this New World our fathers broke away from the precedents of the Old World in both; they said: "The people are the rulers in civil affairs, and the people shall be kings and priests unto God in religion. The state and the church shall forever be separate; Congress shall pass no laws to bind the conscience of any in matters of belief and worship."

It was a tremendous venture of faith and courage to trust all the precious interests of government and religion to the reason and the conscience of the people; but a hundred years ago our fathers stepped out boldly upon that broad platform of the civil and religious rights of man, and time has justified the wisdom of their decision. Naturally enough, with this broad doctrine of the National Constitution, the states became conservative, and some of them passed severe laws against heresy. Virginia long carried a statute making the denial of the Trinity an offense punishable by fines and three years' imprisonment; and one of the New England states made it a criminal offense not to believe in the infallibility of the Bible and a vicarious atonement. But time has modified this severity, and we should all rejoice that an earnest, zealous concern has from the first been felt for the religious welfare of this land.

And now, who were the people of those days—the fathers and mothers of the Revolution—and the founders of this great government? They were a prepared people, a people fitted for such responsibilities and sufferings by the experiences of their ancestors in the countries of Europe. They had back of them the tremendous events of the Reformation and the struggles for religious liberty. The Puritans were fresh from the scenes of the Commonwealth under Cromwell, and the persecutions and banishments that followed. The Dutch had back of them the bloody scenes of the Netherlands and the cruelties of Philip the Second. The Huguenots had not forgotten Louis IX. and the awful massacres in France; and the Swedes had given their fairest sons and great king, Gustavus Adolphus, to save Germany in the darkest days of the "Thirty-years' War." A hundred scholars from the universities of Cambridge and Oxford helped lay the foundations of the early New England settlements.

The progress of the United States in all lines has been a part of the progress of the greatest century the world has ever seen; only we have been more favorably situated to reap its larger results. Unhindered by precedents and constitutions, we started as a nation upon the highway of liberty; the compromise with slavery, of 1776, was settled by the crisis of 1860–'63. Our free, wide territory has invited and welcomed emigration from all lands, and from 3,000,000 a hundred years ago, our population has increased to 60,000,000. The growth of all forms of industry and the increase of wealth have been almost fabulous. Cities have risen up like the creations of magic; enough miles of railroad have been built in this country to reach five times around the earth. It takes 30,000 tons of twine each year to bind the rich sheaves that fall from the reapers that harvest our great fields of grain, enough in length to go around the earth 2,463 times. It is said that the aggregate wealth of this country in 1880 was $43,642,000,000; more than that of the Russian and Turkish empires, and the kingdoms of Sweden and Denmark,

Norway, Italy, South Africa, Australia, South America; and that our wealth exceeds that of Great Britain by $276,000,000. In no land in the world are the people so well fed and clothed and housed. We waste more in this country than the poor of some countries in Europe consume.

And not only in material progress have we advanced so rapidly; we have shared riches in the great world-growth of knowledge; we have built up a mighty system of popular education, of common schools; we have built and endowed hundreds of colleges and universities; we have given scholars, authors, inventors, explorers, travelers, statesmen, warriors, philanthropists, and, best of all, we have honored industry, exalted the home, and crowned wifehood and motherhood; we have crowned woman as queen.

We are not yet perfect; our principles are better than our practice; our theory of government is better than our politics; with our religious liberty and our many sects, half the people are without church homes. The poor in our great cities are crowded into miserable tenements; the criminal classes are increasing, and thousands of neglected children are growing up in ignorance and vice. There is much to do in all the higher directions. We are in one of the world's great transition periods, and it seems as if God had reserved this New World as the stage for the greatest drama of all time. Here, better than anywhere else, can the struggles for the higher equalities of liberty and justice and equal rights in all the great questions of labor and capital find their solution. Here is the field for universal education; and here let church and state remain separate, and the reason and conscience of all be free in the great questions of religion; and here may our public schools be kept forever free from the suspicion even of political or sectarian interference.

"Blessed is the land whose God is the Lord," the land that has the most exalted conception of God, the highest ideal of truth and justice and love, and the profoundest reverence for the good and the right. The higher realizations have not yet come; our world has hardly dreamed of the goodness and the greatness of God, and the possibilities of man as the child of God. Here let us exalt liberty and justice and truth and righteousness, and over all lift higher the flag of union and brotherhood. And beneath all and above all be the ever-precious Cross of Christ, the symbol of suffering, the pledge of victory, the star of hope, and the crown of day.

MR. J. H. McVICKER.

AT THE PEOPLE'S CHURCH.

We are assembled to give our thoughts to those who planted the seed of the harvest of blessings our country is now enjoying, and, so far as in our power lies, to voice the same in praise of the glorious achievements of the giant minds which formed for man a government surpassed only by that whereby the universe is guided and all God's creatures shown the way to happiness.

The inauguration of Washington as the first President of the United States crowned the efforts of men who had built better than they knew, and whose labor, when ended, did not meet with the favor which exists for it now, after the trial of a century. It was the magnetic influence of a military hero's name—he who was first in war, first in peace, and first in the hearts of his countrymen —which held together all factions and discontents until reason took her seat and blended the thirteen into one.

While lauding our forefathers for the blessing they bestowed upon us, let us not fall into the error of believing we have nothing to do for those who are to fill our places a century hence. The men America is honoring to-day did not monopolize all the good in the system they inaugurated, but left much to be done to perfect their work and to eradicate errors which could not be overcome in their day. It should be the work of the thinking men of the second century of American independence to review the past, and while applauding the good done by the contemporaries of Washington and their immediate followers, to ask if nothing has been left undone calculated to cause an unhealthy growth of that which may endanger all.

If we read the signs of the times, shall we not be prompted to be on our guard to prevent the leading sin of mortal life, selfishness, from fastening upon our nation and building up conditions which caused the downfall of ancient republics? The insidious workings of this mortal weakness, if not checked, will permeate the acts of our daily life; it will occupy the pews of our churches, while the pulpits will not be free from it; it will control the press; it will fill places of honor with those only who can buy them, and it will encourage deceit and falsehood in our business methods. At the beginning of our second century the progress of this sin is apparent; it is tending to lower and cheapen American citizenship; through it, and for its use, ignorance is placed on an equality with intelligence, and the welfare of the country is becoming secondary to party prosperity.

If we read the signs of the times and interpret them rightly, shall we not see that the time has come when the emblem of American citizenship should be in the hands only of those who can read and write the language of the nation, the foundation of which should be, henceforth and forever: intelligence, knowledge. "Ignorance is the curse of God; knowledge the wing wherewith we fly to heaven." While ours is the land of the free and the home of the brave, let us define what we mean by those words and make it plain that all who wish to share our blessings must do so as American citizens, having no rights and making no claim on account of birth or previous allegiance.

Having grown rich as a nation, let us not become indolent, careless and wasteful of our inheritance; there is much for us to do. As American citizens we can feel no pride in our municipal governments, which we conduct on political and not on business principles, permitting them to be the nurseries of wrong-doing, indirectly endorsing the fallacious doctrine that governments are instituted only for the material and commercial, and not for the moral welfare of the governed.

While from the evils nurtured in our municipalities we have reason to fear danger to our republican form of government, we seem to lack the courage to correct the error we all admit exists.

As church and state are happily separated in our land, by the action of those we are here to honor, so it should be our work to have municipal and national politics divorced. This is almost a universal belief, and when it becomes an American principle, and enforced, we shall be advancing in the scale of moral manhood, and be more worthy of the country we boast of.

Having freed our country from slavery in one sense, let us remember there is no form of it so abject as that which tends to blunt the intellect and dull the reasoning faculties. As theology loosens the shackles, politics must not be permitted to take them up and so use them as to degrade the unthinking many by making them the slaves and followers of the selfish few; we must be careful that Lincoln's words: "of the people—by the people—for the people," are not paraphrased and become—of, by, and for the politicians.

Here, in our home—in the valley of the great Northwest, where the star of empire is reclining, we must not be content with the material wealth which has been almost forced upon us, and do nothing—or but little—tending to guard the country we profess to love from the danger which Gov. Fifer, in his proclamation, so truthfully pointed to. The desire to build up an American aristocracy, by the concentration of great wealth in the hands of a few—so perceptible in our country—is creating a spirit of unrest and discontent with those whose labor assists in the production of wealth. This condition of affairs must not be left to contending classes for settlement, but should call forth the best efforts of the statesmen who desire to rank with those whom 60,000,000 of people are applauding to-day, as to the best way of meeting the issue with "justice to all and malice toward none." It is a work equal to that accomplished by our forefathers.

The great West inherited none of the jealousies and bickerings which preceded the day when Washington was inaugurated President, and which continued to linger and still strive to cling to life in certain sections, but circumstances have thrust upon it evils as great, and it now stands facing a duty as sacred as that which formed the colonies into a nation. It must not shrink from the work—its voice must be raised against selfishness and selfish sectionalism; against all selfish partyism; against all selfish state sovereigntyism; against all isms of a political nature which in any way tend against nationalism.

We have proved ourselves adepts in all matters tending to our material welfare; let us aim to create a desire for individuality in manhood, which when accompanied with free thought and independent action will become the bulwark of our safety.

While we are justly proud of our system of education, let us reason together and ask if we cannot do more for the people than we are doing without overtaxing those who have perhaps too much. Let us see if we cannot, in our municipalities, lop off non-essentials in our present methods and substitute those of practical value; let us ask if we cannot extend the use of our schoolhouses to parents as well as to children; not in the traditional way of teaching them that twice one is two, but in a system of instruction during the winter evenings which will entertain, while telling them how to live and how to guide their children into a manhood and womanhood which must tend to the moral advancement of the human race. The task is not beset with difficulties, and is in harmony with the nature of our form of government, which, while it cannot be paternal, has been, is, and can be more beneficent, and in more practical ways.

We shall not be able to make this an ideal world, as mortal mind is not prepared for it; but we can better its condition by studying the foibles of mankind and guiding them. Our frivolities will continue to exist and feed on unrealities; the love of pleasure is inherited in our nature, changing in degree from childhood, youth, manhood, and old age, and should not be left for selfishness to feed upon. It should be the aim of government to so guide it as to make it an offset to the asperities and bickerings of life.

Time will not permit of elaboration, but having glorified the past and pointed to work for the future, let us turn our thoughts to the blessings bestowed upon us, and ask which is the greatest that has come during the life of our country; let us look back upon the barbaric rocks of superstition, bigotry, and ignorance, and gaze on the great indentations made therein by liberal thought which has made its way through and from the dark ages, and now, under the banner of a new theology, is breaking down barriers and clearing a path for a better conception of God.

Of all that has come to man this is the greatest blessing of our century—on which there is no patent, no royalty; with which no monopoly can be formed—but free as the air, like which it comes to humanity to strengthen and to nourish. As our retrospective view makes bright the present, so the future is gilded with rays from the star of Hope lighting man's progress onward to the Creative Power of which he is a part.

THE REV. WILLIAM C. DeWITT.

AT ST. ANDREW'S PROTESTANT EPISCOPAL CHURCH.

Let the people praise Thee, O Lord; yea, let all the people praise Thee.
—PSALMS LXVII.: 5.

To-day is in the highest and best sense a civil holiday: the 100th Anniversary of the Inauguration of the first President of the United States. Throughout this broad land, in every state and territory, in every town and village of our great and glorious republic, the 60,000,000 of our American people are to-day alive to the appreciation of the fact that a century of constitutional government is completed, and that the United States of America, though young among the nations of the earth, is recognized as second to none in point of enterprise, wealth and all that goes to make up a prosperous and happy people. The history of the United States in this century past has been unique. No similar epoch in the history of any country, nation or government of the world affords a parallel instance of such rapid progress and development, coupled with stability and actual strength. When George Washington was inaugurated President of the United States ten decades ago he was the executive of less than four million people (about the number of the present inhabitants of this state). And they were a poor people whose resources had been almost drained in the struggle for freedom, for the rights of free men. Seventy-five postoffices were sufficient for the business of the nation, and less than two thousand miles of post routes were traveled by the carriers. To-day the accumulated wealth of the United States is more than $50,000,000,000; 55,000 postoffices are not sufficient to meet the demands of our domestic trade, nor 380,000 miles of post route. Thirty-eight thousand dollars was the postal revenue of the United States in Washington's first year; $50,000,000 in the year just closed. In 1789 Washington traveled from Mt. Vernon to New York by carriage, by boats, horseback and on foot. No such thing as a railroad was known. To-day about one hundred and fifty thousand miles of double steel make a net work from the Atlantic to the Pacific, and from the lakes to the gulf. Nearly one-half of the railroads of the world are in the United States.

These statistics are sufficient to indicate the tremendous rapidity of the growth of this nation which a century ago could obtain little foreign credit, had practically no home manufactories, and little capital to invest.

And let us now inquire into causes. The first that suggests itself to the mind is the natural resources of the country; its mines of gold, silver, iron, lead, copper and coal; its oil wells; its millions of square miles of fertile soil; in short, it is productive of almost everything that is necessary to the well-being and progress of the people. But Washington, in a letter to Lafayette, pointed out another cause. He said: "If I can form a plan for my own conduct, my endeavors shall be unremittingly exerted, even at the hazard of former fame or present popularity, to extricate my country from the embarrassments in which it is entangled through want of credit, and to establish a general system of policy, which, if pursued, will insure permanent felicity to the commonwealth. I think I see a path clear and direct as a ray of light which leads to the attainment of that object. *Nothing but harmony, honesty, industry and frugality* are necessary to make us a great and happy people." It may seem to the student of American history at first thought that the first of these essential characteristics, harmony, has not been especially manifest in our government during the past one hundred years. Even during the two terms of Washington's presidency there was anything but unanimity of opinion and cordiality of support on the part of Congress and the people. Unanimously elected, he was in some matters, like that of maintaining neutral relations with France and England, almost unanimously opposed. He was the victim of as bitter and ungrateful partisan assault as ever was heaped upon any honest man. He was called upon to put down, by force of arms, an insurrection that threatened for the time being the very existence of the new government. He was made to feel the danger of the jealousies that arose from the discussions of the rights of individual states as against the sovereignty of the general government. He saw the clouds of war rising from time to time over various sections of the new confederacy, while at no time during the eight years of his office was this country free from foreign entanglement. And the years that followed, even to the present day, are full of manifestations of apparent discord among the people. But, save in two or three instances, that discord has been rather apparent than real, a discord of opinion rather than of action, stopping short of a strife destructive to the common interests. Where there have been disagreements, there have usually been agreements to disagree, and the minority have quietly and honorably submitted to the will of the majority. The Constitution has been upheld, and the law of the land has been the people's rule of action. Differences of opinion, sometimes developing into bitter opposition, have been the result of sincere endeavor to further ends conceived to be conducive to the common weal.

The honesty of the people is in no better way evinced than by the growth of our national credit; the industry by the accumulated wealth of the nation, by our enormous and productive agricultural and manufacturing interests. It is not so easy to demonstrate the frugality of our citizens by present facts. But up to the beginning of the present generation it would hardly have been questioned. The prosperity of the present is the fruit of the frugality of our ancestors. It was Washington's expressed desire, when he relinquished the duties and honors of the chief magistracy of the United States, that he might retire to his Mount Vernon farm and devote himself to the pleasant duties of a rural life. He expected that he should never exceed a limit of twenty miles distance from his home. In those days, when only one-thirtieth of the populace lived in cities, there was not that superficiality and profligacy, nor the temptation toward it, that there is to-day, when nearly one-fourth of the inhabitants of the nation dwell in her cities, and when the pulse of national life seems to be at its maximum.

The chief natural causes, therefore, for the prosperity of the United States may be found in the natural resources of the ground, and in the harmony, honesty, industry and frugality of the people; and to these may be added the isolation of the states from the immediate proximity and influence of any considerable foreign power.

And yet no man who knows the weakness and fallibility of men can pause here and be satisfied with this catena of causation. We read the history of one hundred years of national life, we see events working together, a thousand effects converging to a central point to bring about an end often unforeseen, which in its turn joins with other secondary effects to cause a glorious culmination in national good. We thus look upon the United States as from a far off point in the heavens. We have a bird's-eye view of the expansion of empire. The events of a century are crowded into a day. We see the manifestation of a mighty physical and spiritual energy; and the harmony of action of a million constituent but various and often discordant parts, forces upon the mind the conviction of one over-ruling power and unseen source of energy. And so we are reminded of the words of our noble first President in his inaugural address. He said : "It would be peculiarly improper to omit in this first official act my fervent supplication to that Almighty Being who rules over the universe, who presides in the councils of nations, and whose providential aid can supply every human defect, that His benediction may consecrate to the liberties and happiness of the people of the United States, a government instituted by themselves for these essential purposes, and may enable every instrument employed in its administration to execute with success the functions allotted to his charge. In tendering this homage to the great Author of every public and private good, I assure myself that it expresses your sentiments not less than my own; nor those of my fellow-citizens at large less than either. No people can be found to acknowledge and adore the Invisible Hand which conducts the affairs of men more than the people of the United States. Every step by which they have advanced to the character of an independent nation seems to have been distinguished by some tokens of providential agency. And, in the important revolution just accomplished in the system of their united government, the tranquil deliberations and voluntary consent of so many distinct communities, from which the event has resulted, cannot be compared with the means by which most governments have been established, without some return of pious gratitude, along with an humble anticipation of the future blessings which the past seems to presage. These reflections, arising out of the present crisis, have forced themselves too strongly on my mind to be suppressed. You will join with me, I trust, in thinking that there are none under the influence of which the proceedings of a new and free government can more auspiciously commence."

If these reflections were so impressed upon the mind of Washington one hundred years ago, in the infancy, upon the very birthday of the republic, how ought they to come home to our minds to-day as we attempt to contemplate something of the grandeur of the estate of the youth into which that infant has developed!

Although freedom of religious belief and worship is guaranteed by our Constitution, the government is distinctly theistic, and has always been. The Declaration of Independence closes with these words: "And for the support of this declaration, with a firm reliance on the protection of Divine Providence, we mutually pledge to each other our lives, our fortunes, and our sacred honor." George Washington took the oath of office upon a Bible, and immediately thereafter, with both Houses of Congress, walked to St. Paul's Church, where they attended Divine services, solemnized by the Rt. Rev. Samuel Provost, Bishop of New York. The deliberations of Congress are preceded by an invocation of Divine blessing; the coin of the land bears the declaration: "In God we trust." We are, in brief, a God-fearing people. And in this fact reposes a source of strength and the first secret of prosperity: "Happy is that people whose God is the Lord." It is by His blessing that we are what we are to-day.

Godlessness in the United States is therefore not characteristic of the statesman or citizen in sympathy with the principles upon which the government was founded and in accordance with which the nation has prospered. It is eminently fitting that the President of the United States, the Governors of the individual states, the Mayors of the cities, and all officers in civil authority over our citizens, should in their various proclamations concerning this Centennial Anniversary recommend to the people as citizens that they should not neglect upon this day to render the devotion of grateful and trustful hearts to their country's God and Beneficent Guardian. Divine worship is, indeed, an essential part of the celebration of every civil holiday. No man can resolve himself into two men, the Sunday Christian and the week-day citizen. If he is a true man he is both at once, and always. He recognizes the rule of God in the ordinary affairs of his business, whether he be farmer, merchant, or statesman; and in contemplating such an event as that which we commemorate to-day, his mind turns not first to the fittingness of processions and popular speeches and pyrotechnics, suitable as they may be, but rather to the propriety of Divine worship. And he who is to-day unmindful of Him by whose beneficent providence we have become so great and happy a nation, but would rather ascribe the honor and praise to the genius of the people themselves, as the causal rather than the coöperative source of our national blessings, but echoes the words of Babylon's king of unhappy memory: "Is not this great Babylon that *I* have built for the house of the kingdom by the might of my power and for the honor of my majesty?" and calls to mind the reply of God which taught him that "the Most High ruleth in the kingdom of men."

Well may we rejoice to-day in our high privilege of citizenship of the United States of America; well may we call to mind and honor the memories of those who ordained with consummate wisdom the course of national progress, and laid the foundation upon which is securely built this wonder and glory of the age; but first of all we would pay by this our act of worship the devotion of grateful hearts, and with one accord ascribe unto Him to whom all honor is due, the only wise God our Saviour, glory and majesty, dominion and power, both now and ever, Amen.

MR. EPHRAIM BANNING.

AT THE EIGHTH PRESBYTERIAN CHURCH.

Notwithstanding occasional glimpses or flashes of light and sunshine, the nations of the Old World for many ages sat in darkness and gloom. The outgrowth of ignorance, bigotry, and superstition, this darkness, gathered through centuries, finally became so deep and impenetrable that it could only be broken through by fierce and deadly struggles, aided by the light of many martyr-burnings. It was in this way, and only in this way, that an entrance could be made for the life-giving light of liberty. But the fiercer grew the struggle the brighter and clearer shone the light, until its intensity and strength became so great that the Old World was found too contracted for the full exercise of its beautiful and powerful influence. Flashing across oceans of space, it then gave birth to the wonderful institutions of our own land, the most important of which we now declare, after one hundred years trial, to be the grandest and most benign government in the world.

After mentioning that "the settlement of New England was the result of the Reformation," Bancroft says: "A Genoese adventurer, discovering America, changed the commerce of the world; an obscure German, inventing the printing press, rendered possible the universal diffusion of increased intelligence; an Augustine monk, denouncing indulgences, introduced a schism in religion, and changed the foundations of European politics; a young French refugee, skilled alike in theology and civil law, in the duties of magistrates and the dialectics of religious controversy, entering the republic of Geneva, and conforming its ecclesiastical discipline to the principles of republican simplicity, established a party, of which Englishmen became members and New England the asylum. The enfranchisement of the mind from religious despotism led directly to inquiries into the nature of civil government; and the doctrine of popular liberty, which sheltered their infancy in the wildernesses of the newly-discovered continent, within the short space of two centuries, have infused themselves into the life-blood of every rising state" in the New World, and have disturbed all the ancient governments of Europe by awakening the public mind to resistless action.

The earnest, progressive character of the Pilgrims who came over in the Mayflower is well shown by the farewell charge of their leader at the time of their departure from the Old World, a charge which, it has been said, "breathed a freedom of opinion and an independence of authority such as then were hardly known in the world." "And so," in the words of one of their number, "lifting up our hands to each other, and our hearts for each other, and to the Lord our God, we departed."

Their departure is thus described by the historian: "The little band, not of resolute men only, but wives, some far gone in pregnancy, children, infants, a floating village, yet but 102 souls, went on board the single ship, which was hired only to convey them across the Atlantic; and on the 6th day of September, 1620, thirteen years after the first colonization of Virginia, two months before the concession of the Grand Charter of Plymouth, without any warrant from the sovereign of England, without any useful charter from a corporate body, the passengers in the Mayflower set sail for a new world, where the past could offer no favorable auguries. . . . The Pilgrims were Englishmen, Protestants, exiles for religion, men disciplined by misfortune, cultivated by opportunities for extensive observation, equal in rank as in rights, and bound by no code but that of religion or the public will."

Before landing they formed themselves into a body politic by a voluntary compact, in which they recited, among other things, that their voyage had been undertaken "for the glory of God and advancement of the Christian faith." This instrument was signed by the entire body, forty-one in number, who, with their families, constituted what has been called "the proper democracy;" and it has been referred to as "the birth of popular constitutional liberty." "As the Pilgrims landed, their institutions were already perfected. Democratic liberty and independent Christian worship at once existed in America."

To the heroism of these brave men and women, which hardly finds a parallel in all history, the country owes a debt of everlasting gratitude. Looking back from the eminence on which we now stand, can we fail to recognize this, and to be thankful for the precious heritage of such an ancestry? And particularly can we fail to recognize the Divine hand—the hand of the Master Workman—that then and there laid the foundation of our present greatness. In all this the guidance of Providence from the very beginning is clearly apparent. The Pilgrims did not come until everything was ripe for their arrival, or, in other words, until the fullness of time. Bancroft says: "Had New England been colonized immediately upon the discovery of the American continent, the English institutions would have been planted under the powerful influence of the Roman Catholic religion; had this settlement been made under Elizabeth, it would have been before activity of the popular mind in religion had conduced to a corresponding activity of mind in politics." In either case the result would certainly have been fatal to the future progress of our country.

Is it any wonder that a century and a half later the children of such a parentage should be found declaring that all men are, and of right ought to be, free and equal? Is it any wonder that, as the fathers braved unknown perils and hardships for the sake of civil and religious liberty, their children should afterward rise up in its defense? In their influence in molding the free institutions under which we now live, the great men of, and immediately following, the Revolutionary period stand next to the Pilgrims of the Mayflower. And it is our privilege to-day, as well as our duty, to be thankful for such men as Washington, Jefferson, Hamilton, and others who stood by them in the great struggle which made us a free people.

But after this second great crisis—the Revolutionary War—came another, not so generally appreciated in the popular mind, but none the less trying in its circumstances or important and far-reaching in its lasting influences. No matter how galling may have been the English yoke, little good could have resulted from simply casting it off. In such case, if nothing better had been provided, what real good, permanent good, would have been accomplished? The question of harmonizing the various and conflicting

interests of the colonies, and of devising a form of government satisfactory to all, and adapted to the wants of all, was a most difficult
and trying one. But, as on previous occasions, the men in charge
were equal to the emergency—to the great work assigned them.
Any one familiar with our early constitutional history cannot fail
to recognize in this a cause of most earnest and devout gratitude.

The history of our country during its first century of constitutional government, also shows at every point that we are a most
favored people—God's chosen people—to carry forward the great
work of civilizing and Christianizing the world. Our borders have
been enlarged and our population increased; from thirteen states
we have increased to forty-two; from some three million inhabitants to over sixty millions; and our general prosperity has been
without a parallel.

The present condition of our country, as compared with other
nations, may be thus stated, in the words of a recent writer:

"The old nations of the earth creep on at a snail's pace; the
republic thunders past with the rush of the express. The United
States, the growth of a single century, has already reached the
foremost rank among nations, and is destined soon to out-distance
all others in the race. In population, in wealth, in annual savings,
and in public credit; in freedom from debt, in agriculture, and in
manufactures, America already leads the civilized world.

"France, with her fertile plains and sunny skies, requires a
hundred and sixty years to grow two Frenchmen where one grew
before. Great Britain, whose rate of increase is greater than that
of any other European nation, takes seventy years to double her
population. The republic has repeatedly doubled hers in twenty-
five years. . . .

"Truly the republic is the Minerva of the nations; full armed has
she sprung from the brow of Jupiter Britain. The 13,000,000 of
Americans of 1830 have now increased to 56,000,000."

This same writer says that our country's wealth is not "altogether due to her enormous agricultural resources, as may at first
glance be thought, for all the world knows she is first in nations in
agriculture. It is largely attributable to her manufacturing industries, for, as all the world does not know, she, and not Great Britain, is also the greatest manufacturing country. . . .

"In the savings of nations America also comes first. . . .
The 50,000,000 Americans of 1880 could have bought up the
140,000,000 Russians, Austrians and Spaniards; or after purchasing
wealthy France, would have had enough pocket money to have
acquired Denmark, Norway, Switzerland and Greece. The Yankee

republic could even buy the home of his ancestors — the dear old home, with all its exquisite beauty, historical associations and glorious traditions, which challenge our love and hold it captive.

"'The cloud-capped towers, the gorgeous palaces,
The solemn temples,'

aye, every acre of Great Britain and Ireland could he buy and hold it as a pretty little Isle of Wight to his great continent; and after doing this he could turn around and pay off the entire national debt of that deeply indebted land and yet not exhaust his fortune—the product of a single century. . . . .

"In military and naval power the republic is at once the weakest and the strongest of nations. . . . Twenty years ago, as at the blast of a trumpet, she called into action 2,000,000 of armed men and floated 626 war ships. . . . Resting securely upon the love and devotion of all her sons, she can, Cadmus-like, raise from the soil vast armed hosts who fight only in her defense, and who, unlike the seed of the dragon, return to the avocations of peace when danger to the republic is passed. The American citizen who will not fight for his country, if attacked, is unworthy the name. . . .

"Of more importance even than commercial or military strength is the republic's commanding position among nations in intellectual activity; for she excells in the number of schools and colleges, in the number and extent of her libraries, and in the number of newspapers and other periodicals published.

"In the application of science to social and industrial uses, she is far in advance of other nations. Many of the most important practical inventions which have contributed to the progress of the world during the last century originated with Americans. No other people have devised so many labor-saving machines and appliances. The first commercially successful steamboat to cross the Atlantic sailed under the American flag from an American port. America gave to the world the cotton-gin, and the first practical mowing, reaping and sewing machines."

All this wonderful development and progress have been the direct outgrowth of the influences above suggested, not the least of which has been that of the constitutional government set in operation by the inauguration of Washington as President one hundred years ago to-day. Looking to the future in the light of the past, should we not fervently pray that this "government of the people, by the people, and for the people, shall not perish from the earth?"

It may have been right, on the ground of expediency, for our government to have at first recognized the legitimacy of slavery and the slave trade. But after all, this was a national sin which could only be washed out in blood, the best blood of the land. But having thus atoned for it, we now stand without a blot in this respect; the blessings of liberty are secured to all, not in name merely, but in fact, and so, with us, it is no longer a hollow form to say that, politically, all men are free and equal. In the old Tower of London, near the dungeons where prisoners were once chained in hopeless darkness, and also near the spot where the executioner's ax ruthlessly carried out the tyrant's will, are to be seen the Queen's crown and royal diadem. In that part of our country where once was heard the clanking of the chains of slavery, and millions sat in darkness of despair, there is now to be seen a more beautiful diadem than that of England's Queen—the diadem of liberty purchased by blood, and given to a people enslaved at the beginning but free at the end of our first century's history.

THE HON. CHARLES CARROLL BONNEY.

AT THE FIRST CONGREGATIONAL CHURCH.

The greatest event in the history of human government was the actual establishment of constitutional liberty by the inauguration of Washington as the first President of the American Republic, April 30, 1789. On that day the original association of the American states was dissolved, and the sovereign powers of a national union established by the people of the whole country were put in actual operation.

The Constitution framed by the convention that completed its work Sept. 17, 1787, under the presiding guidance of Washington, had been submitted to the people of the several states for ratification, and had been approved by the requisite number of states, June 21, 1788. That Constitution, and the laws and treaties to be made under it, were thenceforth declared to be "the supreme law of the land, anything in the constitution or laws of any state to the contrary notwithstanding." The Declaration of Independence did not form the new nation. In that act the thirteen colonies were merely allies in a common cause, and they achieved separate nationalities by the Revolutionary War. The nation was not created till the Constitution was put in force.

Looking backward after the lapse of a century to that convention and its work; to the people and their ratification of the new Constitution; to the first election held under it and the unanimous choice òf Washington as chief magistrate; to his installation in office and the actual organization of the government; to the complex and mighty problems presented for solution and the wonderful success which attended that sublime experiment in free government, we may well declare that such achievements were impossible to man without the providential aid and guidance of Almighty God. Those events constitute and will ever remain one of the mightiest miracles of human progress.

The amendments suggested in connection with the ratification, and soon after made, are treated as practically parts of the original Constitution.

The crowning marvel of the American Constitution of government, is the wonderful equality with which the respective rights of the people, the states, the nation and the several departments of governmental power are protected and preserved. The proper sphere of each is plainly defined and circumscribed; within the limits each finds the domain of its liberty, and we behold how good and how pleasant it is for gigantic rights and powers, interests and duties, to dwell together in unity. Imperial national power, free local self-government, and the largest desirable measure of personal liberty are here united and preserved with marvelous equality and justice; and alike in national and state governments, are protected by adequate barriers against encroachment.

Arbitrary power is banished from the republic. In the laws the people reign, and by public officers their will is executed.

Sovereign Justice is exalted to the highest place, and sits in judgment on the extent and limitations of all the powers of government. Clearly foreseeing the transcendent importance of judicial supremacy as a safe-guard against excesses and usurpations of political or executive power, Washington, in enclosing the commission of the first Chief Justice to John Jay, declared that the head of the judicial department of the government must be considered "the keystone of our political fabric."

The original confederacy was merely an *association* represented by legislative committees. The Constitution is a government of supreme power. The equal and efficient protection of the people, the states and the nation is its one all-comprehensive purpose.

The sublime and far-reaching statement of the objects of government, set forth in the preamble of the National Constitution, is unsurpassed in human history. Let us recall its wise and eloquent words:

We, the people of the United States,
In order to form a more perfect Union;
To establish justice and insure domestic tranquility;
To provide for the common defense;
To promote the general welfare;
And secure the blessings of liberty
To ourselves and our posterity,
Do ordain and establish this Constitution
For the United States of America.

By this Constitution the sovereignty of the people is declared. The unity of the whole people is asserted. The necessary subordination of the several states is made plain. The establishment of justice is set forth as the means of insuring the inestimable blessings of domestic tranquility. The common defense of the whole country takes the place of self-defense by each colony. The general welfare is exalted over all local, sectional, and personal interests. All these provisions are made in order that the blessings of that liberty which is in harmony with them all may be secured to future generations. These safeguards anticipate every assault of foreign enemy or domestic foe, and point out to the people the highway of triumph. The great pyramid of Egypt is called "A Miracle in Stone"; the Constitution of the United States as well deserves the designation of a "Miracle in Words"! It displays a triple trinity of people, states and nation; of executive, legislative, and judicial power; of civil, religious, and intellectual liberty, harmoniously wrought into one complete and imposing structure, against which the storms of invasion, rebellion, and anarchy have beaten, and will ever beat, in vain.

The House of Representatives is made the especial guardian of the rights of the people; the rights of the several states are particularly entrusted to the Senate; peace and war, money and commerce, revenue and legislation, are committed to the two Houses of Congress; and the administration of the government, and the command of the army and navy, are devolved upon the President.

These are some of the leading characteristics of the wonderful system of government put in operation by the first inauguration of Washington as President of the United States.

John Adams was Vice-President, and presided in the Senate. Thomas Jefferson was made Secretary of State; Alexander Hamilton, Secretary of the Treasury; Henry Knox, Secretary of War; and Edmund Randolph, Attorney-General. This was the first Cabinet of the Republic. Its members were indeed illustrious men, and had achieved enduring fame in the struggle of the American colonies for independence, but above them all rose the majestic figure of Washington, their acknowledged leader—calm, commanding, and sublime. Each succeeding generation has added to his fame, and he is now ranked, by common consent, as the foremost of human leaders. A recent political biographer declares that even his letters prove him to have been "the greatest man the earth has yet seen." He was a sincere and earnest Christian. Love to God and love to man were the dominant forces of his character. His integrity and uprightness were as firmly fixed as the everlasting hills. In him a great ambition, and a consciousness of the ability to direct and command, were transfigured, and became the loftiest patriotism and sense of public duty. His intuitive perception of the true principles of free government, and the action demanded by the exigency of any occasion, commanded not only the respect but the admiration of the illustrious statesmen by whom he was surrounded.

The War of the Revolution had established independence at home, but the War of 1812 was required to secure the proper recognition of the new nation throughout the world. The acquisition of the Louisiana territory, Texas, New Mexico and California, gave a geographical completeness to the national domain; but the War of the Rebellion was required to effect the overthrow of slavery and establish the supremacy of the nation.

And now we enter the second century of constitutional liberty, face to face with the remaining vast and solemn problems of free government—the questions of labor and capital; of competition, combination and coöperation; of education and suffrage; of equal rights, privileges and protection; of the free and efficient administration of justice, of public morals and policy, of temperance and domestic tranquility, of law and order. These are the mighty issues which, in the near future, the American people will be called upon to meet and settle. Woe to the political organization that shall put itself in the way of the public welfare on these vital problems of our time, for it will be destroyed by the resistless waves of the advancing tide of a higher, nobler and purer public opinion than the country has seen for more than half a century. Benedictions on every honest effort to promote a wise, speedy and enduring settlement of those great issues, for where the purpose is just, any errors of method will soon be discovered and corrected.

The day of a great advance of the American people is at hand; let us be ready for its dawn. Let us revive the lofty, patriotic and pious spirit of Washington, and in the language of his first inaugural address, declare that it would be, on such an occasion, "peculiarly improper to omit a fervent supplication to that Almighty Being who rules over the universe; who presides in the councils of nations, and whose providential aids can supply every human defect, that His benediction may consecrate to the liberties and happiness of the people of the United States, a government instituted by themselves for these essential purposes, and may enable every instrument employed in its administration to execute, with success, the functions allotted to his charge."

Let us also declare with him, in his glowing words on the same momentous occasion, that "no people can be bound to acknowledge and adore the Invisible Hand which conducts the affairs of men more than the people of the United States, since every step by which they have been advanced to the character of an independent nation, seems to have been distinguished by some token of providential agency."

Above all, let us, on this occasion, recall and take deeply to heart the solemn warning of the "Father of his Country," in his farewell address to the people of the United States, against "the baneful effects of the spirit of party, that distracts the public councils, enfeebles the public administration, agitates the community with ill-founded jealousies and false alarms, and kindles the animosity of one part of the country against another." Let us remember that parties should be the servants of the people, not their masters; that the purpose to be effected is far more important than the political machinery devised to accomplish it, as the harvest is of more consequence than the means by which it is gathered. Let us always be good citizens, faithful to the Constitution and the laws, and devoted to the general welfare; and partisans only so far as may be consistent with the duties we owe to God, to our country, and to our fellow-men.

We are not merely approaching, we are actually in the midst of another great crisis in the development of free government. Anarchy wars against liberty; vagabondism against industry; the saloon against the family; avarice and dissipation against Sunday; infidelity against religion; ignorance against knowledge; vice against virtue; public plunder against honest politics. In this vast and complex conflict every man must finally be drawn to one side or the other, whether it be as an active combatant or merely as giving silent aid and comfort to the side he has espoused. The solemn significance of the general celebration of the first inauguration of Washington consists in its relation to the great moral conflict now in progress.

This celebration will inspire new forces to take the field, and will arouse those already engaged to greater efforts. On a day not far distant a grand advance of the people will be made, and will result in a decisive victory for justice and domestic tranquility; for the common defense and the general welfare; and thereby secure, not only for our own posterity, but, in the fullness of time, through the omnipotent providence of God, for all mankind, the inestimable blessings of *constitutional liberty.*

On this 30th of April, 1889, the American people return, by common consent and universal rejoicing, to the standard of public service and personal character represented by the great name of Washington. Henceforth, if that return be earnest and sincere, the public places of the land, from lowest to highest, will be better filled and their duties more worthily performed. Those who are best qualified for a particular service will be sought out, and solicited for the sake of the general good, to render that service. Party slavery will cease. Men will act with political organizations, or against them, in freedom and according to reason, as good conscience may require. The right of private judgment will be acknowledged to extend even to political affairs. The next presidential election will witness the complete and final overthrow of the liquor saloon as a political power and an enemy of good government, and speedily thereafter attempts to control elections by fraud or force will cease, except as individual crimes, occasionally committed, as are other offenses against the laws.

These great results will be accomplished under the simple rule of common sense, that " *Those who think alike should act together;*" and it will be demonstrated that the dangerous classes of this country constitute only a small and easily controlled minority of the people, and are comparatively powerless when good citizens unite against them. Washingtonian reform is needed, not only in many high places of the country, but equally as much in the humbler fields of public service. Even the policeman should be so intelligent, just, and faithful that he would be worthy to serve in a war for liberty, under a commander like Washington. Even the justice of the peace, within his small realm, should love equity, and do justice, as though a Marshall were coming to inspect his work. Even an alderman should exercise the legislative and political authority entrusted to him, as though a Madison were to examine and pass upon it.

But the true and pure republic is God's government of a free people; and faithfully to serve it is, though unwittingly, to serve Him. Washington, Marshall, Madison, and their great compeers, were great only as they served their country and the world as the apostles of law and order.

The heroism which the great emergencies of to-day chiefly demand is that of a brave and honest ballot. With moral courage to match our intelligence and opportunities, there would forthwith be such progress in reform and the removal of existing abuses and evils as would make the dawn of the second century of constitutional liberty worthy to be remembered and celebrated as the American people this day celebrate the first inauguration of the illustrious Washington. When Washington was inducted into the Presidency he reverently laid his hand upon the open Bible and took the prescribed official oath:

"I do solemnly swear that I will faithfully execute the office of President of the United States, and will, to the best of my ability, preserve, protect and defend the Constitution of the United States."

All legislative, executive and judicial officers, both of the United States and of the several states, are required to take an oath or affirmation to support that Constitution. (Art. VI.) Naturalized foreigners must also take a similar oath. (Nat. Law.) But it was assumed that native-born American citizens would be so impressed by the excellencies of free government, and so inspired by the love of liberty and by sentiments of duty, that there would be no need of exacting a similar obligation from them. Unfortunately, that assumption has not been verified. We all know that the duties of good citizenship have been seriously neglected.

Let this glorious day witness a great revival of civic patriotism! Let us supply by our voluntary act the omitted oath of allegiance. Let us solemnly, sincerely and truly declare and affirm, in the presence of the ever-living God, that with His aid and guidance we will henceforth, to the best of our abilities, perform the duties of our municipal, state and national citizenship, and thereby do our part to preserve, protect and defend that great charter of civil and religious liberty, the Constitution of the United States.

THE RT.-REV. CHARLES EDWARD CHENEY, D. D.

AT CHRIST REFORMED EPISCOPAL CHURCH.

The President of the United States has manifested his deep appreciation of the significance of this momentous day by requesting, in his proclamation, not only a civil but a religious celebration of it. A great writer has said that hate always needs a reason; love, never. That principle is no more true of the love which a good man bears toward his wife or his mother than of the love which the Christian citizen bears toward the country which gave him birth. But if it were needed to assign reasons for a religious celebration of this anniversary, we need not wander far or dig deep in order to discover them. Let me, then, allude to one rarely referred to on such occasions. I mean the *Providential preparations* for the planting of this nation on this Western continent.

Sir Joshua Reynolds was once asked why he set so high a value on one of the productions of his pencil. "It only cost you," said the objector, "a few hours of labor to make that picture." "True," said the great artist, "but it took me forty years to prepare to paint it." The life-time of the American Republic is but a hand's breadth compared with the long rule of the democracies and aristocracies of ancient Greece, the duration of the republics which once fringed the Mediterranean Sea, or the hoary age of the empires and kingdoms of the elder world. But, and I speak with all reverence, it took Almighty God long centuries to make on American soil the Providential preparations for planting here the grand structure of the freest, the most intelligent, the most liberty-loving and law-abiding people on whom He ever permitted His sun to shine. Have you ever thought how the discovery of this Western world bears the marks of Providential interposition, which ought to endear the land to every citizen of the great republic? How did it come to pass that out of the hundreds—perhaps thousands—of adventurous voyagers whose eyes turned longingly across the Atlantic in the closing years of the fifteenth century, only one had the courage and persistency to go begging like a mendicant from court to court of European kings, for help to lay at their feet the boundless wealth of the Western Indies? What power moved the heart of Isabella of Spain to pawn even the jewels of her crown to provide this unknown pleader with the ships he needed? And when the voyage began, and four little vessels faded away from the view of the loungers on the wharves of Palos, was it human skill and courage alone that bore those wretched cockleshells safely over the trackless Atlantic?

It was the stormiest season which veteran mariners could remember. Three out of the four ships were boats destitute even of a deck. The hardy sailors on our Chicago docks would hesitate long before they ventured in such craft to cross from shore to shore of this majestic Michigan. Within was mutiny. Without were the blackness and howling of the storm. Thrice did the rebellious sailors almost reach the point of compelling their great admiral to turn his prow backward toward European shores. Who averted such a disaster? Not Columbus, but an Almighty Hand busied with the preparations to make this continent the dwelling of the American republic!

Go a little further. We often, on occasions like this, talk grandiloquently about our civil and religious freedom, as if the shrewdness and sagacity of ourselves or our fathers had secured us these priceless blessings. But it should always be remembered that it was by what a great historian calls "a miracle of Divine Providence" that this whole continent did not become the scene of despotism in government and of the Inquisition in religion. Francis Parkman, the historian of the early French attempts to colonize the Western hemisphere, declares that " Liberty may thank the savage Iroquois that, by their insensate fury, they averted such a peril. Detroit was a French fort. The passes of the West were guarded by French garrisons. A new France had grown up at the mouth of the Mississippi. Lines of military communication connected the French Gulf of St. Lawrence with the French Gulf of Mexico. Spain held the vast regions of the far South. The British colonies were a broken and feeble line of undefended settlements fringing the waters of the North Atlantic." It was only by a strange interference of Providence that the imperial domain of the vast West was saved from being a French empire—ruled by the absolute tyranny of the Bourbons and under the religious domination of the Jesuits. Why such a scheme failed is a puzzle to the skeptic. It is as clear as day to him who sees in it the Providence of God preparing the place for a people, the corner-stone of whose civil polity should be personal and political liberty, and the corner-stone of whose religion should be the right of private judgment.

Pursue the thought a little further. When Washington, at the end of the Revolution, returned to the enjoyment of the civic honors his sword had won, he distinctly told the American people that it was not the indomitable courage, the military skill or the patriotic consecration of our fathers which had wrought the victory over the tremendous power of the British empire. It was only the strange and extraordinary manifestations of Divine Providence. God was preparing the ground for the last and best experiment in civil and religious freedom.

Nor is the same principle less apparent in the history of our own times. Said a brave Confederate officer, who bears the scars of bloody battles in which he fought to establish a nation based on the principle of human slavery: "I thank God that we failed. It was only His Providence which saved this land from the curse of slavery, and from the worse fate of being split up into bickering and jealous states, wasting their best blood in quarrels with each other." The reverent acknowledgment of God's Providence in the Revolution, which Washington made, was echoed by the nation's martyr amidst the convulsions of our great Civil War. It was only, as he declared in his Gettysburg address, *"Under God"* that the nation was to have a new birth of freedom, and that government of the people, by the people, and for the people, should not perish from the earth.

We measure a gift not by its intrinsic worth. Associations are more precious than gold. The most trifling thing possesses a value beyond all human estimate when we know that loving hands wrought out the gift with the thought of the recipient ever before the mind of the giver. But when the gift was the noblest land and the freest government on earth, and the Giver who wrought it with toilsome preparation was Almighty God, what shall we say? The patriotism of Benedict Arnold was purer than his who can take the gift of the American republic from the hand of God and not love his country with a burning zeal, because of the preparations with which God made ready such a gift for him and his posterity! In days of chivalry, knightly men, on the birthday of our Lord, took the sacrament in pledge that they would defend the right. We have done well to rescue this Centennial of the American Constitution from forgetfulness. But let us go one step further. On this sacred day let us take a sacramental pledge to do our share as individuals to make the nation worthy of its providential preparation. That is the work of the true citizen. That is the living power of genuine love for the American commonwealth. The old Greeks had a legend that when the ten years' siege of Troy was ended, the news of the victory was known in every Greek city before the dawn of another day. On every mountain-top a sentry had been stationed. On Mount Ida a blazing beacon told of triumph. The next peak of the range caught up the message in a glow of fire. Summit after summit, island after island bridging the blue Ægean, sent on the story in letters of flame. The height where our fathers kindled the beacon which told the glad news of a free nation's birth into a world of selfish despotism lies a hundred years behind us. But to-day we stand on another mountain peak and kindle the fire which sends the tidings on. May God grant that each century shall see the flame renewed! May generations of Americans yet unborn thank God for the Constitution, for the example of Washington, and for the birth-hour of a republic which, while time shall last, shall fear God, honor law and preserve liberty on the earth.

THE REV. H. W. BOLTON.

This is an eventful moment in the history of a great nation, the gathering of the people for prayer, praise, and giving of thanks unto Him who honored the heroic faith of 1776 and 1779. Then less than four millions unfurled the flag we honor, and resolved themselves free and independent states. Then it took courage and confidence to declare in favor of independence. Jefferson must have been heaven-inspired when he rose in the presence of that company to read: "We, therefore, the representatives of the United States of America in general congress assembled, appealing to the Supreme Judge of the world for the rectitude of our intentions, do, in the name and by the authority of the good people of these colonies, solemnly publish and declare that these united colonies are and ought to be free and independent states; that they are absolved from all allegiance to the British crown; and that all political connection between them and the state of Great Britain is and ought to be dissolved; and that, as free and independent states, they have full power to levy war, conclude peace, contract alliances, establish commerce, and to do all other acts and things which independent states may of right do. And for the support of this declaration, with a firm reliance on the protection of Divine Providence, we mutually pledge to each other our lives, our fortunes and our sacred honor."

Would to God such a spirit might fill our hearts to-day as sixty millions unfurl the Stars and Stripes over the blossoming earth and beneath a smiling heaven! What means this booming of guns, ringing of bells, and gathering of the people? What! do you ask? It is the gathering of patriots in expression of their loyalty to the flag as the emblem of liberty, equal rights, and national unity. To us patriotism means more than devotion to native land. That is commendable and often strong, even moving the native of Asiatic Islands on beholding a banana tree in the Garden of Plants in Paris, to baptize the plant with tears. Yea, even the Esquimaux becomes so wedded to the frigid zone of his native home as to think the blubber oil and ice-cabin preferable to the gifts of enlightened nations and refined society. Why does the heart so tenaciously cling to that spot on earth where first it learned to live? Because of the friendships and the blessings that were all the world to it. The nations waited for the history of our country to develop the patriotism that should make the sons of all climes and all lands one in defense of the institutions of a free republic. We go not back into ancient history for illustrations of true patriotism.

Speak not to-day of the heroism displayed at Marathon. We have heard of Bunker Hill, Georgetown, Pittsburgh Landing, Fair Oaks, Gettysburg, Lookout Mountain and Antietam. We have seen more than five hundred thousand men leave the shops, mines and schools of our land to fight for the union of states and the maintenance of liberty and equal rights. We glory in the spirit of Lieut. Cummings while passing up the Mississippi, who having had one leg torn from his body, called out as he fell: "Get the ship past the batteries, boys, and they can have the other leg if they want it." Such is the patriotism of American history!

In the fiery furnace of war men have learned to love this, their native or adopted home, more than all others. Yes, the stubborn Englishman, the heroic Scotchman, the enthusiastic Irishman, the hearty German, and the fun-loving Frenchman, join in singing "My Country, 'tis of Thee."

There are good reasons for the strength of our patriotism. This is a home land, a land in which all may find protection in the exercise of a good conscience. Territorially we have room for all who desire to come and share with us. We rank as the third nation on the globe, if we consider only the number of persons dwelling upon contiguous territory, and in less than half a century we shall stand second. Our population is at least fifteen times as great as it was a hundred years ago. I for one entertain no doubt that the sustaining force of the United States is adequate to the support of 1,000,000,000 inhabitants, without any impairment of the enjoyments and comforts of social and domestic life. If we assume the habitable area of the United States to be 2,500,000 square miles, an average population of 300 to the square mile (the present average of the State of Massachusetts) would give an aggregate of 750,000,000 souls. Our capacity may be further measured by considering the fact that if the present inhabitants of the United States could be transferred to Texas the average would not exceed three hundred persons to the square mile.

The diversification of human pursuits, due to science, art and a wise public policy, is making a constant and appreciable addition to the capacity of the globe to sustain human life. The 60,000,000 within our limits are better fed, better clothed, better housed than were the 3,000,000 who inaugurated the Revolutionary War. It is not improbable that this progress may continue for an indefinite period. We have thus in one hundred years rushed to the foremost rank in population, wealth and annual savings. In public credit, in agriculture and in manufactures America leads the civilized world. Her territory is not half occupied. To-day we have in wealth $43,000,000,000, and our manufactures amount to $1,112,000,000, or nearly half as much as those of all Europe.

Again, this rapid growth does not endanger the nation's riches, for God hath stored in these hills, and along these prairies, immeasurable wealth in crude forms. The lead, zinc, copper, tin, silver and gold have only to be searched out; the best and largest quantities are not yet reached. The sunshine of other days when beast and bird occupied the land is now buried in Pennsylvania, Mississippi and Arkansas in 160,000 square miles of condensed light and power, and God hath in these last days shown us how to set the currents on fire all about us. Drive on ye men of thought! Build your mansions, harness the steeds of the sky. We have minerals and power sufficient to make this the City of Gold, with pearly gates and foundations of precious stones.

Again, this is a land of schools and churches. A man cannot escape their influence if he would. As soon as a mother can trust her boy from her presence the bell calls him to school. One hundred and ninety-eight thousand eight hundred and eighty-four schools open their doors to all classes of all nationalities, at the expense of $74,400,000. We published in 1880, 31,789,666 newspapers, with an addition of 4,314 periodicals devoted largely to news, politics and family reading.

Then ours is the land of equality. Here every man has a right to lead and a chance to rule. The log houses of the West are still honored, for out of them come the boys with convictions and a mother's blessing to take the positions of power. We look back on the men whom we have honored. We speak of Washington not as a scholar, but as a man of force and will, such as gave him character and standing; of Jackson, the fighter, who conquered a mother's wish, for she ordained that he should preach; of Abraham Lincoln, of your own state, who rose to shake off the snow that sifted through the splits of his father's house and overcame hosts of obstacles that he might be great. What shall we say of our peerless Grant, our scholarly Sumner, the aspiring Greeley, the historic Garfield, the brave and patriotic Sheridan, and a long list of noble men who have graced our records?

To each and all the gates swing open wide. To gain the brightest honors ever offered to mortals is still possible. In the next hundred years are to be settled grave questions. Temperance and drunkenness, Christianity and infidelity are before us. It is for us to say which shall be honored. No heart touched with divine love was ever in a position to do more than the sons of the nineteenth century. In this great undivided home there are millions to be educated and converted to American and New Testament ideas. Millions of crude, undeveloped natures are to be trained for the race of life. Up yonder there are crowns. Who shall wear them? He who utilizes the zeal and push of his age to guide the dashing train into the everlasting habitation of God.

THE REV. LEE M. HEILMAN.

AT GRACE EVANGELICAL LUTHERAN CHURCH.

We are here to celebrate more than a single day. The 30th of April, 1789, had in it something worthy of remembrance beyond its own sunlight. It was a great day for the infant republic. From Mount Vernon the first President started for New York with a profound sense of duty and of his grave responsibilities. At Trenton, where once the dark clouds of discouragement for the colonies were rent by victory, he passed the arch reared by the enthusiasm of a grateful people. On it was inscribed: "The defender of the mothers will be the protector of the daughters." The alighted chief walks the bridge where women stand and little girls· dressed in white strew flowers of honor in the path of Washington. A boat finally carries him to his journey's end, where an overwhelming crowd awaited him with storms of huzzas. Amidst almost unbounded excitement he came to the stand to take the oath of office as executive of the new-born country. Wearing a suit of dark-brown cloth, white stockings, large buckles on shoes, he stood there a man of august presence, and leaning forward as the solemn vow was to be taken to guide conscientiously the new nation under God just established, he kissed fervently the Book he had learned from a faithful mother to love and study.

That pageant, however, with its heart-touching scenes, is not all that we, after a century, commemorate. There have been richer and more splendid events. Nay, back of and around that day gathered the worth which makes the day memorable. It is the principles that created the occasion which gave the day its value. A single day is not great enough to merit the honor which such a land as ours meets now to lavish on the day a hundred years ago. In it culminated the character of a great struggle for freedom. It was the fruit of terrible war, inexpressible hardships and untold endurance for a cause dearer than life.

First, it is true we affectionately turn to the memories of one man, but it is to a true man. It is a man of worth and highest character. Not far from where he sleeps now Nature has sculptured on a high cliff beyond the harming of human hand a form as of a man's head and shoulders, and which, it is thought, looks like the bust of our Washington. But though so imperishable that picture of rock, the influence of the name and character of Washington will continue more imperishable. Napoleon said: "Posterity will talk of him with reverence as the founder of a great empire, when my name shall be lost in the vortex of revolution." His example shines brightly at the fireside and in the home. As a boy of diligence, learning and practicing the lessons of morality and piety taught by a mother whom he obeyed and revered to her life's end, his name will live in the hearts of America's youth. While in private life he was a man of faith and a communicant member of the Christian Church, he was a man of uncorrupted principle in every public relation. The well-read books lying on his table at death were Sir Matthew Hale on "Mortality," and the Sacred Bible. Our Centennial is made grander to-day because we may proudly point to a genuine man as the leading figure in our history.

And yet what we recall is greater than the day or the noblest man. The principle underlying our government still lives. Liberty to mankind is the soil which, undisturbed in its fertile, inherent force, is our notable inheritance. Its self-governing and self-perpetuating growth has produced a country which in riches and in the entire sphere of prosperity has ascended above all the nations of the world. These principles of liberty have touched and shaken the foundations of monarchical thrones and have tempered the rule of every sovereign on the globe. Nor has the experiment of self-government found the rule of the people an abused power; but liberty's self-generated health has taken anarchy by the throat, throttled it, and cast it into the vortex of death; and rebellion, as is seen in the presence of these veterans before us to-day, has been made a thing of the past. The old doctrines of freedom of a century ago are living; they are firm as adamant. These unchanging things will still give perpetuity to the nation which our fathers reared in sacrifice and with blood, and they will stand the tests of influences which come like ocean-tides against them. I have faith in liberty, and in our institutions founded on truth, and believe that our Columbia will stand as a model to lead the nations to a higher glory.

We, then, review not merely a pageant of a day, or the virtues of a man, or the valor and victory of war, but we call to mind, so that we may also honor them, the distinguished character and the moral and spiritual forces which inaugurated not a single President but a great nation.

And do we not well in such a commemoration? The old aspirations for freedom, that conscience and religion might have liberty, and that the people might flourish, were the pure motives which launched so safely our Union at the beginning, and it is only these aspirations that can perpetuate the nation.

III

EXERCISES IN THE SCHOOLS

EXERCISES IN THE SCHOOLS

In the warmth and enthusiasm of youth are found the best soil for planting the seeds of patriotism. Youth, which is so intense and so imaginative, invests everything with a rosy hue and imparts to every subject something of its own buoyancy and its own earnestness. The patriotism of the youth is different from that of the mature. In the mature it becomes an ideal quality, while in the young it is a creature of the flesh and the blood and the imagination. The mature patriotism is a beautiful patriotism, because it is a tower of strength in itself. It not only begets moral courage, but it supports moral courage. It is a relative aspect of those other qualities of the human mind associated with a love of home, a love of parents, and a love of one's children. There is this difference. Patriotism has greater moral qualities than the other affections, and has a greater hold upon the intellects of men, inspiring them to do some of the loftiest deeds of heroism and personal sacrifice. All history is a record of the promptings of the patriotic impulse. While in the mature it is a greater moral quality, in the youth it is a beautiful one. The child does not appreciate the full significance of patriotism as does the adult. It is one of those qualities of the mind which comes through the operation of reason, and from a sort of intuitive appreciation of the natural condition of things. The germ of patriotism is in the mind of everyone, only requiring the process of years and favorable circumstances to make it bloom into the splendor of the perfect flower.

Patriotism is the bulwark of the nation's safety, and becomes the stronger protection because it is so largely an endowment of every properly constituted citizen. It binds society more closely than law. It is stronger than custom. It is more powerful than any artificial opinion or impulse, because it is so natural. It seems to be a function of every man's nature to express his patriotism, that is, to find an outlet for his patriotic feelings; and it also seems to be a function of the human mind not only to express that patriotism, but to spread the sentiment with the whole strength of one's physical being. Where would we be to-day were it not for patriotism? Was it not this great moral impulse which gave almost superhuman strength to the grand characters of 1776? Was it not patriotism that endowed George Washington with the wisdom of a Solomon, the moral courage of a Socrates, and with a strength that could not be dismayed? Was it not patriotism which gave the little American army the inexhaustible vitality of an Antæus? Was it not patriotism that put down one of the bloodiest wars in all history, our own Civil War? Was it not patriotism that triumphed over the greatest difficulties, that wiped out the blood-stains of our own intestine strife, that has cemented this people into one symmetrical and splendid whole, and has placed us in rank with the greatest and most powerful nations of the earth?

If, then, patriotism is so lofty a quality of the human mind; if it is so necessary to the substantial and symmetrical growth of nations; if it accomplishes so much for the welfare of the community, and so much for the prosperity and protection of the individual, is it not wise to encourage this grand moral sentiment and develop it in our youth? The youthful mind is the proper place to inculcate lessons of virtue and wisdom. It is in a state of receptivity, and the seed that is planted there takes firmer root and grows to a stronger maturity than those seeds that are planted later in life. The mind of the youth, fresh and elastic, is full of hope and full of sentiment. And as the natural elements help propagate a more sterling condition of life, so do the finer sentiments of the mind help to concentrate the more rugged and sturdy virtues. The oak, with its gnarled boughs and umbrageous top, defying the blast of the winds and the stroke of the lightning, comes from a small acorn. That acorn to be an oak must be planted in the earth, the rain must water it and the sunshine invigorate it. By and by it assumes that maturity which has always been the symbol of resisting strength. And so to reach the highest development of patriotism, that patriotism before which all personal interest disappears as mist before the rising sun, before which no personal sacrifice is too great, and no physical suffering worthy to be compared to the results attained —that patriotism must first be planted in the mind of youth. With proper care it will develop into oak-like strength, and what was a charming ebullition of youthful enthusiasm and imagination will become in the man a strong and lofty and unquenchable virtue.

For these reasons the Centennial celebration in the schools of Chicago has a peculiar significance. In the first place, the youth are made familiar with the sacrifices of the fathers of our country, the noble virtues they practiced to attain that which the present generation enjoys, and which is held in trust by them for generations that are yet unborn. It makes them American citizens in the best sense of the word. They join together in celebrating particular occasions, and thus there is a community of sentiment as well as interest. They forget that their parents may have come from foreign lands. They deal with the present in its relation to the past, both of their own and of their adopted country. In the second place, by bringing them face to face with the grand characters of the nation's history, it makes them realize the full beauty of individual patriotism and what it can do for men in extremities. It makes the children understand the strength of this virtue and its relation to the other attributes of the human mind. From the study of this he learns the beauty and the value of virtue in the abstract, and he also learns how much more noble a thing is a lofty virtue than a base sentiment. By placing these in contrast he is taught a lesson in morals. In the third place, the distinction between youth and age is eradicated. The child and the man are merged together. Each feels the revivifying glow of the patriotic impulse, and the imagination in the one case is warmed in the same degree as in the other; and by wiping out the distinction between youth and age, under the influence of the patriotic glow, the child becomes as much an individual in the fabric of society as is the man.

This quality of patriotism, therefore, appeals not only to his sense of moral beauty and to his sense of imagination, but it appeals also to his pride. And, furthermore, he learns this lesson, that his home and his country are interchangeable terms; that if he would defend his home he must defend his country. His country, in its narrower sense, is his home; and his home, in its broader sense, is his country. In being taught to revere his country, he is taught to love his home. He learns that if he would protect his home he must fight for his country. Will not this inculcate a lofty ruggedness of character?

The mind of the youth is the place to engender the virtue of patriotism. Plant it there. Teach the child the full force of its beauty and its strength. Nature will help you. And when he comes to manhood that patriotism will make him respect the laws, will make him love his home, revere his country, and make him realize the full force of the poet's words:

> Nothing so sweete is as our countries earth,
> And joy of those from whom we claime our birth.

This celebration in the public schools of Chicago, if it be rightly understood, possesses something more than mere superficial significance. It is significant because its roots enter deeply not only into the life of the community, but of each individual, child as well as man. And that the people, youth as well as age, fully appreciate the sentiments of patriotism and realize their full import, the celebration in the different schools bears ample testimony.

There are two things that come to mind without effort in contemplating the part taken by the school children in the celebration of this Centennial anniversary. The first is that youth is naturally patriotic, and that it needs only time and occasion to find its full expression. The second thought is that patriotism obliterates the line of nationality. Look over the names of the children who took part in these ceremonies. They come from sunny Italy, from Scandinavia, France, Germany, Ireland—in fact, nearly every country of Europe is represented in the list. It is a most gratifying showing. It shows that the spirit of liberty has as strong a hold on the adopted citizen as on the native; that the institutions of this free land are so alluring that a man who comes to our shores is certain to be anchored with us and to throw himself heart and soul into the customs and institutions of his adopted country. And that so many foreigners have become a part of the fabric of our society, is the strongest evidence to be secured that America is indeed the land of the free and the home for the oppressed of all classes. In this Centennial celebration the children took no insignificant part. For several weeks the little ones had been undergoing the necessary training preparatory to the due observance of the day. The brightest pupils in each of the classes were selected to read original compositions or to declaim the finished orations of the foremost men of the country during the century just closed. All classes were taught to sing the patriotic songs which inspired our soldiers to many noble deeds on the eve of many a bloody battle. They had daily lessons in the constitutional and political history of our country, and, judged by the results of this celebration, the teachings were of the greatest value. The essays, on the whole, indicated considerable study both of the Declaration of Independence and the Constitution, and the manner in which the gems of American oratory were delivered by pupils not out of their teens showed that the infantile mind had grasped the true significance of American patriotism. Dressed in holiday attire and carrying small flags in their coat lapels and knots of red, white and blue in place of the usual corsage bouquet, the boys and girls trooped to their respective schools in happy spirits. Most of the class-rooms were gaily decorated with flags, streamers and bunting. The sternness of school discipline and the dull routine of school life were conspicuously absent. It was a holiday with a purpose. There was considerable similarity in the character of the programmes arranged for the day, but this was incident to the day and could not have been otherwise. The programmes were well rendered, and there was no hitch in their fulfillment. Each number was redolent with the aroma of patriotism and the highest duties of citizenship; and as the little ones told of the brave deeds of the forefathers of our nation, hundreds of aged visitors felt the blood run faster through their veins, and they thought involuntarily of the years past, when the few surviving heroes of the Revolutionary epoch had told of the times that try men's souls, and listened with rapt attention to the recital of those deeds in which they had taken such an active part. The addresses were by men who had won distinction in professional and commercial life. The speakers showed their youthful hearers the beauties of a government of the people, for the people, and by the people. At the close of the exercises each pupil was presented with a medal in commemoration of the event.

Below is the programme as arranged by the committee having the matter in charge:

I.

1. Appropriate devotional exercises.
2. The national flag to be displayed from all school buildings.

II.

1. The pupils of the high schools meet in the halls of their respective buildings at 10:30 o'clock a. m.
2. Singing of patriotic songs.
3. Essays and declamations on patriots and patriotism.
4. Recitation of historic facts pertaining to the formation and adoption of the Constitution of the United States.
5. Recitation of patriotic quotations from the speeches and writings of the founders of the nation.
6. Addresses suggested by the occasion by speakers appointed by the committee.
7. Presentation of memorial medals.

III.

1. The pupils of the primary department and of the lower grades of the grammar department assemble in the rooms or halls of their respective school buildings in charge of their own teachers as 10:30 o'clock a. m.
2. Singing of patriotic songs.
3. Recitation of patriotic quotations.
4. Reception of memorial medals.
5. Singing of "America" in conclusion.

IV.

1. The pupils of the higher grammar grades assemble in their school buildings in charge of their regular teachers at 10:30 o'clock a. m.
2. An appropriate song.

3. Recitation of historic facts concerning the organization of the Government of the United States.

4. Recitation of Whittier's "Centennial Ode."

5. Song, Keller's "American Hymn."

6. Recitation of patriotic quotations.

7. Addresses by speakers designated by the committee.

8. Presentation of memorial medals.

9. Song, "America."

CELEBRATION IN THE VARIOUS SCHOOLS.

NORTH DIVISION HIGH SCHOOL.

At the North Division High School the exercises were of an interesting character. There was no attempt at decoration or display, and a spirit of earnestness marked all the proceedings. The audience filled every inch of space in the large auditorium. The young ladies wore small white flags in place of the usual badge, and the younger pupils were decorated with knots of the national colors. The exercises began with the singing of the "Star Spangled Banner." The Governor's proclamation was read, and then followed in their turn essays, dialogues, and songs. The Hon. A. M. Pence delivered an effective address on the necessity existing among mankind for self-government, and explained wherein the government of the United States was the best mankind had yet devised. The Constitution was the organic law of the country, which the Supreme Court had been instituted to sustain. The Rev. Dr. McIntyre was the next speaker. He pitied the man who, at this time of celebration, could do nothing better than indulge in croakings, and was not satisfied with the social, moral, and material conditions with which he was surrounded. Such a man was out of harmony with the spirit of American institutions. He was the cause of discord in the body politic. Never in the history of the country were there better men or purer women. The world was constantly growing better despite the pessimistic views of many, preachers included. America, the youngest of nations, paved the way for peace. It is fighting the battle for freedom for the whole world, and will succeed unless the people become demoralized and give the reins of power into the hands of boodlers and political thieves. A brief address by Mr. Henry S. Boutell closed the programme. Mr. Boutell told of the advantages of the constitutional form of government to the people at large. Those pupils who participated prominently were: Lillie A. Burtheimer, Fred W. Niblock, Jennie Franklin, Howard H. Davenport, Walter C. Rain.

SOUTH DIVISION HIGH SCHOOL.

The exercises at the South Division High School passed off in a happy manner. The decorations were unusually complete, consisting of flags and bunting, while over the Wabash avenue entrance was a large banner. The national colors were displayed wherever it was possible to show them. The feature of the celebration at this school was the presence of an orchestra composed entirely of the young men of the school, as follows: First violins, Henry Mitchell, Charles Iverson, Willie Bond, George Stonham, Benjamin Enhale. Second violins, Clarence Willett, John Kelly. Cornets, Edward Griswold, Frank Hanson, Samuel Barnes, George Stein. Miss H. Simmonds was accompanist. Shortly after 11 o'clock the exercises of the day were opened with a short prayer, followed by a selection from the orchestra. Mr. J. Lipsohn read the Governor's proclamation. Clarence T. Miller read an essay on "Patriotism and Honor," and Miss Kate Reed one on "Two Inaugurations." They were both scholarly efforts and were received with many manifestations of pleasure from the large audience. Patriotic addresses were made by Mr. D. L. Shorey and the Rev. Dr. J. H. Barrows. Principal Slocum distributed the celebration medals. He compared 1789 and 1889 as two piers and said that the present occasion was a bridge that spanned the chasm between. Speaking of the medals, he said that it was not their intrinsic worth that gave them their value, "but may the memories called up remind you of the grandest events in your country's history, and beget an honest and joyful pride that you are an American." Music was interspersed throughout the programme, the whole serving to make an enjoyable occasion.

WEST DIVISION HIGH SCHOOL.

One of the features of the celebration at this school was the presence of Gov. Fifer and his staff. These distinguished visitors were under the charge of the following committee: Mr. George E. Adams, Mr. S. D. Kimbark, Mr. W. H. Harper, Mr. Fred L. Forch, Mr. Graeme Stewart. The gentlemen occupied seats on the platform and took great interest in the exercises. There were over one thousand flags and much bunting displayed. But more indisputable than these evidences of a gala day was the enthusiasm of the pupils. Marshalled by their respective teachers, they marched up stairs, where seats had been provided for them. At the head of each school room walked two little misses bearing aloft the Stars and Stripes. Each pupil carried a small flag or wore the national colors in badges, scarfs or hair ribbons. "I am proud of this day, young ladies and gentlemen seated before me," said Gov. Fifer, turning to Mr. Stewart; "this is indeed an inspiring sight, and I am glad to be here." The exercises began with the singing by the pupils of the "Ode to Washington," written by Supt. Howland. The programme was an interesting one. Principal Wells delivered the welcoming address. Mr. Robert Shaw followed with "What Constitutes a Citizen." Gov. Fifer delivered an address to the children and so did Congressman Mason. There was music, a poem by W. M. Paine, presentation of a handsome flag, and a charming representative tableau of the "States," by forty-two young girls, with a grand solo.

AT THE KEITH SCHOOL.

At the Keith School every pupil took some part in the exercises of the day. The schoolhouse was thronged with visitors, and the rooms were artistically decorated with festoons of flags, evergreens and flowers. Portraits of prominent men of Revolutionary fame were a noticeable feature, and the whole was set off with shields and escutcheons in colored crayon, making a very pretty effect. The larger children recited patriotic sentiments which were culled from the poetry and prose of prominent authors, and the dialogues were arranged so that a number could take part in them. The little children, under the leadership of Miss Perdue and Miss Fletcher, gave a military drill with flags,

and the little ones sang with much intelligence and good execution the songs, "The Red, White and Blue," "Columbia" and
"America." It is not necessary to state that the singing of the
little ones created much enthusiasm. Another noticeable feature
in the entertainment of this school was the recitation, in Miss
McGrath's division, of a composition entitled "The Story of the
Day," written for the occasion by Miss Meta Wellar of this
school, and recited by thirty-nine pupils. The little ones seemed
to enter heartily into the spirit of the piece. In another room
"Miss Columbia's Tea Party," in which all the states were represented in costume, was a unique idea. In Miss Nelson's room
"Liberty's Call," a dialogue in costume, was the principal attraction. Thirty-eight prettily attired young girls, robed in the
emblems of our national Union, were received by Liberty; while
four little misses rapped for admission and were invested with
the honors of statehood, completing the galaxy of forty-two
stars. Perhaps the centre of attraction was to be found in Miss
McConville's room, where the largest audience was gathered and
where an interesting programme was given. In this programme
was included a dialogue of the original thirteen states. The
pupils of Miss McGarren and Miss Wellar gave their exercises in
room No. 1, which was liberally decorated for the occasion. The
musical programme was unusually excellent. An interesting
debate in the Continental Congress was given by boys in
costume. Mr. Adams of Massachusetts, Mr. Bartlett of New
Hampshire, Mr. Dickinson of Pennsylvania, and other famous
Revolutionary characters made stirring speeches for liberty, and at
the close signed the Declaration of Independence, winning prolonged cheers. A blooming young miss in costume, with her
hair powdered a snowy white and wearing an old-fashioned russet
silk, read an eulogy on Lady Washington. A composition
entitled "Advocating the Constitution," participated in by eighteen girls, was composed by Miss Meta Wellar.

After the regular programme had been finished, Mr. E. G.
Keith delivered a very interesting address, which was listened to
with profound attention by the entire audience. Mr. Keith
opened his address by referring significantly to the occasion, and
quoting the memorable lines of John Adams to his wife on the

3d of July, the day before the adoption of the Declaration of Independence by the Congress: " This day should be commemorated as a day of devotion by solemn acts of devotion to Almighty God. It should be celebrated by pomp, shows, guns, bells, bonfires and illuminations from one end of the land to the other from this day forward forever! You may think me transported with enthusiasm, but I am not. I am well aware of the toil, blood and treasure that it will cost us to maintain this declaration, and to support and defend these states. All through the gloom I can see the rays of light the clearer. I can see the end as worthy of more than all the means, and that prosperity will triumph, although you and I may rue it, which I hope we shall not." Taking this as his text, Mr. Keith went on to show how America has more than fulfilled the bright prophecy of Mr. Adams. He said:

In 1789 we were a nation of 3,000,000 people, many of whom were slaves. To-day we number 60,000,000 or more, all free. During the Revolutionary War John Adams wrote to his wife to take care that the children do not go astray. Cultivate their minds, inspire their ways, raise their wishes, fix their attention upon grand and glorious objects. Read to them from the lives of illustrious thinkers, widen their minds, and make them good and manly; teach them to scorn injustice, cowardice, and falsehood. Teach them to revere nothing but religion, morality and liberty. And it is in this spirit that I ask you to-day to turn your thoughts toward these illustrious sentiments when you come to bear rule as citizens of this mighty republic. First of all, do not fail to cast a conscientious vote; and for you, young women, who cannot vote, you can at least teach some one to vote right. Strive ever to put the best and purest men in public office; and those habits which you now form in your school life, if made part of your every-day existence, will prove the best for you and the highest happiness for your fellow-men. It has been said that patriotism is a weak plant, and thrives best on need and on self-sacrifice. We regard that of little value which we obtain without struggle, and if we would continue to prosper as in the days of our fathers, we must study their heroic lives, that we may be stirred by them to noble deeds. Study your country's history until it becomes as familiar to you as your own lives. Read the story of the virtues and self-sacrifices of Washington, Hamilton, Adams, Jay, Franklin, Webster, Lincoln, and Grant; knowing their lofty aims and contemplating their virtues, we shall uplift our own lives to their splendid standard; emulating their lofty examples, we shall partake of their exalted patriotism.

THE RAYMOND SCHOOL.

At the Raymond School a large audience gathered to participate in the celebration. A very interesting programme was
offered. The large hall was tastefully decorated with pictures,
flags, flowers, and bunting, and each of the pupils seemed to enter
heartily into the spirit of the occasion and performed his or her
respective part very well. The two addresses were made by Judge
H. M. Shepard and Mr. George C. Ingham, both of which were
scholarly and patriotic efforts, and were highly appreciated by
the large audience. In the course of his remarks Judge Shepard
referred to the cause of the delay in the adoption of the Constitution. The first confederation of the states was without power to
enforce its mandates and for nineteen years was represented only
by the Continental Congress. The first idea was to present all
common grievances to the King, and there was no thought
of separation from the mother country. Speaking of the patriotism and self-sacrifice of the heroes of the Revolution, Judge
Shepard said: "To us at this day it is apparent that it was
through the lessons of early self-government that we owe the
scheme of government embodied in that remarkable instrument
of liberty adopted one hundred years ago, and which we celebrate to-day; and proud indeed must any member of this school
be who to-day can trace his descent from one of the illustrious
men of that early time." The speaker concluded his remarks
with the following words:

The union of federation and local self-government has been
declared by two of the most celebrated politico-historical writers of
the day to be nothing more than the grafting of the old Connecticut
system of local self-government on the stock of the old federation,
a union of the commonwealth and town rights, represented in the
union by a combination of national and state rights. In the colonies there had always been much freedom in purely local matters.
The people of these days had become accustomed, long before the
Revolution, to interest themselves in the affairs of practical government. Long war and the experiences of the Continental Congress had shown the need of union, and had given an insight into
what was necessary to make the government effective. It was not,
therefore, as remarkable as at first appears, that such men should
frame a Constitution the wisdom of which has been demonstrated
by the experiences of one hundred years. To you, young men and

women, this precious heritage of a free Constitution will soon be handed down. The old men will soon give place to you. It was said of New England, many years ago, that she was poor in all things except men. And the best crop that any land can raise is that of industrious, thoughtful men. Each generation of men, like every crop of grain, must be equal to the demand, or disaster will follow. Don't beguile yourselves into a sense of security. The national freedom for which your fathers fought will only remain with you at the price of eternal vigilance. Believe in the proverb that the might of right will prevail. Study the Constitution of your country and the causes from which it sprung, and appreciate and love its majesty; and the stupendous necessity of maintaining it at any cost being fully revealed to you, posterity will owe to you the same debt of gratitude which you owe to those now gone before.

Those pupils who took a prominent part in the celebration exercises, were Hagar Metz, Susanna Madden, Ida Becker, Helen Maine.

HEADLEY SCHOOL.

The new school flag was unfurled at the Headley School in the presence of patrons and friends who assembled to witness this interesting ceremony at 10 o'clock in the morning. An entertaining programme had been provided, in which singing and patriotic selections formed an interesting feature. The exercises connected with the unfurling of the flag occurred in the open air. Mr. Charles J. Sundell of the Chicago Board of Education, delivered the oration. " This is beyond comparison," he said, "the grandest anniversary of the nation's history, and should receive special celebration in the hearts of every true American. The younger generations in our free public schools should glorify this day, and should learn from it a new lesson of lofty patriotism in every true American feeling, into which no foreign sentiment should be allowed to find place. While other nations have had their great men, from Alexander to Bismarck, they have all of them been animated by a desire for conquest, for subjugation of their fellow-men and for the gratification of personal vanity; while Washington and the framers of our Constitution were actuated by the noblest feeling of the human breast, that of making the American people free and independent in a government the most natural of all, namely, a government 'of the people, for the people, and by the people.' Through this war the people achieved one of the grandest acts of power that a single mind in its moral condition can perform, that of instituting a new government and making free a new country. It was on this day one hundred years ago that Washington was inaugurated and took the oath of office at Federal Hall in New York City, in the presence of the first Congress, civic and military parades and a vast concourse of people. First in war and first in peace, he was installed in the foremost position of leadership in the Union, which was soon to become, as it has become, great, grand and glorious, and which shall remain one and inseparable now and forever more! Let us keep constantly in mind the memory of our fathers, the greatness they obtained in the history of our country, in the ages of mankind and in the story of civilization."

Mr. Sundell's address concluded, the pupils went to their various rooms, where they listened to the different programmes prepared for them. In Room 1 was displayed a portrait of George Washington, draped with the national colors and presented to the school by the graduating class of 1889. It was presented by Mr. J. Reichmann on behalf of the class. The Rev. Mr. Scott pronounced the benediction.

SKINNER SCHOOL.

The Centennial Celebration at this school was a noteworthy event. At 10:30 in the morning the pupils formed in procession and marched to the school yard, each child carrying a small flag, and each class led by a pupil carrying a large flag. At 11 o'clock the national colors were unfurled with hearty cheers from the large audience present. The song "America" was sung, the Governor's proclamation read, and interesting addresses delivered by Judge McConnell and Mr. James S. Harvey. The following is an abstract of Judge McConnell's speech:

It is well for us to-day, both young and old, to try to fully appreciate the occasion of which this is the hundredth anniversary. We cannot tell of it, we cannot contemplate it, without such contemplation giving us greater loyalty to our institutions, greater devotion to our country. After long trials with the primeval forests, after many hardships, after eight long years of bloody warfare, after innumerable trials and misfortunes, a great man, whose honor we celebrate to-day, led our armies to victory one hundred years ago. Washington was great as a soldier, wise as a statesman, and admirable as a private citizen, and every boy and girl should be familiar with his noble character and the history of his great achievements. We are also celebrating the hundredth anniversary of federal representation under the terms and limitations of a free Constitution. It has been left for our ancestors to make the great experiment, and through their bravery to earn for themselves a "government by the people, for the people, and of the people." It is for us to preserve, and when necessary to improve, this government. Both young and old should feel this responsibility. We must try to be good citizens. We cannot be so unless we understand our institutions, and are brave and sincere in our efforts to be good citizens. I trust that while we celebrate we may in time become more and more active citizens. We can pay no higher tribute of worth to Jefferson, Madison, Hamilton, Clay and Franklin than in our esteem and resolution to be good citizens in a Union that came to us through the practice of their zeal, their patriotism and their wisdom.

Following is an extract from Mr. Harvey's address:

The celebration which we honor to-day is the grandest in the whole world. Throughout this broad land sixty millions of people cease from their toils and celebrate the birthday of the nation. With the discovery of the New World came three conquerors, who disputed the possession of the soil. Spain came for plunder, France for glory, but England's sons were attracted by another motive. They came as individuals who desired the privilege of worshiping God according to the dictates of their own consciences and what they believed to be right. They turned the prows of their ships toward New England, that they might find there freedom of common conscience. The colonies grew, thrived and prospered; and when the country at home awoke to their importance, they attempted to draw tighter the reins of government and undertook to exercise it without the people's wish or interest. After six years of hydra-headed authority the people again assembled in convention, in order to form a more perfect union, establish justice, insure domestic tranquility, provide for the common defense, promote the general welfare, and secure the blessings of liberty to ourselves and our posterity. To do this they ordained and established this Constitution of the United States. And this is the Constitution under which we live to-day. If we would appreciate the liberties for which our fathers fought, toiled and tried; if we would gain a clearer appreciation of the twin oaks of freedom, liberty of conscience and liberty of government toward all mankind, we should strive as reverently as did our fathers one hundred years ago to make His word and His spirit our guide in all we undertake.

After the address the formal programme was completed and "America" sung by the audience amid much enthusiasm. The interior decorations of this school merit special commendation. They were entirely the work of the pupils.

TILDEN SCHOOL.

At the Tilden School the regular programme, singing and recitations, was varied by some very pretty patriotic tableaux, one representing "Columbia and the Original Thirteen States," and the other representing "Additional States." Twenty-three pupils also helped with the formal exercises, reciting patriotic quotations. The addresses were delivered by Dr. J. R. Corbus and Dr. Carlos Montezuma. Dr. Montezuma spoke in substance as follows:

There has been a period of nearly one hundred years in our nation's history since George Washington was inaugurated President of the United States. Soon followed a great war for liberty, freedom and just rights. And all this was not obtained until we had filled over a hundred thousand graves. Wonderful indeed has been the history of America. We hear to-day the hum of the spindle, the clang of the hammer, the rattling of the printing press, the roar of the railroad train, the rush of the steam engine, and the clash of machinery by means of electricity. We also have our educational institutions and our churches where one may worship, where we exercise liberty of conscience, and where none dare molest us. It is for us to decide who shall direct our institutions, who shall form our opinions. Shall we be ruled by men who love their country, or shall we be governed by men who gratify only their own selfish desire and seek to gratify only their own ambitious ends? Shall we be ruled by foreign lands, or shall we see order and freedom in this land, so that when a foreigner steps on our shore, in a little while he shall say: "Let me then remain among you, with your people as my people, your God as my God." The flag of our country is the emblem of peace, the emblem of security, and the emblem of strength for time and eternity. Rejoice and be glad, for the Lord thy God hath not dealt so with any other land.

Dr. Corbus's remarks were, in substance:

One hundred years ago the first Continental Congress met in New York. It was the 4th day of March, 1789. The government was not in full running order until April 30. It was on that day that George Washington was made President of the United States of America. During the century which has intervened from Washington to Harrison, a tremendous change has been wrought in our country's history. Great indeed has been the advance in science, trade and the arts through the wonderful inventions of the past hundred years. The name of George Washington has sounded down the century past, and the music of that name now fills every breast. It is lisped by prattling babes and eulogized by our greatest men. Reverently we speak it. Judge Marshall, in his wonderful words on Washington at the time of the latter's death in 1799, rightly called him "first in war, first in peace, and first in the hearts of his countrymen."

MOTLEY SCHOOL.

At the Motley School the celebration was confined to the general programme arranged for the occasion. There was singing, recitations, essays on "Patriotism," "George Washington," also two dialogues, one "Uncle Sam and His Supporters," participated in by twenty-four boys, who represented Uncle Sam and the twenty-three Presidents from Washington to Harrison; and the other, "Across the Years," twenty girls, ten representing 1789 and ten 1889. A large audience enjoyed the exercises.

ROGERS SCHOOL.

After singing Keller's hymn, "America," the children marched to the school yard, where the regular programme was given, and much enjoyed by the large audience. Noteworthy among the special features were the following: "Paul Revere's Ride," by fourteen children; patriotic quotations from Evarts, Patrick Henry, and from the letters of Washington. The singing was good and the essays were given with much spirit.

ANDERSEN SCHOOL.

The pupils of this school commenced the day's programme by singing the "Battle Hymn of the Nation," after which the regular programme was given. In the rooms of the smaller children appropriate speeches were made, with patriotic quotations interspersed between. Each child had a flag and a rosette, and at the close all were sent home wearing the souvenir medals prepared for the occasion. The children gathered in the hall, which was crowded to its utmost capacity. The programme included singing, essays, and patriotic quotations from John Adams, Washington, and Pickering. Excellent addresses were delivered by Mr. Frank Wenter and Senator B. A. Eckhardt.

KINZIE SCHOOL.

Over five hundred persons gathered at the Kinzie School and lustily shouted when the national colors were given to the breeze, at once joining in the stirring song "Rally Round the Flag, Boys." The little ones and their friends then marched to their various rooms, where they listened to music, singing and addresses. There were some very beautiful dialogues and essays which showed considerable thought. The address by Prof. Matellini was of great interest. Said he:

To us who find ourselves pupils or teachers in public schools, permit me to remind you of the grandeur of this day. Its greatness, its strength is largely due to these same public schools. You well know the great part education plays in the history of the country, and therefore I exhort you to foster and sustain the public school. Education will make good citizens. Without it there can be no good citizens. Education has done more for civilization than wars. Strive to make your lives worthy of your country, so that your names will be as venerated and honored as those now gone before.

PEARSON STREET SCHOOL.

The exercises at the Pearson Street School were in accordance with the formal programme. There were essays on "Washington," on "Liberty" and on "Freedom," singing, dialogues and patriotic quotations. The programme, while an ambitious one, was well rendered, and seemed to be heartily enjoyed by the large audience present.

PICKARD SCHOOL.

At the Pickard School the exercises were opened with a very pretty drill by thirty young girls dressed in red, white and blue, headed by three waving the national colors. The school sang "O Columbia, the Gem of the Ocean," and as the flag was unfurled prolonged cheers burst from the 800 assembled guests. In the various rooms the regular programme was followed. The decorations were very tasteful, consisting of bunting, pictures, flags and an elaborate ship of state. In Room 3 the programme was varied by an interesting exercise of sixteen pupils, eight on one side of the room representing 1789, and eight on the other representing 1889, and each one carrying a Harrison banner. The exercises in the lower rooms were very commendably performed.

The blackboard decorations were done by Thomas Jehnek.

OAK STREET SCHOOL.

At the Oak Street School there was much patriotism awakened by the programme, not only among the pupils, but in the audience as well. Washington was considered from every point of view, and his high moral courage, his noble patriotism and his beauty of character plainly brought out to every one present. The music was excellent and the recitations very creditable.

COTTAGE GROVE SCHOOL.

The pupils assembled at 10:30 in the school-yard and broke into lusty cheers when the national colors were hoisted on the main building. Cheer followed cheer as the flag ran up. The pupils then formed themselves in a double column, and led by "Columbia" and the original thirteen states, filed into the hall, where "Columbia" and the original thirteen took seats on the stage. The formal programme consisted of essays, songs, speeches on Washington in childhood, as Commander, as President, and the influence of his life on contemporary times. The unique drill of twenty-four girls in red, white and blue, with light blue sashes, was a pleasant diversion from the formal programme. Worthy of special mention was the tableau of the thirteen original states. The states, headed by "Columbia," marched to the stage, where they formed themselves in a semi-circle, with "Columbia" in the centre. Bits of history, patriotic sentiments and appropriate quotations were recited, the interesting exhibition closing by pretty grouping of the thirteen states.

Judge Doolittle delivered an address on Washington, declaring him to be a preternatural man clearly sent by heaven to relieve us in our dire distress.   America seemed above all to be favored by God, for from time to time great men have arisen at times of great crises and led us forward over the exigency.   The Rev. Jenkyn Lloyd Jones spoke to the children.   He placed Horace Mann, William Lloyd Garrison and Louis Agassiz before them as high types that the country had produced.

The following pupils filled prominent parts on the programme in the highest seven rooms, which joined in holding a general celebration: Hiram Patterson, George McBean, Harris Forsythe, Robert Forsythe, Minnie Bushnell, Edith Boake, Cyrus Tollman, Mabel Richards, Grace Fiedler, Louise Kraus.

GRANT SCHOOL.

The assembly hall of the Grant School was crowded to its utmost capacity.   The pupils gathered in their various rooms and listened to the programmes prepared for them.   The recitations were well read and the songs well sung.   Addresses were made by Robert A. Childs, Dr. Wallace, and Mr. J. H. S. Quick.

These pupils took part in the Centennial exercises: Annie Sternberg, Florence Traye, Olive Prica, Sadie Briggs, B. White, Nathan Guest, James Buffton, Mollie Rue, Walter Ayers, Lillie Parker, Abe Frankenstein.

HURON STREET SCHOOL.

The first feature of the exercises at this school was the unfurling of the flag in the presence of the pupils, patrons and friends. Following this was the singing of the song "Our Country's Flag." Capt. C. C. Merrick delivered the address, saying:

We meet to-day to celebrate an event which could only have been brought about by a people imbued with patriotism   We meet to celebrate that true devotion and sturdiness which makes true citizenship, and to render homage to those who sacrificed their lives in the faith of their country.   Especially do we commemorate the self-sacrifices of our ancestors and the splendid system of universal education through them made possible, so that to-day in our free land our youth may acquire whatever is necessary to fit them for any station in life.   This is a day to be commemorated by the old as well as the young.   Ours is one flag, one land, one people, the grandest nation on the face of the earth.

Those who took part in the formal exercises were: Grace Verrill, Gerty Worth, Charles Slip, Mammie Meyers, Edith Stafford, Louis Egir.

JONES SCHOOL.

The exercises at this school were of a very interesting character. Those of the pupils who took active parts were, in Room 1: I. Brinkworth, Ella Derrick, M. Raymond, N. Schiefstein, C. Corrigan. The Rev. Dr. W. H. Bolton spoke in half a dozen rooms, the scholars being under the charge of their own teachers. Mr. Fernando Jones, after whose father the school was named, and whose picture adorned the walls, said, pointing to the picture of Gen. Washington, which the speaker had presented to the school, that it was from a painting by Stuart, and gave a very correct likeness of Washington. Washington's character is one to study and reverence. We should formulate our lives upon Washington's character. The nearer we come to being what Washington was, the nearer we come to living lives marked by nobility and patriotism. A touching incident in the celebration at this school was the rising in her seat of Mrs. R. Elam, an old lady, who said that for more than fifty-six years she had watched the progress of this school, and that she had known the school from the time it was a log hut on the edge of the wilderness. She was intimately acquainted with the founder, Mr. Jones, and she wished to see the school live and prosper in the future as it had done in the past. The exercises in the lower rooms were of an entertaining character. In Room 16 Sig. Camillo Volina delivered an address in Italian.

BURR SCHOOL.

At the Burr School at 10:30 the pupils of two rooms met in the hall and the group thus formed in the various rooms held each its own exercises, consisting of patriotic songs, quotations, recitations and essays. The rooms were decorated with flags and bunting, and the blackboards with patriotic drawings. Every room had its own speaker. These were assigned as follows:

Room 1.—The Rev. Wilbur Satterfield.
Room 2.—The Rev. Thomas Collins.
Rooms 3 and 4.—Mr. Horth.
Rooms 5 and 6.—Mr. R. A. Haase.

Rooms 7 and 8.—Mr. George Warr.
Rooms 9 and 10.—Mr. Mossup.
Rooms 11 and 12.—Mrs. Montgomery.
Rooms 13 and 15.—Mr. George Hopkins.
Room 14.—Mr. Thomas Bolger.
Rooms 16 and 19.—Mr. John Nuveen.
Rooms 17 and 18.—Mr. T. P. Jones.
Room 20.—Mrs. Whiffenbeck.
Rooms 21 and 22.—Dr. Fanny Leake.
Rooms 23 and 24.—Mrs. E. Page.

At 11:30 o'clock the pupils, their friends and patrons, to the number of three thousand, assembled in the school yard, cheering lustily as the national flag was unfurled. Mr. Millard B. Hereley delivered the address, speaking as follows:

It gives me great pleasure to-day to see so many happy faces that live under the stars and stripes, and that have gathered to do homage to the nation's anniversary. This is indeed the land of the free and the home of the brave. Many of your fathers came from homes beyond the sea. Did you ever note how many people come here to make their homes from foreign lands, while so very few ever leave here to seek a new home in other lands? Why is this so? It is because our country insures perfect freedom, which is of more value than life itself. We should never forget those who one hundred years ago offered their lives that we to-day might be free.

CENTRAL PARK SCHOOL.

The exercises at this school were preceded by a flag-raising and salute. This was decidedly the feature of the occasion. The pupils gathered first in their respective rooms, then formed in line and marched, grade by grade, from the front hall down into the yard, where friends and patrons had gathered. Many of the girls were in special costume, some dressed in Martha Washington style and others representing the original thirteen states. The singing was conducted by Nora Condry, one of the pupils, and by the cornetist, Harry Robinson. After marching back to their respective rooms the pupils rendered the exercises, composed of speaking, recitations, reading of compositions and singing. In one room "Martha Washington's Tea Party" was given by a little girl in ancient attire. In another room the thirteen original colonies made their appearance before a modern audience. In another room Martha Washington herself appeared, seated by a small tea stand in a position of honor on the stage. Mr. George W. Spofford delivered the address, visiting the various rooms for that purpose. His address was filled with patriotism and good advice. The rooms throughout the building were tastefully decorated.

OAKLEY SCHOOL.

At 10:45 the exercises were opened with an address and singing, after which the pupils repaired to their several rooms, where the formal exercises were held. A large audience assembled to listen to the excellent programme. The decorations consisted of flags, bunting, and patriotic sentiments written on the blackboards. Mr. Philip Stein delivered an excellent address on the Constitution, explaining its object and purposes. Those who took part were: C. C. Dodge, Bertha Piper, James Castello, Clara Bennett, Glenn Hall, Allie Whittell, Cora Lynthcombe. A number of visitors also made remarks to the pupils.

GARFIELD SCHOOL.

In front of this school building a large red, white and blue banner waved, and one hundred of the little ones sang "Three Cheers for the Red, White and Blue." The chorus was led by two young violinists, and proved a very enjoyable feature of the occasion. Room 1 was tastefully decorated with flags, banners and pictures. The seventh and eighth grades united in giving an excellent musical and literary programme. Thirteen young ladies, dressed in the national colors, represented the original thirteen states, and marched under the leadership of Miss Ella Pearson, who personated "Columbia," singing "O Columbia! the Gem of the Ocean." Among those who participated were the following: Mollie Crouse, Kate McMahon, Emma Lingenberg, Ada Young, Lizzie Finn, Frank Campbell, Abraham Addleson, Miss Baker. The addresses were made by Judge A. N. Waterman, the Rev. P. F. Matzinger, Mr. Frank Wenter, and Mr. H. H. Thomas.

HEALY SCHOOL.

The exercises at this school were opened with the formal programme prepared by the committee for this occasion. The singing of patriotic songs, recitations and speeches formed the principal features of the day.

LINCOLN SCHOOL.

At this school the exercises were listened to by a large audience. The unfurling of the new school flag was the first feature of the day. Short speeches were made by Dr. Johnstone and Mr. Frank J. Loesch. The programme was followed out in a creditable manner.

SHERIDAN SCHOOL.

The pupils, friends and patrons of this school joined in singing "Our Flag is Still There," while the national colors were thrown to the breeze. The address of the day was made by Mr. John M. Southworth, who said:

We look back to-day upon one hundred years of national progress and success such as no nation on the face of the earth can furnish an equal example. One hundred years ago to-day the United States took its place among the nations of the earth, George Washington, the leading patriot of his time and the most illustrious man, being inaugurated President of the United States. This liberty, which is insured by the Declaration of Independence and granted by the Constitution, was only to be made a living reality in our land by dreadful harvests of death. As a people we enjoy more liberty, justice and equal rights than any nation on the face of the globe. We are a people imbued with the spirit of liberty, and are the fairest minded people in the world. No foreign power can ever prevail among our free people. To you, young persons, I would say, imbibe the spirit of liberty, study our institutions, learn the Declaration of Independence and contemplate the conditions under which it was issued. It is the greatest public document ever signed. Study the Constitution of your country. Remember that to you will soon be confided the great duties of its execution and preservation, and remember when you look upon the bright stars and broad stripes of your country's flag that no flag has ever enriched a people by the truth it represents as has ours. Our country is the harbor of the oppressed of every country across the sea, the haven into which they are received to homes of happiness. Our flag has been the emblem of armies noblest of the noble and mightiest of the mighty, yet never in any war has it been given to a foreign foe. In entering upon the second century of our nation's history, we should be thankful that we live in a land of equal rights, equal privileges, under the Constitution which we should maintain perfect and unimpaired, proving under it and under our form of government that the rights of many and the rational enjoyments of millions may be realized and enjoyed, that through its attributes of divinity, its liberty and justice, the human race will rise to the highest degree of civilization and the greatest perfection attainable on the face of the earth.

The pupils who took leading parts were: Minnie Casey, who assumed the rôle of Columbia, while those who represented the thirteen colonies were: Mamie Phalon, Clara Lippart, Charles Kriper, Frank Sweeny, Jessie Hawkins, Frieda Brown, Catherine Sweeney, Thomas S. Grimke, Eva Edmunds, Charles Drueck, Emma Bowting.

FROEBEL SCHOOL.

At this school the exercises were opened at 10:30 with the singing of "America." After this the pupils went to their various rooms, when the formal programme, prepared for the occasion, was rendered. Mr. Edward Roby and the Rev. Dr. S. F. Smith, the venerable author of the hymn "America," carried out the programme, which was replete with good features. The pupils who took prominent parts were: Lizzie Lindstrom, Albert Sandquist, Alice Watson, Edwin Volk, Clara Falvey, Katie Adams, Julia Haighberg. At the request of the principal, the venerable author of the national hymn was asked to address a few words to the young. In introducing him, the principal, Mr. Henry C. Cox, said, "that he had sung 'America' as a boy, had sung it in camp, had sung it in Andersonville prison, had this morning sung it as a salute to the flag, had sung it in church, and would sing it again as a closing piece to the day's exercises. It was his wish," he said, "that not only might his pupils have the distinguished honor of seeing the author of the hymn which had inspired so much patriotism in every land, but might have the more distinguished honor of hearing him speak."

After gracefully acknowledging the compliment, Dr. Smith said:

Since you have just sung the hymn "America," perhaps you would be interested in knowing something of its composition and the circumstances which led to its origin. In 1832 Mr. William Woodbury returned from Germany, where he had been studying the systems of music in use in their schools, bringing back with him a great pile of the books used to teach the youth the elements of music.   The books were given into my hands with the instruction that if I should see anything worthy of copying I should translate, if not I should write.   I took the books and began turning the leaves until I came upon a song which impressed me in a peculiar way.   I sang it through and at once wrote down on an old scrap of paper the hymn, "My Country, 'tis of Thee."   As it appears to-day, so it was written in the first draft.   Could I have realized at the time that the song would be taken up by millions, I certainly would have spent some time in revision.   But it is as it is, and the people have made it theirs.

Mr. Roby delivered an eloquent and impressive address, which was heartily appreciated by the large audience.

VEDDER STREET SCHOOL.

The flag unfurling, followed by the singing of a patriotic song, opened the exercises at this school, after which the pupils went to their respective rooms and listened to the formal programme prepared for the occasion.   The rooms were prettily decorated with red, white and blue bunting, pictures of Washington and Harrison, and flags.   The programme inspired considerable enthusiasm and was heartily enjoyed by the whole school.

THROOP SCHOOL.

The formal programme was closely followed at this school.

There were three speakers: Mr. D. F. Bremner, Mr. Adolph Kraus and Mr. F. W. Young, whose addresses were good.   Mr. Young said:

It is difficult, if not impossible, to find perfection in anything human, but the system of government given us by the men of the Revolution is as nearly perfect as anything human can be.   When it was first established the royalists of England predicted its early downfall.   The 100th anniversary of its birth we celebrate to-day, a hundred years full of changes, and it is here yet.   Will it be here a hundred years from now or will it pass away, to be followed by despotism?   The answer to a great extent lies with the children of this generation.   It depends in a great measure on the conduct of the little boys of to-day and the influence of the little girls of to-day, whether the people of the country one hundred years from now will enjoy the rights of free government.

MOSLEY SCHOOL.

At this school there was no attempt at a special exhibition, but each class gave its own programme. There was the unfurling of the flag before the assembled pupils in the school grounds. Quotations were read from history, selections from the poets of the Revolution and pictures drawn on the blackboards, illustrating the principal events of the last hundred years. In the eighth grade the children, dressed in colonial costume, gave an interesting representation of Washington's inaugural. An eloquent address was made by Bishop Cheney. Another speaker was Mr. W. D. Roys, an extract from whose remarks is as follows:

In the first hundred years of our national history we have developed scholars, heroes and martyrs, and we have learned to look upon our Constitution as that perfect model which united the discordant elements in the confederation into more fraternal relations. Washington's memory lives and is celebrated by this national pageantry to-day by sixty millions of people. He builded for the future, and to-day we are building for the future under that flag which he unfurled in the wide extent of the heavens, and which is to be the emblem of constitutional liberty forever. We shall never look so far into the future as when we look into the past and seize upon some ideal life and place it high in the heavens as a fixed star for our guidance and direction. Dean Maitland cried from the pulpit "Oh get innocency!" and to-day Washington cries to us from the lofty heights of undying fame "Oh keep loyalty!" Thus shall every star emblazoned on our national banner shine resplendent forever.

In the seventh grade the pupils in their exercises made the study of Washington a special feature of the celebration.

FRANKLIN SCHOOL.

Long before the hour set for the commencement of the exercises of this school, a large crowd had gathered before the school building. At 10:30 the enthusiasm of the pupils was increased by the unfurling of the national colors, the band playing the " Red, White and Blue." After the song a short address was made by Mr. Francis Walker, standing upon the steps of the building. He paid a touching tribute to the founders of the nation, spoke impressively of the price at which liberty had been bought, of the protection afforded by the American flag, and unfolded the advantages of a free country in which all men are equal. His desire was to impress on the children the importance of realizing the splendid future of this great country, who in a few years would become the voters of our land, and to whom would be confided the care of its institutions. With a knowledge of the history of past events we would be actuated by new objects and by patriotic feelings of the highest advantage to our country.

At the conclusion of the address, "Hail Columbia" was sung, and the children and the invited guests went to their several rooms, where the programme prepared for the occasion was finely executed by the pupils. The decorations consisted of small flags and blackboard drawings of American eagles, American shields, and, in fact, everything American.

McCLELLAN SCHOOL.

Immediately after the cheering at the unfurling of the national colors had subsided, the teachers, friends, patrons and pupils of this school filed into the room in which the exercises of the day were to be held. The rooms were tastefully decorated with flags, bunting, pictures of Washington and Lincoln, and other appropriate designs. In two of the highest grammar grades all the grammar grade pupils were assembled. The speeches of the day were delivered by the Hon. John F. Finerty and Mr. C. W. Martin. Both of these gentlemen delivered eloquent addresses. Mr. Martin concluded his address as follows:

I have already made mention of the man who was more intimately connected with the foundation of the government than any other. We first knew him as a young lieutenant, saving the king's armies from destruction; next as a member of the Continental Congress; then commander-in-chief of the colonial forces; chairman of the committee that framed the Constitution; lastly, first President, twice unanimously elected. What shall we call him—warrior, patriot, or statesman? George Washington is without a parallel in the history of the world. While the successful leader of a great revolution, his patriotism was without ambition. Cæsar made himself perpetual dictator, and Brutus slew him for ambition. When Cromwell's Ironsides had placed England in his power, he placed himself at the head of a commonwealth with more power than a king. Napoleon, the offspring of the French Revolution, was not content with the kingdom of France and fell striving to make all Europe his empire. But George Washington, when his enemies had been conquered, and he himself might have been king, disbanded his army and withdrew to his quiet home at Mount Vernon. Regretfully he left it to guide for a time the Ship of State as no other man could have done; and he left as a final legacy to his countrymen those sage suggestions contained in his farewell address. Grand, inspired and patriotic, George Washington stands unrivaled in all history. To some the future was doubtful, to him it was sure. He formed plans that have assured to you and to me this great American republic.

In the course of some eloquent remarks on the life, character and influence of Washington, Mr. Finerty declared that Washington stood preëminent in the world's history as personating high moral courage and immortal patriotism. Washington's achievements in arms were noble, modest and of unparalleled unselfishness. Called by his country, and placed at the head of the young republic, he did not conspire to murder its liberties, but rather to preserve and perpetuate them. He laid down the powers of office at the expiration of his term as President, as willingly as when supreme commander during the Revolution, he had disbanded his armies and had laid down the sword of sovereign command. The speaker then contrasted present conditions with those of 1789, and pointed out the beauty of maintaining a grand free country, united under one free flag, and guarded by a free Constitution. He paid a tribute to the free American system of public schools and the proficiency of the pupils, whose exercises he had witnessed. In the youth of America, as in the youth of nations everywhere, is to be found the hope of the future, but the American youth has more to fire his ambition than the youth of any other country. Born in the travail of a great Revolution; baptized in the blood of a fierce warfare, whose storm has rather strengthened than weakened the grand structure of our Union, our country has forever blotted from the pages of American history the foul stain of human slavery. He hoped that in the year of grace 1989, our children's children might join in the celebration of the second century of the perfection of the republic, and like their fathers before them, give thanks to the God of Liberty that they still dwelt in a country in which ruled no tyrants and pined no slaves.

NEWBERRY SCHOOL.

The day at this school was celebrated in patriotic style. From every corner and window of the building floated the glorious Stars and Stripes. The main entrance presented a handsome appearance, draped as it was with the national colors. First, the large audience gathered in front of the building, where the exercises were commenced with the unfurling of the national colors. At a signal from the principal, the school sang "America," accompanied by two cornetists, O. J. Muellenbacher and Howard O. Snyder The pupils then fell into line, and with the cornets playing the "Stars and Stripes," marched into the building and into their several rooms. The divisions below the sixth grade had entertainments in their own rooms, while the five higher divisions gave a special programme in the assembly hall. The hall was handsomely decorated with flags, bunting and patriotic designs. Short addresses were made by the principal of the school, Mr. C. P. Stowell, and by Mr. Edgar Madden.

WELLS SCHOOL.

At this school the celebration was marked by much enthusiasm on the part of the large audience. In the seventh and eighth grades the programme was quite a pretentious one, being made up of studies of leading patriots, quotations and extracts from the writings of these great men. Ex-Mayor Roche and the Rev. Dr. Severinghaus delivered stirring addresses. Admirable musical features enlivened the occasion.

OGDEN SCHOOL.

No attempt was made at this school to gather the pupils together on account of the lack of accommodations, so the little ones assembled in their separate rooms, where the exercises of the day were held in a patriotic manner. The decorations were handsome, consisting of bunting, flags and festoons of evergreens. The blackboards were covered with patriotic emblems in colored chalk, representing important events in the first hundred years of our national history, scenes from the Revolution, and portraits of the great men of the day. Among the decorations were four handsome steel engravings, given to the school by Judge Elliott Anthony, and representing the signing of the Constitution, and portraits of Washington, Webster and Lincoln. The addresses in every room were delivered by Judge Anthony, Mr. William Vocke, Dr. S. W. Stryker and Gen. Stout. The programme was rendered by Charles Stevenson, Ira Bauer, Lilian Mallory, Nettie de Billbrass, Maude Rounseville, C. Anderson, Bertha Sloan.

SCAMMON SCHOOL.

The pupils of this school assembled in front of the building to listen to the addresses of Mr. Thomas Cratty, Mr. Anthony Culver and Mr. David Felsenthal. The flag being raised, Chud-leigh Perry stepped forward, saying, "We salute our flag," and the large audience of 2,000 responded with cheers. Mr. Cratty closed his address as follows:

Revere our flag, love it. If any little one should see any one disrespectful to our flag, place your little fist under his nose and say "stop." If you see the flag of any nation friendly to America respect it; but if you see the flag of anarchy, socialism or communism, stamp on it, tear it down and trample it in the dust.

The formal programme was given in a creditable manner, bringing these pupils forward in leading parts: Kittie McNeil, Josephine Rice, Charles Perry.

THOMAS HOYNE SCHOOL.

The celebration at this school was opened by a reading of the Governor's proclamation by Miss Nellie Baines. After this the school flag was run up, amidst hearty cheers from the large audience. Principal Léech then addressed the pupils, dwelling on the importance of the occasion and the events it commemorated. He urged the pupils and their friends to ever uphold our flag and our institutions and to foster American ideas, chief among which he placed the public schools. The rooms in which the exercises were held were suitably decorated. Gen. Joseph B. Leake, Mr. Lawrence M. Ennis and Mr. William G. Beal delivered the addresses.

BROWN SCHOOL.

The Brown School presented a gay appearance on Centennial Day. There were flags in every window, a banner floated from the pole in the yard, while the desks and rooms were decorated with flags and bunting. On the blackboard were crayon drawings

of the heroes of the Revolution. The pupils all wore some
patriotic emblem. The little girls wore Columbia hats, red,
white and blue ribbons and turbans. The boys were as patriotic in their dress as the girls. Some wore cocked hats, others
the continental garb, while others displayed the tricolor. A good
many of the girls were dressed as Martha Washington, with
powdered hair, flowing sleeves and buckled slippers.

A large number of visitors attended the exercises. The
room in which the programme was carried out was decorated
with hundreds of small flags which festooned the wall. Large
bouquets of tulips and Easter lilies on the piano served to
heighten the effect. There were patriotic scenes and tableaux.
The first tableau represented the inauguration of Washington.
Mamie Mithe represented Martha Washington, while Willie
Greenleaf represented the immortal Father of his Country.
Then came the cherry tree incident, with Walter Greenleaf as
the father and little Frank Ellis as the truthful wood-chopper.
Washington on the Delaware and at the Battle of Trenton were
the other subjects. The first address was given by Congressman
William E. Mason. His address was directed to the children and
was much enjoyed by them. He loved to study the history of
his country and the scenes, incidents and lives of the founders of
the nation. Here is where he drew his inspiration and intensified his love for free America. It was that which had united
federal and confederate and had made them forget their enmities.
The country, while scarcely a hundred years old, was grand
beyond belief. Its church spires are against the sky, its free
schools on every hand, its people most fully blessed with prosperity and peace.

Patriotic addresses were also given by Mr. M. J. Dunne, the
Rev. Dr. W. M. Lawrence, Mr. Mallory and Mr. R. E. Jenkins.
Following is an abstract of Mr. Dunne's remarks:

I suppose you scholars are not at all pleased in being disturbed
at your studies to-day and having a holiday. But the event you
are commemorating not coming again in a hundred years, it is best
that you celebrate it now, for you will then be too old to enjoy it.
I therefore counsel you to enjoy it as best you can. You take
great pleasure in celebrating the Fourth of July, with flags, processions and burnt fingers, and as this day only comes once in a

hundred years, you should rejoice one hundred times as much as on the Fourth. When this government was formed only a small part of this land was inhabited by the white race. A small strip of land along the Atlantic was occupied, while the rest was given over to the vast unbroken wilderness, wild beasts and savage tribes. Since then the land from the Atlantic to the Pacific, from North to South, has been brought into one grand government. I counsel you to keep in mind the glorious occasion which this day commemorates. Remember with pride the early days of this republic, and the gallant, wise and noble conduct of the fathers of our country. Cultivate in your own hearts, in your own children, a love for your country, a love for liberty. If you do this as you ought, then this country will grow in greatness and power and strength, until, one hundred years hence, when our posterity celebrate the beginning of our second century, the prophecy made by John Bright in England in 1862 will more than have been realized. He said: "A broader vision comes before my gaze. It may be but a vision, yet I will cherish it. I see one vast confederation stretching from the North in one unbroken line to the South, from the wild billows of the Atlantic westward to the calmer waters of the Pacific main; and I see one people, one language, one law and one faith, and over all this wide domain, freedom for the oppressed of every land and of every clime!"

The following is a brief extract from the remarks of Dr. Lawrence:

It gives me pleasure to accept your invitation to-day and to speak from my heart to you. Not that it is necessary for me to say anything, because you have had the pleasure of hearing two very carefully prepared addresses which I myself did not hear. I hope this day will lead you to cherish your country. There is some disposition to encourage everything foreign in America to-day. I have no objection to our country's improving itself and importing into our own American life that which we find of service in the lives of other nations, but when it comes to throwing what we have away and replacing it with what is no good in the lives of others, I feel a species of indignation that we have a tendeney to be such servile imitators. I feel what it is to be an American. As the days go by and you go out into life, may the memory of this celebration remain not merely as a great incident in your school life, but as something to inspire and cultivate loyalty in your hearts.

The following pupils took leading parts: Minnie Hickey, Miss Shepherd, Willie Hold.

DOUGLAS SCHOOL.

At this school the Board of Education arranged to have the formal dedication of the building in connection with the regular exercises of the day. Over 1,500 people were in attendance. The speakers were Mayor Cregier, Mr. Stephen A. Douglas, Mr. George Howland, the Hon. J. R. Doolittle, Jr., and Mr. Henry V. Freeman. Mr. Howland's address, which was admirably brief and to the point, is as follows:

My young friends of the present generation, I, as a representative of the generation of the past, am glad to welcome you into the beautiful new building on this great day in the nation's history. This day begins the second century of the greatest constitutional republic the world ever saw; a nation in which all avenues to success are ever open to intelligence, industry, and unswerving integrity, and whose highest pride and greatest faith is in her public schools. The present century is demanding more schools. Our course of study should be broader, richer, deeper. Alongside of our high schools and parallel with them we are having industrial and trade schools, schools of the mechanic arts, schools of science, and schools of art. I am only sorry that an important previous engagement will prevent my being at this school at the next celebration, one hundred years from now, when our great-grandchildren of the Douglas School, then ennobled by a long line of graduates as statesmen, or in the arts, and professions—as men, women, fathers and mothers—will celebrate with higher power and holier splendor.

The Mayor told the little ones that soon they would be called upon as voters to maintain the successes of the past. "Not one of you here but may be called to some high office. Now is the time to prepare yourselves for the future. Where else in the world can you get such a privilege of becoming educated if not in our free public schools? I hope you will improve your opportunity and always keep the government free and united, as I believe this is the greatest nation on the face of the earth."

These pupils took individual part: Warren Everett, Laura Gleason, Louis Head, D. Turner, Kate Hinkley. The programme included music, recitations, and declamations. A calisthenic drill by forty-eight boys, waving the Red, White and Blue, was a feature of the occasion.

Mr. Henry V. Freeman, in his very able address, gave an

excellent review of the events which preceded the inauguration of George Washington as the first President, the deplorable condition of the country under the articles of confederation, and the unspeakable blessings which "a more perfect union" conferred upon the country. He portrayed the peerless character of Washington in eloquent terms, and closed with the following beautiful peroration:

To-day a hundred years have gone since first the nation's life began. The infant of that day stands a strong man, acknowledging no superior among the nations of the earth. The century has been filled with momentous events. Revolutions have shaken the thrones of Europe. Empires have risen and fallen across the sea. But the union of these States has grown always stronger and more vigorous. The noise of battles and the tramp of armies have come to us not only from afar. We have had our own experiences of war, at home and abroad. The Constitution of a hundred years has been assailed from without and from within. But, like the mountain oak, it has gained strength and vigor from the tempest, and stands to-day a proud monument to its founders, the rock of national unity and strength. Under it we and our fathers have for a century past enjoyed the blessings of liberty controlled and regulated by law. Under it, let us hope, the same blessings may still be enjoyed by generations yet unborn, who will stand upon the now silent shores of the far-off coming time.

Upon you who are boys and girls to-day the fate of these coming generations will largely depend. You may not be called on to engage in the conflicts of arms, as your fathers have been. But you will have to fight battles no less serious. Each generation must fight its own battles, and every generation finds new battles to fight. It is still as true as it ever was that

> "We are living, we are dwelling
> In a grand and awful time—
> In an age on ages telling,
> To be living is sublime."

This, my young friends, is *our* country. That flag is our flag. Think what it has cost to defend it. That flag has been bathed in the blood of heroes. It is the emblem of our liberty, the symbol of national unity and power. It represents home and friends and freedom and country. Many a man among us has seen it floating above the smoke of battle.

> "Many an eye hath glanced to see
> That banner in the sky."

Land of liberty, "May peace be within thy walls, and prosperity within thy palaces! May there be no decay, no leading into captivity, and no complaining in thy streets. May truth spring out of the earth and righteousness look down from heaven."

DORE SCHOOL.

At this school an interesting address was made to the pupils by the Hon. E. B. Sherman. The programme included the singing of " Old Uncle Sam." The song had a special significance for this occasiom. It was written by Col. Putnam, the son of the nephew of the Revolutionary Putnam, who settled in Marietta, Ohio, and who took an active part in the War of 1812. The pro. gramme included singing, declamations, quotations and essays.

HOLDEN SCHOOL.

The celebrations were held in each room of this school edifice. There was no general programme on account of the lack of suitable accommodations. Addresses were made by Judge Baker, Col. D. W. Munn and J. P. Ahrens. The programmes were of great interest and were well rendered.

HARRISON SCHOOL.

To the music of flute and piano, the pupils of this school marched to the large hall. The exercises were opened with singing Keller's American hymn, by a chorus of 250 voices, and after this the programme prepared for the occasion was followed out with fidelity and intelligence. A good feature of the programme was the appearance of the forty-two states, represented by forty-two little girls with crowns and badges. Another feature was the wand exercise, given by girls, the wands being trimmed with red, white and blue. The speakers were the Rev. Dr. Utter, ex-Mayor Carter H. Harrison and John Foster. Mr. Harrison was received with great applause. He told in an eloquent address of the duties of citizenship. In the course of his remarks Dr. Utter said:

It is a strange mingling of seed with which, two hundred years ago, this land was planted. There were Pilgrims and Puritans, Separatists, Brownists, Quakers and Scandinavians, beside other heretics and heresies with which the age was rife. There were the Dutch at New Amsterdam and on Manhattan Island. The French were out West in the wilderness, and ever since the people have been coming from many foreign lands. We do not need any more people now from foreign lands. Let us mould into one union now, if we can, what we have already got. In union there is strength. This day one hundred years ago they gave us a constitutional government and selected that grand man, Washington, as our first President. Before the Constitution was written it was in our hearts. The nation has written it there to-day. That Constitution written in our hearts makes us a nation. It fuses this widely differing people into one grand nation. Love, reverence and never be untrue to your flag. With all its grandness it means our good, freedom and its blessings.

The pupils who took a prominent part were: A. Guerner, G. Quinlan, W. Johnstone, G. Cohn, E. Saunders, George Schroeder.

BRAINARD SCHOOL.

This building and its various rooms were very tastefully decorated for the Centennial occasion. Every one connected with the school entered enthusiastically into the work of preparation for the proper observation of the anniversary of Washington's inauguration. The address of the day was by Samuel Parker, who spoke on "A Goodly Heritage." He said:

There may be advantages, benefits, enjoyments to be derived from belonging to other nations, but there is no nation that can compare with this one; and the statement thus broadly made by thousands of orators and speakers to-day will stand unchallenged. In this highest of free government you feel nothing of those selfish conditions that influence others not so highly favored. It is for the purpose of still more stimulating to a loftier appreciation of the one who more than any one else framed this government, that we have set aside this day as one of celebration and rejoicing. It seems that the fathers builded wiser than they knew, and indeed through that wisdom which always comes soonest to those who earnestly ask it, they have brought to you and will soon pass to your hands for safe keeping the grandest and best government ever devised for serving the best interests of all. If out of the wrecks of former efforts from which to form and found a great republic, and to perfect it through years of effort, our fathers have brought this government to us one hundred years old, we with our advanced surroundings should cherish and protect it, and always strive to pass it on to others improved, if indeed it can be, and so on and on and on to the outermost verge of time.

LANGLAND SCHOOL.

The rooms of this school were prettily decorated with bunting and flags. In the lowest rooms and primary grades the exercises included music, singing, recitations and selections in harmony with the day. In the highest rooms the formal programme was given with great fidelity. Those who took part were: J. Patterson, O. Bendixon, Florence Sylvester, C. Delposse, G. Walker, Ella Klatscher, Nellie Stephenson, Howard Richards, Eddy Irwin, H. Pieser, A. Moore, M. Rosenthal, M. Schulze. The address of the day was delivered by Dr. J. Rosenthal, who spoke in substance as follows:

It has been truly said that the American Declaration of Independence was the beginning of a new age, and changed the condition from redress of grievances to a self-governing commonwealth, which thirteen years later developed into the government of the United States, the centenary of whose existence we are now celebrating. In reviewing the history of the time we find that there was no one man so absolutely necessary to the government of the time as was Washington, whose noble wisdom, frankness and character alone were able to sustain him with any prospect of success in the strange duties and responsibilities of the new and untried office of President. The century of suspense has passed into a pleasant retrospection. From thirteen states we have advanced to three times that number. We have grown from the infant cradled in mother Columbia's arms to a free nation. It is a noble lesson, and should be conned by all. If you need further inspiration, think what has been done in free America. Remember that you have an equal right to rule with any other man in the commonwealth. Think of all these privileges. I think often of them and then thank the Creator that I am in free America.

CARPENTER SCHOOL.

The exercises at this school were of unusual interest. Flags, bunting and evergreens beautified every part of the different rooms. The programme included the rendering of excellent music, selections and recitations. The following pupils took part: L. Thoen, L. Ross, D. Quinlan, T. Baker, L. Colburg, L. Brinkworth, Kate Cashiere, Clara Larsen. The address of the day was delivered by the Hon. T. C. McMillan. He sought to show how much the world owes to its poor men. Washington was born in a log cabin in the wilderness, and the campaign of 1840 revived this log cabin of the father of his country. Lincoln lived in a humble log cabin, and in that humble home out on the prairie had read the few books in his possession by the fitful glare of the log fire. Mr. McMillan alluded to the fact that the nation is greatly indebted to its great men. He also spoke of the interest the celebration of to-day would have for the children when it became the celebration of yesterday.

HAVEN SCHOOL.

The exercises at the Haven School were of a most interesting character. Separate programmes were prepared for each room. Those in the higher grades were very praiseworthy, and were executed with intelligence and spirit.

HUMBOLDT PARK SCHOOL.

The exercises at this school were very entertaining. The regular programme of songs, dialogues, patriotic quotations and essays was followed. The addresses were made by Col. A. C. Higgins and Mr. Edward R. Sweet. Col. Higgins said, in concluding his address:

It was Washington's hand that placed the five-pointed star in the flag of our country. As Hamilcar led Hannibal to the altar, and made him place his hand on the sacrifice and swear by the gods of Carthage that he would forever be at enmity with her enemies, so let us place our hands on our national flag, on this the hundredth anniversary of her birth, and swear perpetual enmity to national disunion. We may then rest assured that this land of Washington will become the greatest among the nations of the earth, and we may thus offer our salvation and our freedom to the oppressed of every nation under the sun. Columbia's free institutions will offer an example to the world, so that the people everywhere shall rise up and deliver themselves from the hands of their oppressors. The throned despot will tremble beneath Columbia's law, the scepter unsheathed shall fall from the tyrant's palsied hand, and men everywhere shall stand erect and right-minded and regenerated before the American Union and the Constitution of the United States.

HAYES SCHOOL.

The Hayes School was gay with flags on the morning of the celebration. A large flag waved over the main entrance, while forty-eight smaller flags floated from the windows. Within, the various rooms were appropriately decorated with flags and bunting, and the blackboards filled with drawings and quotations. The Godfrey Weitzel Post, G. A. R., with its colors, helped to do honor to the celebration. In the ninth division the dates 1779–89, formed in small flags, drawn by the pupils in colored crayon, each child drawing a flag, were placed on the blackboard. The exercises were held in every division except the third. In this the pupils combined with the others. In the first division the Godfrey Weitzel Post occupied seats of honor on the stage and sang G. A. R. songs before the exercises began.

Addresses were made by the Rev. J. Vilas Blake and Dr. Lyman. There were several interesting features of the programme, one consisting of patriotic quotations and exercises in calisthenics entitled "Our Flag." The music was good, the recitations were excellent and so were the essays.

In the second, third and fourth divisions the pupils met in Room 3, where they followed the same programme as in the first division. Commander Wray of the Godfrey Weitzel Post made an extemporaneous address. In the eighth division a little girl, Lizzie Jensen, not quite thirteen years old, recited a poem "One Hundred Years Ago," composed in three and four line stanzas by herself. Another little girl, Hetty Thatcher, recited two poems composed by her grandmother, Mrs. A. L. Thatcher. In the thirteenth division quotations from Halleck's poems were read by ten little girls, each one bearing a letter of Washington's name and reciting an appropriate verse. In the sixteenth division one little girl asked questions concerning Washington and the other pupils answered them. Those who took leading parts were Carrie Walters and John McCune.

LA SALLE SCHOOL.

The celebration at this school was highly interesting. Some of the rooms were very liberally decorated, particularly the eighth grade, where were displayed many of the European and colonial flags. There was also much bunting and many pictures presented by the different classes. In one of the latter rooms the children were costumed in colonial style, with wigs, silk breeches and lace. The regular form of programme was followed in each room. The exercises closed with a tableau and the national air. The addresses of the day were delivered by the Rev. F. M. Bristol and Mr. William J. English. In the course of his remarks Mr. Bristol said:

Washington, the ideal patriot, the ideal American, we are assembled to-day to honor his memory and praise his work and worth. He was inspired by a high purpose which makes character and moral excellence, and he was actuated by the teachings of a divine religion. As we look back upon the origin of this people, this nation, let us commemorate the Divine Providence which prepared this country for the grandest civilization. When Columbus leaped from his ship of discovery and first touched the virgin soil of this new world, he fell upon his knees in a prayer of gratitude to that God whose providence had guided him over trackless seas to this new land. When the Pilgrims sprang from the Mayflower to the bleak New England shore, they fell upon their knees in prayer that God had led them over storm-tossed waves to a country where they might worship Him in accordance with the dictates of their own conscience. If to-day we would crown anew the name and brow of Washington with gems of tribute, let us place in that crown the sublime words of Lafayette, "Washington is the grandest man;" take the grand exclamation of Fox, "Illustrious man, deriving honor less from the splendor of the station than the dignity of his name;" then take the eloquent encomium of Webster, "I would cheerfully put the question to the intelligence of Europe and all the world, what character of the century on the whole put in the pages of history, is the most sure, the most respected, the most sublime; and I have no doubt but that by a suffrage approaching unanimity the answer would be—Washington." Then place among the gems of eulogy the stirring words of John Bright in the English Parliament: "Washington stands alone and unapproachable like a snowy peak rising above its fellows in the clear air of morning, with a dignity, constancy and purity which has made his name the ideal type of civic virtue to succeeding generations. Each one turns to Washington, and if the people were called upon to contribute to his glorious renown, from millions of grateful hearts would be poured tributes of devotion and praise to gem his resplendent crown of fame."

Mr. English delivered a very interesting address, a tribute to the Declaration of Independence. He said:

The Constitution has shown to other nations that they are

deprived of many of their God-given rights. In England the Declaration introduced free discussion, thereby rendering the government more liberal. France stands greatly indebted to our country. When the Declaration of Independence was first made the lower classes in that country were just beginning to feel their power, and were trying to make French rulers respect them, and our Constitution induced them to strike. At this time a solemn duty rests with every citizen to support the laws and obey the Constitution in order to strengthen the government. This sacred duty has long been slighted and treated with contempt. Would you see despotism overwhelm us? Would you desire anarchy to extinguish liberty? Then trample on the Constitution, resist the laws, instill in the young mind a wholesome contempt for their obligations. But we hope that such will never be; that men now in possession of influence will use it rightly; that they will not swerve from duty and give up substantial benefits for some wild chimera.

KING SCHOOL.

At the King School the Hon. W. H. King delivered an address to the pupils, of which the following is an abstract:

One hundred years ago to-day George Washington was inaugurated the first President of the United States in New York. The country at the time contained probably four millions of people. It now contains perhaps sixty millions. Then there were no railroads or telegraphs on the American continent. Now of the 290,000 miles of railroad in the world, the United States contains 135,000, nearly one-half the railroads in existence. Of the 600,000 miles of telegraph wire, more than one-fourth is in the United States. Our progress has been unprecedented in the history of the world. No where are educational facilities equal to ours. In this free country of ours industry and economy will secure a competence for all if they practice these virtues. And there is no good reason why people should not be contented and happy. Twice since the day, the centennial of which we now celebrate, have we been engaged in foreign wars, once with Great Britain and once with Mexico. In 1861 an unholy rebellion was inaugurated for the purpose of destroying this Union. Many armies were raised and the clash of arms resounded on many a bloody battle-field. It was claimed that this was not a union, but a kind of conglomeration of states and that each might withdraw at its pleasure. It required four years work to subdue that rebellion. The rebels were taught an instructive lesson. This Union is the enemy of anarchy in any of its forms. If there is any one here who does not like the laws and customs of our country they are at liberty to leave on the next train out. Such as these we do not want. The soil seems to be indigenous for producing men eminent in the professions and all business callings of life, and our women are the most intelligent and beautiful on the face of the earth. Of Washington, the first President, it is not necessary to say that he was the Father of his Country. Let us ever reverence his name. Stand by the old flag, boys; stand by the old flag, girls! It is our flag handed down to us unimpaired by our ancestors. We must transmit it to posterity in the same unimpaired condition.

IRVING SCHOOL.

At the Irving School the address of the day was delivered by the Rev. Charles Conklin. After touching lightly on the political history of the early republic, he said:

Grave indeed must have been the thoughts of that grand, good man, as on that calm bright morning one hundred years ago to-day he placed his hand on the sacred book and took the oath of office. What was this man? What the occasion of so great a trust? Noble in bearing he must have been. Lafayette declared, on seeing him in the procession that day, that he was the grandest man he had ever seen. Washington was well fitted intellectually for the position he so greatly honored. He graduated not from college or academy, but from the field school, a small log cabin on his father's estate. He was largely a self-cultured man, yet his knowledge was great and was acquired with patience. He was a man of the finest nature and purest life. This is why he was equal to a trying war. The day suggests its duty. The nation is our heritage. We hold in trust this noble estate. We must enrich it as it passes through our hands down to posterity. Teach the children to love Washington and to be true to their flag and their country. Should dangers encompass our Union, should foes within or foes without strive to make null and void the great principles of Washington, our Constitution and our ancestors, let the memory of his spirit and devotion rise in your hearts and make you stand in defense of your hearthstones and ancestors.

CALUMET AVENUE SCHOOL.

Mr. Charles Kozminski was the orator at the Calumet School. The programme was an interesting one, music contributing to the general interest. He spoke in substance as follows:

Where we now stand one hundred years ago the wild Indian

was hovering for prey and the white man's scalp, while in the City of New York one of the greatest events in the history of the world was taking place.   Our forefathers have fought bloody battles and brought great sacrifices for freedom and liberty, the fruits of which we to-day enjoy.   This is the great heritage left to us by men who above all else loved their country, at the head of whom stands the great George Washington.   On this day one hundred years ago he stood and took the oath of office to support the Constitution of the United States of America; and as to-day, then also the great flag was hoisted, but with only thirteen stars where now we find forty-two in this grand emblem of liberty and freedom, the emblem of the greatest country on the face of the earth, where everyone is sovereign.   The framers of this Constitution, which to-day fills the hearts of all true American children with joy and happiness, acted in accordance with and were inspired by the will of God, who knows no difference between his children, be they born in the hovel or born in the palace of the rich.   How insignificant, therefore, must they appear to us, who, while proud as American citizens, draw a line between the poor and the rich, who inspire a prejudice against their fellow beings, because they are either not blessed with riches like themselves, or they have been free to worship differently, or destiny has colored their skin darker than others.   People with such feelings deserve our pity.   They are not true Americans in the sense of our great ancestors and in the great inheritance left to them, and which they now in selfishness and self-esteem enjoy.   They neither love their neighbors as themselves nor understand the solemn obligation taken by George Washington for them.   And for such our great Abraham Lincoln and U. S. Grant and many thousands of our best citizens spilled their life's blood; and if ever a dark cloud has rested on this country, the Emancipation Proclamation of Abraham Lincoln has wiped it out.   And as one people who love our country without distinguishing race, color or religion, we are here to-day, united as Americans to love the day for our country and for its Constitution.

ARMOUR STREET SCHOOL.

At the Armour Street School the address of the day was delivered by Mr. Geo. L. Stone, who spoke in substance as follows:

What a glorious morning is this, the 100th anniversary of our first President's inauguration!   We have met with joyous expressions of gratitude upon our lips and in our hearts that Almighty God has vouchsafed to the sturdy colonists His signal favor, and gave to this country that incomparable chief, "First in war, first in peace and first in the hearts of his countrymen." We have met also to revive our solemn obligations. We have also met to pledge ourselves that we will transmit this priceless heritage, in all its original splendor, to generations yet unborn. The most prominent part of a nation's history is its military record. When all other mementoes of remote time have passed into oblivion, when authors, statesmen and jurists, merely as such, lie forgotten, the memory of battles lost and won, of valor on sea and land, of great captains and heroic soldiers, will retain its fragrance—ay, shall gather brightness as it rolls down the stream of time, scattering sparks of inspiration among the generations as they come and go. Like the lights in the Jewish sanctuary, this sacred fire is not permitted to grow dim, and from the remotest past it burns a holy flame to guide the student traveler from age to age—a light to warm the patriot and warn the traitor. It was kindled anew upon these shores, and lit up the continent from the hills and plains of already historic states. Nor let us forget those by whose prowess the inestimable gifts of civil and religious liberty vouchsafed to our fathers, and transmitted through the fires of two wars to a splendid posterity, are bequeathed by a sublime struggle to this generation. I prefer to think of the heroes of '76 and '61 as not separated in spirit. The touch of the vanished hand I can almost feel. Their voices still seem to break in sweetness on my ear. Soldiers and sailors, heroes all, your deeds are enshrined in a nation's heart, and the memory of your sacrifices shall be cherished as long as ocean's billows roll, while flowers in beauty bloom and rock-ribbed hills endure, as jeweled and most precious possessions.

OTHER PUBLIC SCHOOLS.

The celebration at the Von Humboldt School was witnessed by over one thousand pupils and by an equal number of patrons and friends. Alma Burgh, of the graduating class, addressed the school in a feeling manner, after which Keller's American hymn was sung and three rousing cheers given for the national colors. In the different rooms different programmes were prepared for the entertainment of the audience. The speakers were Mr. Paul O. Stensland and Mr. Scharlau.

A large audience listened to the exercises at the Sheldon School. The programme was opened by the unfurling of the national colors and the singing of "America." The exercises included singing, recitations, dialogues and music.

The exercises at the Kosciusko School were begun with a flag-raising and followed by the singing of "America." The same programme was followed in all the rooms, and considerable enthusiasm on the part of the audience as well as the pupils characterized the day. Each room in which exercises were held was decorated with flags, pictures of Washington, evergreen, and red, white and blue bunting. There was singing, essays and interesting dialogues from history. The programme was an ambitious one and was well rendered.

The Polk Street School was liberally decorated with flags and banners, and over every window and door with streamers and bunting. Over every door was a picture of Gen. Washington, with cross-swords and flags. The blackboards were covered with patriotic drawings made by the pupils and teachers. Most of the pupils in this school are from foreign lands, a fact which gave additional significance to the Centennial Celebration. In the larger room were seventy-five Italian children from six to fifteen years of age. Most of these were unable to speak English. They were addressed in Italian by Sig. Rouga. The older children carried small flags. Thirteen little girls recited selections from the Declaration of Independence and twenty-one little boys from the Constitution of the United States.

At the Russell School the children, their patrons and friends opened the day's exercises with singing "America." A unique feature was sixteen boys contrasting 1789 and 1889, led by the comedietta entitled "Old Maids," in which thirty little girls went in search of husbands, wanting none better than Washington. The address of the day was delivered by Mr. Higgins.

At the Hoffman Avenue School Miss Kohler read Gov. Fifer's proclamation and Willie Monroe spoke a short piece on the Constitution. Nelly Nolan with "The first Inauguration," Alma McNeil with Whittier's ode, and Nellie Richter with "Examples of Washington," were good examples of school oratory.

The Wicker Park School had similar and interesting exercises consisting mainly of music, the day being closed with a charming Martha Washington tea party.

Bishop Fallows and Mr. C. C. Kohlsaat addressed the pupils at the Clark School. The rooms were all decorated with flags and bunting, but exercises were held in but four rooms of the grammar grade.

At the Washington School the exercises were unusually interesting. The part taken by the school consisted mainly of songs, essays, recitations and dialogues. The flag drill was an interesting exercise, and was much enjoyed by all who witnessed it. The speakers were Mr. Frank Wyley, Mr. L. P. Meech, Mr. John E. Dalton and Mr. F. G. Colby.

Bishop Samuel Fallows delivered an address to the older pupils at the Marquette School, dedicating the day to the children of America. The address proved highly interesting, and the only regret was that on account of the limited size of the room many were prevented from hearing it.

Patriotic addresses and recitations by the children and speeches by the Rev. H. W. Thomas, Mr. E. Nelson Blake and Mr. John MacLaren comprised the programme at the Hendricks School. The celebration was in every particular an unqualified success.

At the Lawndale School the day was observed appropriately. The exercises were opened by the singing of "America," after which Miss Brayton read the Governor's proclamation. The following pupils took part in the programme, which included some very interesting features: Etta Lynn, Edith Gumbell, Pauline Roberts, Otto Schulz, Alice Hawkins, Edith Burnham, Charles Watson, Rester Anderson, Bryn Dodds, Bertha Billings, Maude Merrill. The recitations and essays were confined to the revolutionary subjects and eulogies of Washington. The Rev. Mr. Bell closed with an address on the day and the responsibilities thereof.

MISCELLANEOUS CELEBRATIONS.

The Cook County Normal School, the Illinois Industrial School for Girls, the Chicago Manual Training School, and other schools and institutions, united with the public schools in celebrating this occasion. The programmes were a little more varied in character than those in the public schools, but the general trend of the exercises was the same.

At the Cook County Normal School the programme included music and the recitation by Mrs. Parker of a poem delivered at the inauguration of Washington. Six girls, dressed in white, represented the welcome given to Washington by the young women of that generation. Washington's escort was composed of thirty-two boys in colonial uniform. Extracts from eulogies on Washington, some admirable music, a flag raising, and recitations showing the spirit of 1775, and the growth of the sentiment in favor of union, comprised the exercises. The address was delivered by Mr. C. S. Cutting.

The Illinois Industrial School for Girls, at South Evanston, opened its programme with music, after which the following recitations by scholars were given: "Landing of the Pilgrims," "Sketch of Washington," "Independence Bell," and others. Two addresses were delivered, one by Mr. Albert Dunham, the other by Mr. N. L. Stowe. Mr. Dunham delivered a stirring address, picturing in eloquent language incidents connected with the inauguration of Washington, dwelling with hope upon the fact that the public schools are taking such a large part in the Centennial Anniversary.

The Manual Training School of Chicago distinguished itself with a very simple yet effective programme. The pupils assembled in the lecture-room, where the exercises were held. The themes of the essays were assigned to the pupils a month before the celebration. The design was to get a connected idea in the words of the pupils of the important events which characterized the early history of our country. Those which were read, with the names of the pupils, were as follows: "Critical Period in American History, 1783–89," Warren H. Lewis; "Washington as President and as a Citizen," Carl Fairbanks; "Washington the General," G. T. Sigwell; "Washington's Journey to New York, 1789," Louis Howell; "Washington's Inauguration," Frank S. Pagin; "Washington as a Statesman," C. H. Toby; "Washington and His Cabinet," Otto Scheible; "1789–1889," — — Belfield; "A Day in 1989," Robert Currer. The address delivered by the Hon. E. B. Sherman was marked by patriotism and eloquence.

The pupils of the German Theological Seminary met at St. Mark's Evangelical Church, where the address of the day was delivered by the Rev. Dr. S. J. Severinghaus, who spoke on "One Hundred Years of National Life" and the value of the moral education of our youth.

At the schools of the Cathedral of the Holy Name the celebration of the Centennial by the Catholic schools took place. Solemn high mass was celebrated at 9 a. m., which was attended by the guards of the parish in full uniform. At 10:30 the exercises began in the school hall. The programme included songs, essays, recitations and tableaux; also a piece entitled "Washington's Marching Song," in which thirty children in the costumes of George and Martha Washington took part. Miss Reidy sang a song and Miss Tiefenbrun played a composition by Liszt for the piano.

The St. Margaret's School exercises were held at the Church of the Epiphany. They were opened by a prayer by the pastor of the church, the Rev. Mr. Morrison. This was followed by the singing of "Columbia, the Gem of the Ocean," in which the entire school took part. The thesis of Miss N. Williams won applause. Miss Rosa Greenbaum sang "The Star Spangled Banner," and Mrs. Ella F. Young addressed the students of the parochial schools. The exercises closed with the singing of "America," joined in by the entire audience.

The exercises at the Academy of the Sacred Heart were opened with a piano number by Misses Walsh and Cavanaugh. The concert recitation that followed was rendered by Misses Becker, Lynch, Powell, Clara and Julia Ernst, White, Donovan, Gitman, Carney and Raitton. Then came a chorus sung by the school. Miss Amanda Massauer and Miss Telia Doniat read essays. Miss A. Walsh played an instrumental solo, after which there was the distribution of the ribbons and medals. The exercises closed with the singing of the *mater admirabilis* and the solemn opening of the month of May.

At St. Columba's School the address of the day was delivered by the Rev. D. P. O'Brien. The programme included music, recitations, and two excellent essays by Miss M. Shelly and Miss M. Shea.

The pupils of St. Aloysius School listened to a Centennial address by the Rev. J. Prince, S. J. The programme at this institution was an attractive one. It opened with an instrumental duet by Misses Nellie Lynch and Nellie McCarthy. The chorus "Columbia" followed, with Miss Jenny O'Heron as accompanist.

There was also a recitation by Miss Nellie Powers, and an instrumental duet by Miss Katie Ryan and Miss Jennie Doover. The recitation by Miss Nellie O'Neil closed the exercises.

The programme at the Holy Angels' Academy offered many attractions. It was opened with a *march militaire*, piano duet by Misses M. Boyer and Ryan. This was followed by the Centennial hymn, sung by the entire school. Judge Thomas A. Moran next delivered an entertaining address. Master J. Farrell recited a "Tribute to Washington." Next, a medley was sung with Miss W. Joice as accompanist. Maj. Allen followed with an address, which in turn gave way to a duet, "The Golden Star," by Misses Hayes and M. Carey. Miss H. Hutchinson recited " Margaret of France." Mr. W. Hayes recited "The Dandy Fifth." Then came a duet by the Misses M. Joice and M. Riley. Next followed an essay entitled "Our Republic's Birthday," by Miss M. Farrell. The programme closed with the chorus "Columbia," sung by the Centennial Chorus.

At the Chicago Home of the Friendless the day was appropriately observed. The school room was beautifully decorated with flags, the national colors, evergreen and pictures of Washington. The school sang patriotic songs, after which came an entertaining piece entitled "Columbia's Tea Party." Fifty pupils and old people took part, each wearing a badge on which was the name of the state represented. Columbia invited all her children, the states and territories, to come home and celebrate with her her hundredth birthday. At the close of the exercises "Columbia" was sung by Dr. Belle Reynolds.

The rooms of St. Xavier's Academy were prettily draped with flags, bunting and flowers. The new flag was unfurled from the entrance. The religious services were held in the chapel. High mass was celebrated by the Rev. J. McCann, and a solemn *te deum* was chanted by the pupils of the academy. The patriotic exercises prepared for the occasion took place at 3 p. m. Archbishop Feehan and the Rev. S. McDonald addressed the pupils. The Archbishop talked to the children in a familiar way, explaining the beauties of our Constitution, and declaring that we should thank God for its preservation, as well as for the material prosperity of our country. Those who took part in the programme were: Miss Mary Marble, Miss Alice Shannon, Miss L. Hesslein, Esther Glenn, Maggie Murphy, Annie Hudson, Olive Lewis, Susie Bonfield, Edith Maslin, Delia O'Malley and Pearl Hunt.

Three hundred little orphans in holiday attire filed into the chapel of St. Joseph's Orphan Asylum at 6:15 a. m. and listened to a solemn high mass celebrated by the Rev. J. McNamee. The reverend chaplain endeavored to impress on the minds of the pupils the significance of memorial day. The programme closed with the singing of patriotic songs, after which the little ones were feasted on candies and good things to eat.

At the Chicago Free Kindergarten the children observed the day in an appropriate manner by singing patriotic songs and by marching with guns and flags. The little children seemed to enter heartily into the spirit of the occasion.

The pupils of the Angel Guardian and Chicago Industrial School celebrated the day with a solemn high mass. The Rev. Father Pancratius delivered an appropriate address on the duties of the pupils to God and the country. Patriotic songs were sung and the Centennial pieces spoken. Afterward the children visited the parochial school.

The celebration at the Dearborn Academy was an attractive one. Patriotic songs were sung. Miss Halsey recited Webster's reply to Hayne. Patriotic quotations were related by twelve young ladies. Miss A. Reeme gave an essay, "A Cup of Tea at Mt. Vernon." May Coffeen recited "Stars of my Country's Flag," and an essay on the "Daughters of 1789" was recited by Miss Edith Moss. Mary Barrows recited the "American Flag," and Miss Fannie Wells "Woman's Duty to America." The address of the day was delivered by Mr. George W. Needham.

The exercises at the Sacred Heart Convent were witnessed by 800 girls, all attired in white, with gracefully draped red, white and blue scarfs. The school hall was tastefully arranged with the national colors, with a generous intermingling of flags. The programme was an interesting and varied one. It was opened by an instrumental duet by Misses T. Byrne and A. Rogers. Then came a recitation by forty-two girls. This recitation consisted of facts connected with the history of our country. The most

striking passages from the speeches of our orators were given
with spirit and made an excellent elocutionary drill.   Bryant's
lines "On Washington" were given in concert by the class.   On
the announcement of the surrender of Cornwallis, the school sang
"Yankee Doodle."   A recitation of the origin of the "Star Spangled
Banner" was followed by the singing of the "Red, White and Blue"
by the whole school.   Then came patriotic songs and recitations.
Miss Bryan played an instrumental piece, "The Star Spangled Banner" and the Goddess of Liberty and her forty-two states appeared,
bringing the programme to a close.   The address of the day was
delivered by the Rev. Father Otting, S. J.

The celebration by St. Pius's girls was begun at 9 o'clock, the
holy sacrifice of the mass being conducted by the Rev. Father
Hackett.   Next the Rev. Father Kelly of St. Cecelia's Church
delivered a patriotic sermon to an appreciative and large congregation, after which the children of the choir sang the hymn of
thanksgiving.   The mass concluded, the children, dressed in the
national colors and all carrying flags, marched in procession to the
gymnasium, where the exercises took place.   Miss Ella McAuliffe
delivered an address, which was received with great applause;
the senior class sang several national airs and Miss Mollie Carroll
read a paper on the life and character of Washington.   The little
St. Pius cadets attracted no little attention by their musical performances, which formed a most cheerful feature of the occasion.
The medals were distributed by the Rev. Fathers Hackett, Don-
nelly and O'Sullivan.

The day was opened at St. Francis' School by the singing of
"America."   The addresses were delivered by the Rev. Mr.
Cavalary and Mr. Peacher.   The first class boys joined in an
interesting exercise and sang "Marching Through Georgia," and
the second class sang "Our Flag," the girls following with
"George Washington" and "Liberty Bell."   The other classes
gave interesting exercises.

At Messrs. Schobinger & Grant's Harvard School, 2101 Indiana avenue, the pupils met at 11 o'clock, together with their
teachers, parents and invited friends.   The hall was handsomely

decorated with flags and bunting, and well filled. The platform was occupied by an orchestra formed by pupils of the school. The exercises were opened with prayer. Then followed the singing of " America" by the pupils, supported by the orchestra. The Rev. Thomas C. Hall next addressed his youthful hearers in an appropriate speech well calculated to rouse their patriotic fervor. Then " Hail Columbia" was sung. Mr. M. Guerin and Mr. Julian Nolan, members of the school, next read their essays, the subject of the former being the successive steps that led to the formation of the Constitution of the United States, the latter an account of the inauguration of the first President of the republic. The medals were then distributed. The singing of " The Star Spangled Banner" and other patriotic songs closed the exercises. On separating, every one, young and old, carried along memories of an exceedingly successful and spirited celebration of " Our Nation's Birthday."

At Fick & Schutt's German-English School, 621–623 Wells street, the exercises were highly interesting and impressive. The fine school building was gay with streamers; in the assembly hall the German colors were entwined with those of America, and the blackboards showed the names of the foremost Americans, together with choice patriotic quotations. A handsomely printed programme bore in bronze color a portrait of Washington and a selection of extracts from the Constitution and from Washington's Farewell Address, as well as mottoes shown in the procession of New York a century ago. Mr. Henry H. Fick, in his opening remarks, spoke of the virtue of patriotism as inherent in the German character, and gave the names of men like Muhlenberg, Steuben and Kalb as evidence of the support which Germans lent to the establishment of the government in this country. If the German thinks fondly of the realm where his cradle stood, he turns with no less affection to the land which gave him a home, and for it he is ready to yield his life, if needs be. The order of exercises embraced songs, recitations and readings, both in German and in English, the distribution of the Centennial souvenirs and the presentation of a fine flag by the pupils of the school.

Among the many excellent selections recited by the pupils, Hezekiah Butterworth's "The School House Stands by the Flag," received the warmest applause as the last stanza was rung out:

> The blue arch above us is Liberty's dome,
> The green fields beneath us Equality's home,
> But the school-room to-day is Humanity's friend—
> Let the people the flag and the school-house defend!
> 'Tis the school-house that stands by the flag,
> Let the nation stand by the school;
> 'Tis the school-bell that rings for our Liberty old,
> 'Tis the school-boy whose ballot shall rule.

IV

THE MASS MEETINGS

THE MASS MEETINGS

The popular interest in the centennial celebration was particularly manifested in the mass meetings. The committee had contemplated a public gathering in one of the city's large halls, but long before any definite plan had been decided upon it became evident that one meeting would be entirely inadequate to the demands of the occasion. Two meetings were accordingly decided upon. But the public interest kept growing. The two meetings were abandoned in favor of three; the three became four; grew to five and six. Still the barometer of public sentiment continued to reveal the increasing pressure of an atmosphere surcharged with patriotic zeal. It soon became evident that the committee could not make its arrangements on too large a scale. Finally, to relieve the pressure which must inevitably come upon a few meetings, no matter how large and commodious the halls in which they were held, it was decided to issue a call for eight mass meetings, one in each of the big auditoriums afforded by the Exposition Building, Central Music Hall, the Cavalry Armory, Battery D Armory, Farwell Hall and the Board of Trade, and one in each of two mammoth tents to be erected on the Lake Front. As it afterward turned out, even these accommodations were not up to the requirements of the occasion. Of the great crowds gathered at each of the appointed meeting-places, thousands were turned away, unable to get even within sight of the entrance doors.

In order to further divide public interest and to prevent undue crowding at any one of the conventions, information as to where the different speakers of the day would hold forth was kept secret. The names of all the orators were published, but no one in the great audiences assembled on the day of the celebration knew which of the speakers he was to hear. The wisdom of this manœuvre was subsequently demonstrated by the impartial manner in which the public patronage was distributed among the different gatherings.

At 3 o'clock—the hour set for the opening of the doors—each of the appointed meeting-places presented a scene of wild enthusiasm. The enormous crowds which began to gather as early as 1 o'clock were under the contagious spell of the general excitement. Every slight incident which could be made the pretext was greeted with applause and cheers. When the doors were finally thrown open, the huge throngs surged in with the irresistible rush of so many tidal waves and took instant possession of all available space. Even then those who were forced to remain outside did not go away, but hung around the entrances, seemingly quite as ardent and cheerful as their luckier fellows within. Finding themselves barred from participation in any other way, the majority of them stood the proceedings through, reëchoing every cheer and joining in every song. At Dearborn Park an "overflow meeting," formed largely of those unable to gain admission to the other gatherings, was organized. The crowds which clustered around the entrance to the Exposition Building were summoned by a bugle call to the park. Here ex-Mayor Carter H. Harrison, acting as chairman of the meeting, Prof. A. C. Geyer of Indiana, the Rev. Jenkin Lloyd Jones, and Mr. C. W. Martin of New York, delivered eloquent addresses to as appreciative an audience as assembled anywhere during the day. After listening to speeches for over two hours it was still unsatisfied, and in response to repeated demands Mr. Harrison arose and delivered a second speech, to the great apparent satisfaction of his auditors.

At the Exposition Building, where a throng of over ten thousand people had assembled, the spectacle was truly magnificent. The immense interior was packed to its utmost capacity, and when a stir of applause grew out of those near the platform and swept swiftly over the big concourse with increasing strength, the very walls seemed to vibrate. At the Board of Trade every inch of standing room was occupied, and the graduated "pits" where bidding is carried on could only be located by the little turrets and cones of humanity which surmounted them. The effect was that of a fantastic architectural design worked out in human forms, with a rococo ornamentation of bunting and flags. The crowds which gathered at Central Music Hall and Farwell Hall were the largest ever assembled in those buildings, and at all the meetings every block of space into which a human figure could be squeezed was occupied.

In all the different halls the decorations had been made a unique feature of the occasion. The national flag and the tri-colored buntings were displayed in profusion. The speakers' platforms were lavishly decorated. Flowers, plants, wreaths and festoons were used in abundance and in every manner which ingenuity could suggest. These floral thrones were surmounted by large portraits of Washington. Placards bearing the profoundly democratic motto, "Government of the People, for the People, by the People," were imbedded in masses of flowers and flags. The two tents on the Lake Front were ablaze with bunting and rows of little flags were strung between the tent-poles.

The programme of exercises was in the main the same for all the meetings. Care had been taken to provide the different conventions with good musical organizations, and the singing and playing of the national airs was a notable feature of the day's celebration. It was shortly after 3 o'clock when the meetings were called together by their respective secretaries, who at once introduced the chairmen appointed to preside. At Central Music Hall this office was filled by the Hon. Robert T. Lincoln, who was vigorously applauded from the moment of his entrance. Judge Walter Q. Gresham occupied the chair at Battery D, the Hon. Joseph Fifer, Governor of Illinois, presided at the Exposition Building, Senator Farwell at Tent B, Mr. E. Nelson Blake at the Board of Trade, Justice John M. Harlan at the Cavalry Armory, Judge Richard S. Tuthill at Farwell Hall and Mayor Cregier at Tent A. The introductory addresses delivered by the chairmen were very brief. Judge Gresham made no address, merely prefacing the exercises with a neat sentiment:

It is proper and natural that the national sentiment and love of country should find expression to-day. We never could have become the great nation that we are under the Articles of Confederation. Our unexampled growth is due to the "more perfect union" which was formed by the adoption of the Constitution now one hundred years old, and our continued happiness, prosperity and safety depend upon the unselfish devotion of the people to the Union and its preservation at all hazards through all times.

The applause evoked by the addresses of the chairmen was hushed as the chaplains of the different meetings were introduced and with bowed heads raised their voices in prayer for the continued prosperity of the nation. The playing of national airs by the bands was in all the meetings the signal for a tumultuous outburst. The people arose, waved thousands of little flags, and united their voices in a grand and impressive chorus. When the enthusiasm had somewhat subsided, congratulatory messages exchanged between Chicago and the cities of Minneapolis, Pittsburgh and Springfield were then read.

The simple greeting sent out by Chicago was as follows:

Eight hundred thousand Chicago citizens send greeting to Minneapolis, with the wish that, guided by the experience of a century of our national life, our second century may show a record still more glorious.

Minneapolis sent the following reply:

Minneapolis, on this memorable occasion, sends fraternal greetings to her sister city, Chicago. Together our people return thanks to the Almighty God for the blessings embraced in a century's growth of civil and religious liberty, and earnestly pray that the reign of Presidents begun this day one hundred years ago, may only end with time. When Washington was inaugurated first President of the United States, the site of your city was an unknown morass. The spirit that plucked up half-drowned Chicago by the locks, filled her streets with the ceaseless tread of commerce, and poured the wealth of nations into her lap, had its twin virtue only in the patriotism of her people. Constitutional liberty has no braver defenders nor more watchful guardians than the sons of Illinois. When our grandchildren repeat this celebration may the same flag float above them, no star effaced; symbolizing then as now the broadest freedom and the greatest happiness to men; and may they be found still possessing and still transmitting the virtue of Washington, Lincoln, and Grant.

From Springfield the following response was received:

The capital city of the empire state of the West sends greeting to the great metropolis of the Northwest on this Centennial natal day of constitutional government. The infant nation then born grew rapidly and strongly, but not healthily. It was inoculated with the virus of slavery. This poison well nigh produced death. Under the good providence of God there was found in our little city a man whose wisdom met the peril. It is well, then, that Springfield, that Chicago, that Illinois should rejoice on this Centennial anniversary of the founding of a government by Washington, the father of his country, which was preserved in the hour of peril by our Abraham, the savior of his country.

The greeting sent by Pittsburgh was as follows:

Pittsburgh sends greeting to Chicago as a token of the high esteem, deep friendship, and broad admiration this gateway of the West holds for the Queen City of the Lakes.

The citizens of Pennsylvania, where Washington, the young militia colonel, performed his first public service, assembled in mass meeting to do honor to his memory on the Centennial anniversary of his first inauguration, say to the citizens of the West: "Follow in the footsteps of the fathers, and hold fast to what Washington gave you."

The following messages from prominent men throughout the nation were also read:

FROM LEVI P. MORTON, VICE-PRESIDENT OF THE UNITED STATES.

There is a peculiar appropriateness in the observance of this Centenary of the birth of this great nation by the residents of Chicago. The minds of the throng that surrounded Washington on April 30, one hundred years ago, were fixed upon the possible future of the nation. They foresaw, not as dreamers, but as practical men, that population and wealth, highroads and canals, and cities would be multiplied on this new and fertile continent, under a free government, and while it is true that their visions of material progress fell far short of the reality which we have lived to see, and of which Chicago is one of the more remarkable illustrations, yet in the dim future they saw the Chicagos that were to be.

It is, therefore, but befitting that Chicago should now be thinking of them and celebrating the memorable event which marks the beginning of the history of the United States under the Constitution.

FROM SIR JOHN MACDONALD, PREMIER OF THE DOMINION OF CANADA.

I greatly regret that the sitting of the Canadian Parliament prevents me from accepting the invitation. Had it been possible it would have given me great pleasure to assist on this most interesting occasion.

FROM THE REV. DR. R. P. STORRS, DAY'S CHAPLAIN IN NEW YORK.

I rejoice that this day is to be worthily commemorated in the city whose swift and splendid growth is itself a magnificent tribute to the protecting power and inspiring impulse of a government whose establishment was completed one hundred years ago.

FROM JOHN BOYLE O'REILLY, BOSTON, MASS.

Your kind invitation to attend the Chicago Centennial celebration is most gratifying, and I deeply regret that other engagements prevent my acceptance. But it does not matter much on that day where the American stands, or under what conditions he may be placed, he is part of your celebration as you are part of his. Our liberty, our law, our order, our members and power and prosperity, our growing homogeneity as a nation, our regard for the rights of each other, all these are the elements of the Centennial of Washington's inauguration. The lights from city to city across the continent on that day are only one light—from the hearts of the whole American people, love and respect and veneration for the name of the great man who was the first President.

FROM CARL SCHURZ, NEW YORK.

We cannot worthily commemorate the practical beginning of our constitutional government without doing homage to the man who was the first and highest illustration of its character. Popular hero worship is to be commended and encouraged when it consists in the admiring contemplation of conspicuous virtue and wisdom. The memory of George Washington is, and will always remain, one of the most important and precious possessions of the American people.

His services in the War of Independence were inestimable. But as the head of the civil government he conferred a benefit upon his people which stands unsurpassed, if not unequaled, in the annals of mankind. It consists in the fact that the first President of the United States was the model President. Whenever the American people wish to consider what the Chief Magistrate and the government of this country should be, and when a President wishes to make it clear to his own mind by what rules of political morality he should regulate his conduct, by what motives he should be guided, and upon what principles he should act, he can find a model perfect and complete in the teachings and example of the first President. The more clearly those teachings and that example are understood, the more faithfully they are followed, the purer, the stronger, the more glorious will this republic become.

FROM EDWARD EVERETT HALE, ROXBURY, MASS.

If anybody in the world should celebrate the presidency of Washington, it is the people of Chicago.

It is very interesting now to see that, more than any man in America, George Washington understood the infinite wealth of the valleys of the Mississippi and of the lakes. His schemes for uniting those valleys were worthy of the best sense that your Chamber of Commerce has to-day; and in the midst of a thousand other cares, he steadily carried them forward. Among a world of dreamers he was the only one whose vision in the slightest degree approached the great realities of the future; and in his presidency he did not forget his vision. If anybody ever writes the history of the United States even tolerably well, his interest in the West will be brought out as it never has been.

FROM THE REV. BROOKE HERFORD, BOSTON, MASS.

The old Romans were accustomed to celebrate their victories with what they called a "triumph;" and they never thought their procession was complete unless they could drag along in it some captive specimen of the vanquished people. May I be allowed to be that captive specimen? I am, however, a very willing captive, drawn not in fetters of iron, but in bonds of admiration and love.

So far as I represent England, I represent not that old England which Washington defeated, but the new England which recognizes that the defeat was right and a blessing to the world. Nay, more, by personal descent, I represent the nobler England which, even in those days of struggle, lifted its voice for America, protesting against the attempt to coerce the colonies as the war of the king, and not the war of the people.

To-day, however, there is only one England on that whole matter. We think of Washington, and the strong men who gathered around him, as among the noblest characters of modern history; and we rejoice with the great Nation whose foundations were laid in such a broad spirit of liberty, and such a grand trust in human nature.

FROM HANNIBAL HAMLIN, BANGOR, ME.

I sympathize with Chicago most fully in its noble and patriotic commemoration of the event named. It is a duty of the American citizen to know and keep alive the great services of George Washington to our country, as well as to the whole world. And Chicago may be appropriately commended for its wise and patriotic action.

FROM THE HON. L. T. CHAMBERLAIN, BROOKLYN, N. Y.

I congratulate Chicago on her thoughtful patriotic observance. The lesson of this hour, as of a hundred years ago, is devotion to principle, citizen fealty, the supremacy of law. Ideas have power, right is stronger than force. God is over all. I say, with John Adams, "Independence forever."

FROM HORACE WHITE, NEW YORK.

The occasion which you celebrate is distinctly the inauguration of George Washington as the first President of the United States. Therefore the interest of the day centres in the personality of that great man. I think that all persons who study the history of the revolutionary period minutely will agree that without George Washington there would have been no American republic at the time when it came into life and being as an established fact; that he it was who gave force and effect to the Declaration of Independence; that while it was not he alone who did this, yet that if he alone had been absent it would not have been done. His Atlantean shoulders held the weight of a sinking cause in many a desperate hour when no other could have sustained the load. If we are allowed to make comparisons between him and his greatest successors, I think he who bore the storm, first in the field and afterward in the cabinet, earned the double meed of glory which we, of the later generation, have gratefully apportioned to Lincoln and Grant.

FROM THE REV. ARTHUR LITTLE, BOSTON, MASS.

Living under the very shadow of Faneuil Hall, the birthplace, and the old South Meeting House, the cradle of liberty, and within sight of Bunker Hill Monument and Dorchester Heights, it gives me exceeding pleasure to send cordial salutations and congratulations on this auspicious occasion to a large number of stanch patriots in the metropolis of the West, who are making a more desperate effort to preserve liberty than our fathers did to secure it. Your magnificent celebration put sleepy old Boston, which is living on its past achievements, to shame.

The arrangements for the celebration of that day in Chicago are simply ideal. What an object-lesson for the children. Chicago does nothing by halves. By anticipation, I am already beginning to feel the inspiration of this superb event, and to feel the thrill of enthusiasm and patriotic fervor which, centreing in Chicago, will pervade every home and every hamlet throughout the entire Northwest.

The American spirit, the American flag, the American idea, the American hope, may these find a new interpretation and awaken new devotion and zeal in their maintenance and realization on this memorable day.

The following lines from the Hon. Robert C. Winthrop, who made the address at the laying of the corner-stone of the Washington monument at its completion, were also read:

I.

Illustrious names in each successive age,
Vying in valor, virtue, wisdom, power,
One with another on the historic page,
Have won the homage of that little hour
Which they adorned, and will be cherished still
By grateful hearts till time shall be no more.
But, peerless and supreme, thy name shall fill
A place apart, where others may not soar.
In "the clear, upper sky," beyond all reach
Or rivalry; where, not for us alone
But for all realms and races, it shall teach
The grandest lesson history hath known,
Of conscience, truth, religious faith and awe,
Leading the march of liberty and law.

II.

Yes, century after century may roll,
And bury in oblivion many a name
Which now inspires the lip and stirs the soul,
Giving promise of an endless fame;
Yet still the struggling nations from afar
And all in every age who would be free,
Shall hail thy great example as the star
To guide and cheer their way to liberty—
A star which ever marks, with ray serene,
The path of one, who from his earliest youth,
Renounced all selfish aims; whose hands were clean,
Whose heart was pure, who never swerved from truth;
To serve his country and his God content,
Leaving our Union as his monument.

After the reading of the messages, the following resolutions, drawn up by the committee, were read and adopted by acclamation:

WHEREAS, The inauguration of President Washington was also the inauguration of our present form of government, and therefore the harvesting of the results of a century and a half of democratic impulse, hope and struggle, and secured to America and to the world the political and religious and industrial liberty that our famous colonies had developed and fought for in that long period of separated life; and,

WHEREAS, The republic which Washington and his compeers established was at that time the grandest experiment ever projected in behalf of the democratic principle and the boldest claim ever made in the name of Democracy, repudiating the necessity for any and every form of irresponsible or centralized government and widening the capacities and facilities of democratic institutions to equal the area of any possible nation, and to answer the demands of any possible stability; and,

WHEREAS, Looking back over one hundred years of peace and war, of political controversy and conservative constitutional development, we see the growing success of the great government established by the men of 1789; and,

WHEREAS, Although this vast political success, although this recognized demonstration of the ability of the people to govern themselves when they are sixty millions as easily as if they were a Greek city or a Swiss canton, although this justification of democracy is the greatest treasure of this hundred years, we can also congratulate ourselves upon an unprecedented industrial development that has sensibly raised the well-being of all our people, and upon a social development that has conspicuously raised the intelligence and the happiness of our own people and of all mankind; and,

WHEREAS, This great history has been made more illustrious by the eminence of a great company of incomparable men, who are not the least inheritance of the heirs of our wonderful one hundred years; therefore,

Resolved, That we will bear constantly in mind that important teaching of our history, that our institutions depend much more upon our faithful support in times of peace than even upon our devotion in time of war.

Resolved, That as we have to-day undertaken to impress upon the memories of the school children of this city the far-reaching importance of this red-letter day, so we will hereafter strive, by a course of education in our public schools, to fill the minds of our children with a knowledge of our history and with a veneration for our great men, that they may grow into an habitual knowledge of what American republicanism means and into an habitual sentiment of patriotic obligations.

Resolved, That we will ourselves set our children the example of a conscientious study of our history and institutions, and go before them in following the impulses of a sincere patriotism.

Resolved, That we cherish the teachings of Washington even as we commend them to our children, and that we especially will both teach and imitate that characteristic national spirit which lifted him whenever the occasion required safely above mere considerations of party into the serene and exclusive contemplation of the public good, and that we will also teach and imitate the reverential spirit which was at all times a characteristic of Washington, recognizing in our national prosperity a result of the guidance of a divine wisdom and imploring for the future a continuance of the blessing of Him in whose invisible hand are the destinies of nations.

The adoption of the resolutions completed the first part of the programme and paved the way for the orators of the day. Two speakers had been assigned to each meeting, as follows: At Central Music Hall, the Hon. J. M. Thurston and the Rev. S. J. McPherson; at Battery D, the Hon. John M. Langston of Virginia and the Hon. Peter Hendrickson of Wisconsin; at Tent A, the Hon. Richard Prendergast and Bishop Spalding of Peoria; at Tent B, the Hon. Albert G. Lane and the Hon. William E. Mason; at the Exposition Building, the Hon. C. C. Albertson and the Hon. J. R. Doolittle; at the Board of Trade, the Rev. Frank W. Gunsaulus and the Rev. Robert McIntyre; at the Cavalry Armory, the Rev. Dr. Barrows and Judge Otis; and at Farwell Hall, Mr. L. D. Thoman and Rabbi Hirsch. As the speakers came forward to deliver their addresses, they were met with round after round of applause. A spirit of unbounded enthusiasm permeated the great crowds and swayed with its magic both orators and audience. Every well-rounded period, every eloquent flight and every rhetorical climax was greeted with cheers and plaudits before it had fairly left the speaker's lips. Every mention of the name of Washington was the signal for renewed cheers, and throughout the time in which the speeches were being delivered the vast throngs alternated, with that strange unanimity of movement with characterizes excited crowds, between intensely silent attention and clamorous applause.

As the addresses came to a close, the chairmen at each of the various meetings stepped forward and asked those present to rise and join in singing "America," to which the author of the hymn, the Rev. Samuel Francis Smith, had added a centennial stanza:

> Our joyful hosts to-day
> Their grateful tribute pay—
> Happy and free—
> After our toils and fears,
> After our blood and tears—
> Strong with our hundred years—
> O, Lord, to Thee.

It was with no faint voices that the multitudes took up the well-known strain and the air was still reverberating with its echoes when the people filed out on their way home.

There were two features of the meeting at Battery D Armory which are entitled to separate mention. The first was the presence of the Rev. Samuel F. Smith, author of "America," who had come by special invitation to participate in the celebration, and who joined with the audience in singing the hymn which he wrote in his youth, but which has become the property of the nation. The second was the singing of Prof. S. G. Pratt's centennial hymn, by Dr. P. H. Cronin, who, four days later, was enticed from his home on an errand of mercy and brutally butchered by a gang of fanatical assassins. To those who, on Centennial Day, listened to the mellow tones of his voice, the discovery of his mutilated body in a sewer, where it had been thrown, like the carcass of a dog, to rot, was peculiarly shocking.

CENTENNIAL ADDRESSES.

THE REV. F. W. GUNSAULUS.

AT THE BOARD OF TRADE.

The inauguration of George Washington, and the adoption of the Constitution of the United States, are two flowers, brilliant and simultaneous, which grew upon a stalk whose roots ran down deep into the very eternity of God. No great event in the world is extemporaneous; no little event is born of a moment; and an event, such as that which gathered the powers of democracy into a single state paper, and incarnated the hope of the future in a single great personality, has wide sympathies and large relationships which run everywhere into the whole past. It is interesting to-day to think if ever before on this planet there occurred so large a celebration of any political event. I have thought of the crowning of Charlemagne in the midst of the darkness of the Middle Ages; and then my mind went back to that one event in the history of Rome, the coronation of a Cæsar as the one possible event that might have moved at one time such large populations with songs of joy. How different to-day is this scene! No Cæsar sits before us enthroned upon the rights of the people, but the memory of George Washington is enthroned by all the affections and all the hopes of the American people.

When the Western end of the Roman Empire fell it was certain that the human race had decided that Cæsarism was done forever. Rule by force, sovereignty by power, had passed forever out of men's hope and thought. No longer possible was it to erect upon men's consciences and brains any sort of empire which was not supported by their voluntary and loyal allegiance. The whole problem of history, from the fall of the Western end of the Roman Empire until the day of the inauguration of George Washington, was to find out what kind of government human conscience and human thought would agree to. Through all the long Middle Ages it was one continuous contest between Christian thought of government and the thought of the Cæsars. Living right there in Rome, under the Roman eagles, with every opportunity for Roman sovereignty, there had come into the world a man of the name of Jesus of Nazareth. That Man had attacked the national institutions with the heart and conscience of humanity. He had told the old aristocracies of the past that there was to be a new aristocracy, and it was to be the aristocracy of character and truth. He taught men to pray a prayer—"Our Father"—which lifted every man out of his individualism into social relationship with every other man, and made the picture of a common Father above the head of plebeian and aristocrat. It was the thought of this Man, in that prayer, of the Fatherhood of God and the brotherhood of man which went through those dark centuries with such tremendous power and such constant victory.

He also taught the world a new conception of liberty. Before His coming, for the most part, man had supposed that liberty was a concession; that a throne, or a kingdom, or a scepter, or a crown, had the sole right of giving liberty to mankind. This man came and said, in the very presence of Rome, "Ye shall know the truth, and the truth shall make you free." He came to teach men that by so much as they took truth into their brains and hearts and consciences by so much they were free. He came also to teach another thing. The world was full of ancient institutions; there had come out of a very venerable past a large number of very reverent traditions from old institutions, that were all moss-grown and covered with the memory of ages. This Man immediately said in every single operation of His life, in every line of His thought, that the valuable thing in this universe was not institutions, but man's soul. He began to teach humanity that the most interesting thing in the world to God was not what man made, but man himself; that every institution, like the temple, like the state, like laws, like thrones, might be thrown down, and that Man touched the most venerable institution in all his time—the Temple. He told them that it would fall before their gaze, and when He died the veil of the Temple was rent in twain from the top to the bottom. He came to tell men that man was more valuable than institutions; and when He died He died with the thought in the minds of His disciples that He had died for all men, bond and free, black and white, rich and poor, high and low. And, ladies and gentlemen, it was not in some club of infidelity, it has not been upon the platform of some infidel society, but it was at the cross of Christ, where one made all men equal, that your democracy and republicanism were born. For ten hundred years these great principles had a continuous fight, and all the way along through these centuries they led armies and re-created civilization.

Rome was a perfect chaos at the close of the fifth century. The question was what power should come into the world and take hold of those battered and broken fragments and make civilization out of them. The great problem was what power should go into that chaos and bring order and government forth. You know of the long fight. You can see the battle-fields as you read your pages of history. You stand there on the battle-field of Chalons and see Attilla, the dread of the world, meet these new ideas. You go a little farther and you see the great Charles Martel marshaling Christians with his sword and encountering the hosts of Mohammedanism, and telling the world that the West belongs to Christ and not to Mohammed. You look still farther and you see a battle between brothers upon the field of Fontenoy. You go still farther into history and you are standing with Harold and his legions against William the Conqueror, at the battle of Hastings. You go into France at a still later period and you are standing with Joan of Arc at the gates of Orleans, from which she hurls the English hosts and makes France and France's future secure. And just at that time there seems to burst upon the world a tremendous glory of morning. The dark ages have gone, but these splendid ideas have ruled. There is John Wickliffe, who has translated the Bible. There in the heavens is John Huss, who has died for that Bible. There also by his side is John Gutenberg, who will print that Bible. There is Martin Luther, the leader of a great reformation, and at last here is Christopher Columbus, who comes and gives to the principles of that Bible a new world for their perpetual empire.

There were other contests, as you know, ladies and gentlemen, but we must see this background of history to understand the leader of the American republic. Great visions of the matchless breadth and height of the possibilities within the soul, great visions of the incomparable possibilities of the land he calls his country without, are met in his spirit.

Only as the eye of the American turns within, and accustoms itself to the depths of conscience, is there power enough in it to reach the horizon of his country without. The American eye was in training when an outcast of Galilee made all men equal before His cross, when King Alfred wrote the treaty of Wedmore, when the Army of God wrested the great charter from John in the meadows of Runnymede, when Savonarola ruled Florence, and when John Hampden refused to pay the ship money. When Cromwell refused the kingdom, it had so learned to look into the depths of conscience that, in the shadow of his pilgrim contemporary, Bradford of Plymouth, you may see the prophecy of one who should not only decline a kingdom, but also found a republic. An eye for duty within and for opportunity without—this characterizes the American. There was nothing so vast to Washington, the Virginia boy, as the great continent without, save the imperial domain of conscience within his soul. In the joy of his ardent youth, I note that the first moment of a real Americanism within him is recorded, when he writes this rule for his conduct: "Labor to keep alive in your breast that little spark of celestial fire called conscience." To keep conscience is to let it reign. What, then, has been and what is left of Americanism have come because a boundless material opportunity, which we call our country, has been met thus far, in critical hours, by a limitless spiritual perception of the value of man's personality, which in the young Washington grew as he wandered amid these forests and traveled along the feet of these mountains. How the vision within—which had made Luther and Gustavus Adolphus—must have luxuriated and expanded, as the Virginia surveyor heard the splash of the distant cataract, or saw the peerless queen of night watch the mighty territory so long beneath her, a single field for statesmanship and of such magnificent dimensions. The sublime spoke to the sublime. Deep called unto deep. The very sweep of the vision without harmonized in hues of profound suggestion with the vision within. "What a mighty stage does man require," dreamed the young Washington, half unconsciously, as he saw what man was, in the vision of his imperious conscience. "What a mighty man does such an opportunity demand," spoke the shining rivers, the enormous valleys, the luxuriant forests in the unmeasured empire around him. There was the silence, and that was the mystery in which the mind of Washington grew.

We are transported to other days in which this sort of Americanism had its earliest trial. It is 1775. This policy of trusting truth absolutely has been for a century and a half, in an atmosphere whose currents have gone from Plymouth Rock to the Carolinas. It has been sung by the child of the Pilgrim and Puritan in New England, on the Hudson by the child of the Dutchmen who sheltered the Pilgrim in Holland, and the child of the cavalier and Huguenots has taught its melody to the south wind. Many souls less sublime than that of the young surveyor has known with him the vision within of man's possibility, and the vision without of man's opportunity. The democracy of truth has been making men democratic. The very skies have inculcated these large views and this serene faith. Every breeze has had the breadth of a continent, and has forbidden little things. In Harvard, Samuel Adams had supported the affirmative of the question: "Whether it be lawful to resist the chief magistrate if the commonwealth can not otherwise be preserved," and in Virginia the clarion of Patrick Henry has sounded. It is now a continent over which the same sky seems hovering, as that which, a century and a half ago, was over

England when Milton was Latin Secretary for Cromwell and Eliot went to prison. Those who left England's revolution brought inside the Mayflower with their faith a grand revolution for their children's children. And now the hour has come when the music which the world did not hear at Marston Moor, Dunbar and Worcester, should break forth in larger power.

The air was full of Americanism and this is the hour when Americanism must incarnate itself. Where is the person in whose life and spirit move freely these visions of what man has for America and what America has for man, these two dreams of power and opportunity? Where is the soul whose hopes are as lofty as those which these mountains seem to hint, whose thought is as broad as these areas can inspire, whose sentiments are as rich as these magnificent valleys can suggest—the man, where is he, whose spirit is great enough to include such variety of power and possibility, such enthusiasm of youth, such generous sympathies, such dauntless faith as must ever live on this luxuriant soil between these singing seas? It is not the king yonder who rules the colonies. They are broad, courageous, magnanimous; he is narrow, obstinate, conservative. He only can rule who can head this tide. It is not Grenville, prime minister. The times present too great a problem for his dogmatism or cautious doubt. Townshend's eloquence has charmed Walpole, but neither nor both of these may entertain such prophecies of man as move in the air above Concord and Yorktown, restless for incarnation. Not even Burke or Chatham, no man in England fully comprehended at that hour what that spirit was whose swift feet flashed from this side of the sea.

That spirit was true Americanism. She had from within a vision of the dignity of man, from without a vision of the fearless opportunity before him. She had found the truth of the right of self-government; she had courage and trusted it absolutely. Unseen, she stood undismayed before the awful shadow which English strength threw upon American weakness, until out of that shadow, at Cambridge yonder, stepped George Washington. His sword flashed with the old immortal idea. Again Charles I. must meet his Cromwell. The Mayflower had faithfully borne her unseen freight. But a century and a half had gone, and Americanism had now become incarnate for victory.

> "Never to see a nation born
>   Hath been given to mortal man,
> Unless to those who on that summer morn
>   Gazed silent when the great Virginian

Unsheathed his sword, whose fatal flash
Shot union into the incoherent clash
Of our loose atoms, crystalizing them
Around a single will's unpliant stem,
And making purpose of emotion rash."

At last Americanism had the triumph, at last a watchman traversed the streets of Philadelphia shouting:

"Past 12 o'clock and a pleasant morning.   Cornwallis is taken."

The brain of England at last recognizes Americanism triumphant in the sword of Washington. But even now, one man alone can save Americanism. It may fail here. The tide of feeling toward Washington is ocean high. It rolls upon the coast of a new-born nation with resistless power. It flashes with each succeeding breaker; nothing can stop it. Desperation of soul adds its pathetic strength in a weary army. "A crown for the hero! Washington must be king!" There stands your great American at Newburgh. A scepter waits; a throne invites him. Again, it is Cromwell called to a kingdom. Shall he, like "the Lord of the Fens," advise, consider, wait and postpone decision? Nay, nay! the Americanism of Washington spoke. Instantly he declined it. Like a Gibraltar, he hurled back the ocean tide and the sea was still. Could he fully trust the truth? Did he really believe in self-government. He answered doubt as to his faith in Americanism by returning to Mount Vernon to finish for posterity the portrait of the true American. Other duties, however, call him from private life. All through that stormy past Washington, with other true Americans, had seen the weakness of the Confederacy. Americanism, he saw, did not allow itself to reside in "joint-stock company" made up of states with no sovereign will, more than in a throne. And when the necessity for a national government was apparent the convention of 1787 came and the Virginia delegate was chosen to the President's chair. Washington's Americanism shone like the North star. Against Anglicism on the one hand, against all theories of confederation on the other, the man who had met a monarchy and who knew in battle the inefficiency of the Continental Congress, battled for a nation, as at Monmouth and Yorktown. It was to perpetuate those victories that he, who understood them, labored with other far-seeing patriots; and at last the Constitution came. It was the record of a noble Americanism, and yet it was not so noble as the Americanism of George Washington.

In its compromises, the eye of the prophet saw evil and danger. Already he could hear the voice of nullification and he could see the slave-power rise for secession. At last those fears were realized; but the Americanism of Washington carried the nation through the peril and stands yet to-day pointing the way for us. There is a pathetic grandeur in his figure at the close of the Revolution. He must do more than Cromwell; for he must insure the sovereignty of those principles which had been won at so mighty a cost. During that convention, it was a question whether the larger Puritanism which had left England in Cromwell's time, to win the triumph here, should continue in the state what it had gained on the field. This American Cromwell had also fought against the idea that a king was irresponsible to the people he ruled. Was he also to be a leader whom the next generation would decline to follow? Like the great Englishman, he, too, had seen glitter on his sword the recovered rights of freemen. Must that truth have an army for its parliamentary defense, or go out of sight for a time? He had refused a despotism at the hands of an army. Should he need to become the protector that he might keep either anarchy or some young Charles II. from the throne?

How decisively all these questions were answered! Yea, they were answered so well that the compromises of the Constitution could not foil the march of Washington's Americanism through our country. Years after his death did this Americanism have its severest trial and surest triumph. For we now look back to the day when the genius of Calhoun had staked all on nullification, and the dissolution of the nation seemed imminent, to see the form of Washington standing in the shadow of Andrew Jackson, as he says: "The Union must and shall be preserved." In the hour when Hayne repeats the philosophy of his great teacher and thrills the Senate of the United States with his eloquent words, the Americanism of Washington steps into the shoes of the defender of the Constitution, and Daniel Webster makes the spirit of disunion tremble in its castle. It is in this hour of his communion with the soul of the great leader, that the orator understands Americanism, and he says, "I was born an American, I shall live an American, I shall die an American, and I expect to perform the duties incumbent upon me in that character to the end of my career." Washington's Americanism saw the danger in slavery. On with the growing crisis does that spirit travel, until at last Robert Toombs proposes to call the roll of his slaves on Bunker Hill. Warren did not die to consecrate that soil to such a purpose. Nay! Nay! And soon the Americanism of Washington is incarnate in the person of Abraham Lincoln, who says, "I believe that this government cannot endure permanently half slave and half free." Again the sword of Washington gleamed in the fire of war, nor did it rest till the old Union was saved. Two centuries had gone and the larger Puritanism was victorious.

Washington's value to us lies in his Americanism. Napoleon died with the hope that his reign might be considered a dictatorship; Washington, with the hope that an American dictator was rendered impossible. One is the typical autocrat; the other the typical republican. There is a republicanism in duty, for every man has its privilege and its cares. Napoleon had no duty but his glory. Washington had no glory but his duty. There is a republicanism in every honest, reverent effort to win success. Every man has these inspirations and opportunity. Napoleon's destiny was autocratic; the destiny of Washington is vouchsafed to every man. The genius of Napoleon is solitary and has a monarchy all its own; that of Washington seems only the large perfection of that which every man feels is in him. The influence of one is imperious, dazzling, dictatorial; that of the other genial, inspiring pervasive.

In the forefront of a nation's life, it is of deepest significance that there may stand one who shall invite into largest life the peculiar characteristics of the national spirit. There is the greatness which humiliates and there is the greatness which inspires. Under the spell of Napoleon's influence there can be no self-government; every man must feel how weak he is. Under the benign influence of Washington self-respect rises; there can be no tyranny; every man sees his own power in the larger power of his leader. The triumph of Napoleon would have made that of his successor impossible; there was that in Washington which, though it had been defeated in him, would have been victorious in the next generation. To-day the loftiest with the lowest looks up to him and cries: "My father, my father, the chariots of Israel and the horsemen thereof!"

THE REV. S. J. McPHERSON.

AT CENTRAL MUSIC HALL.

The two ruling ideas of American history are liberty and order. By their propitious interaction as the centrifugal and centripetal forces of political astronomy they have struck out the wide astral orbit of our national career.

Liberty, the herald of order, was born with human nature itself, as the inherent, God-given right of man. But it only reached its majority when it landed an exile on the bleak coast of New

England.   Centuries of medieval darkness and despotism had shadowed and shriveled it.   The dim, interior light of its patient, self-consciousness had been barely kept alive by the hostile breath of tyranny.   Eternal twilight had fitfully dawned upon it with the horizontal sun of the sixteenth century.   Then, discovering the friendly wilderness of the virgin West it had leaped glad-hearted across the sea to enjoy at last its congenial day.   Here, for the first time at home, rescued from fictitious hardships, it became indigenous in the New England town meeting and school and church.   Heroically it wrested autonomy for the young colonies from sweeping maternal oppression.   Resolutely it reserved substantial rights to the succeeding states.   Enthusiastically it dictated the epoch-making Declaration of Independence to the discerning mind of Thomas Jefferson, and the supplementary emancipation proclamation to the great heart of Abraham Lincoln.   And the stars in their courses are still fighting for liberty against every siserary.   While cherishing hard-won treasures, local self-government and free play for the individual, it shall yet bury out of our sight forever the repulsive carcass of Mormonism; shall yet grant the full rights and duties of moral manhood to all dependent races and souls within our borders; shall yet irradiate and so eradicate the last vestige of alien systems which may menace freedom on our soil; and, ringing out like a bell let down from God, shall yet "proclaim liberty throughout all our land unto all the inhabitants thereof."   This glorious idea measures the whole circumference of our possibilities as a nation.

Excepting the approaching Centennial of the Supreme Court of the United States, its natural sequel and supplement, this Centennial to-day is the last of that august series which began fourteen years ago at Concord and Lexington.   The Centennials of the Declaration of Independence, of the various battles of the Revolutionary War, of the formation and adoption of the National Constitution, of the Ordinance for the Government of the Territory Northwest of the Ohio, culminate in the present anniversary of the actual organization of the government of the United States.   The Grecian Confederations, the Venetian Republic, the Geneva of John Calvin, the Commonwealth of Cromwell, were among the faint foreshadowings of our real self-government.   The colonization period was our exodus from slavery and our long wilderness march toward the land of promise.   The preliminary wars and the Revolution itself were its decisive conquest.   But with the inauguration of George Washington ended the weariness of hope deferred, ended even the practical anarchy of our iron age, which occupied the interval following the great war, and in which every incipient state did what was right in its own eyes. Hence, the current Centennial is the summary and climax of all that have preceded—in value and significance it is the greatest of them all. Greater than the Fourth of July, the evangel of freedom; greater than the 17th of October, Yorktown's death-knell to despotism, stands the 30th of April, the covenant of order and the beginning of national life. The emphasis of this occasion, thank God, is placed, not upon a rebellion which because it was both just and successful is called the Revolution, not upon a passive scheme of political ideas like Plato's Republic or More's Utopia, not upon the abstract political system of a paper constitution, but upon concrete and practical action which assumes its freedom as already secured, which realizes its lofty ideals and sets the machinery of its government in actual motion. The first President looms before our eyes to-day as the typical flesh-and-blood embodiment neither of empty liberty nor of brute force, but of vital organism and creative order.

In the marvelous organization of this young commonwealth what awe-touching displays of providential control! He who, on this uplifting anniversary, can not look toward heaven and say: "Thou hast multiplied the nation, Thou hast increased their joy," must ignore the plain lessons of history, must be blind to the key-stone of our miraculous structure. He must, as a degenerate son or successor, be out of sympathy with the Huguenots and Hollanders, the Covenanters and Puritans, who in the name of God and of man colonized this new world of hope; out of sympathy with the constructive geniuses who built the framework of our constitutional government; out of sympathy with Benjamin Franklin, who proposed prayer as the one remaining avenue of escape from the insuperable difficulties of the famous Convention in Philadelphia; out of sympathy of the Father of his Country, who developed his first inaugural address around this sacred sentiment: "No people can be bound to acknowledge and adore the Invisible Hand, which conducts the affairs of men, more than the people of the United States."

Our history shows that for once, at least, Providence was on the side of the weaker battalions. First of all, His great and wide sea was made our ally. The barrier of the Atlantic Ocean, wider than a dozen deserts, deeper than a hundred Jordans, buttressed this new chosen people against Egyptian contaminations and assaults, and left us free to work out our own destiny unhindered.

Providence endowed our country with natural resources in comparison with which the old land of promise was barrenness itself. By carrying out the ancestral policy, we have now a heritage greater in area than the whole of Europe, and estimated to be capable of sustaining, by agriculture alone, a thousand million of inhabitants. Our mining industries eclipse those of Great Britain or of all the remaining portions of the world. In manufactures and in commerce, as in population, we are barely second among the civilized nations. Such things as these put upon us greater responsibilities than ever nation sustained before. O, we look upon our broad and rich domain, producing nearly every known variety of plant and animal; we look down into the depth of our soul at forests of coal, oceans of oil and treasure-troves of precious metals; we look up to our two lordly mountain systems, spanning the continent, and lifting it out of the waters like the twin buttresses of some gigantic bridge; we look out upon an endless system of inland lakes and rivers, which drain and feed our continent like the blood system of the human body; we look abroad over our two great ocean highways, indenting our shores with admirable harbors and spurring us on to compete for the commerce of mankind; and, as our hearts dilate with gratitude over the exhaustless resources of this prodigal land, we may well exclaim: "The Lord hath not dealt so with any nation."

Providence favored our forefathers by giving them a new world for their majestic experiment in civilization—a world new and therefore unbiased by hostile precedents. How blessed it is that the colonies had not first been petrified, like yearning France, by ages of monarchical habits before they devised their peerless republic. If they had left the undertaking to us our country, I fear, would still be but a pale duplicate of Canada, whose parts are provinces of a foreign realm. Certainly the difficulty of the task would now be immeasurably increased.

Providence favored us with an unique commingling of peoples and ideas. This fusion of itself alone must inevitably have issued in a novel economic composition. No one race controlled. If British blood fortunately predominated, its insular prejudices were largely neutralized by strains of continental transfusion.

It was a parallel Providential benefit that the various nationalities thus thrown together were swiftly forced to make common cause with one another by the blind folly of the mother countries. God made the wrath of man to praise him. European neglect or abuse hastened American unity. Similarly it was no accident that Old World persecutions, ecclesiastical or civil, had compelled so many men of the noblest type to seek a haven in the New World. Europe was not worthy of them, and lo, they turned to America.

We are all debtors to the fact that they brought with them a natural hatred not only of tyranny but also of that ignorance which makes tyranny possible. In order to found their Republic, they first built colleges in the woods, and from Scotland and Holland they transplanted common schools two hundred years before England had any. However surprising to Tocqueville and Bryce, is it strange to us that urged on by common sufferings and a common faith, our fathers made intelligence, equality and uniformity characteristic of our country? Is it strange that the nation became rich in strong, good men?

Where else in all the topography of time will you find such a galaxy of minds gifted with so lofty yet practical a genius for government? When I consider what the forefathers accomplished with their most meagre external resources, I stand uncovered before them. Dr. Edward Everett Hale, complaining that we have retired George Washington to the realm of myths, appeals from Washington the soldier, the statesman, the President, almost the demigod, to Washington the man. One can sympathize with that sensible effort and yet continue to be conscious of the reverence which renders the effort so difficult. Measured by my standard, this Timoleon of America was a superlatively great man. Yet, after all, it is only his matchless radiance that eclipses the splendid luster of such colleagues as Jefferson, Hamilton, Madison and Adams. Our highest gift from Providence is found in these wonderful men who first rehearsed their principles and tried their experiments in the colonies, and finally, when God's hour struck, furnished forth these United States.

Fellow-citizens, if we are studious of American history, devoted to the ruling American ideas of liberty and order, reverent toward Divine Providence and molded by the example of our transcendent fathers, the America of the future, great beyond our fondest dream, will be secure with the intelligent and patriotic posterity to whom our dear heritage must be handed down.

With the venerable author of our national hymn, "America," who honors our Chicago celebration with his presence to-day, we may all devoutly join in this fresh tribute of praise and prayer:

> " The century ends—our hosts in peace
>   Hold the broad land from sea to sea,
>   And every tongue, and every breeze,
>   Swells the sweet anthem of the free.
>
> " Still may the banner of Thy love
>   O'er all our land in glory rest,
>   Our heaven-appointed ægis prove,
>   And make the coming centuries blest."

THE HON. JOHN M. THURSTON.

AT CENTRAL MUSIC HALL.

The inauguration of George Washington as President of the United States put an end to the divine right of kingly rule. Despots still hold in subjugation the lives and liberties of unwilling subjects. Emperors still surround with the splendor of courtly pageantry their crumbling thrones. Kings, shorn of their royal prerogative by the gradual encroachment of parliamentary power, still wield their puny scepters, and in imagination govern as of old. But the saintly mask no longer hides the hideous face of oppression, and the clamor of the great bell on Independence Hall awakened the whole world to the glad knowledge that the divine right of government is in the people.

When Paul Revere rode through the night, rousing the sons of liberty with the cry "To arms!" he not only summoned the patriots of Massachusetts to the unequal struggle and martyrdom of the morrow, but he summoned the genius of universal freedom to the revolution of humanity against the injustice and oppression of a slave-crushed world. That revolution did not end with the surrender of Cornwallis at Yorktown. It still goes on wherever some desperate martyr hurls his bare breast against the bayonets of despotic power and with his life makes way for the liberties of his fellow-men. It still goes on wherever some great constitutional leader dares to combat the prejudices of political associates that government may be administered to all alike. It still goes on wherever the mighty engine of a free press scourges injustice with its scorpion lash. It still goes on wherever eloquence and song have power to stir the souls of men. It still goes on wherever from Christian pulpits is preached the living word of God. And this mighty revolution will be carried on by every people and in every land until the glorious sunrise of its victorious day rests with equal splendor upon all the earth.

On this Centennial occasion our hearts are filled with gratitude to those great men whose inspired patriotism, lofty courage and sublime sacrifices wrought out the miracle of American independence. They toiled and struggled not for themselves but for all future generations. They did not dream what mighty strides would mark the nation's onward path. They saw but dimly through the mists of years the possibilities of time.

They sought no honors, asked for no reward. They laid their lives as willing offerings upon the altar of duty, content to know that what they did was for the sacred cause of right. Who can fitly commemorate the courage and devotion of those patriots and heroes of '76? What pen can write, what tongue can speak their fitting mede of praise? History has immortalized 300 Spartans who, at Thermopylæ, kept the gateway of their country until all but one had died. The chivalrous devotion of Napoleon's old guard, who at Waterloo made absolute verity of their watchword, "The old guard dies, but never surrenders," has filled the world with wonder. And the song of Tennyson has thrilled the hearts of all mankind with the story of the noble six hundred who at Balaklava charged an army. The minute men of Lexington and Bunker Hill, the defenders of the old log fort in Charleston harbor, the refugees of Valley Forge—yea, every "ragged rebel of them all"— should be canonized as saints in the cathedral of liberty, and the memory of their glorious deeds will live undimmed forever.

And not alone by those who drew the sword for freedom are the laurels to be worn. There were great men of peace, whose wisdom and statesmanship guided the struggling colonies, armed, equipped and maintained their armies, brought order and union out of the chaos of conflicting interests, and finally confirmed by wise constitutional provision the victories of war. Such names as those of Adams, Franklin, Jefferson and Madison have reached the full stature of immortality.

Having gained their independence and formulated their constitution, the people of the new union were called upon to select a chief magistrate. Our ancestors, in the barbaric ages of the past, when victory had blessed the prowess of their arms, raised upon their bloody battle-shields the greatest hero of them all and crowned him king. The same spirit of hero-worship elected George Washington our first President by unanimous choice. He might have made himself a dictator, and perhaps a monarch, but he only accepted the exalted presidential office for the purpose of more certainly establishing constitutional government in the land, and for the people his sword made free.

We stand at the close of our country's completed century. In place of the original thirteen colonies there are now thirty-eight populous, thriving, magnificent commonwealths, while four new stars already cast their dawning glory across the azure of the nation's flag. From less than four millions, who struggled through the desperate night of revolution to the morning of constitutional freedom, we have grown to sixty millions of happy people, all in the full enjoyment of individual liberty; all in exact measure protected by the law of the land; all with equal opportunity pursuing the prosperous paths of peace.

The wilderness of the new world has indeed been made to blossom with the roses of civilization. Into the depths of the primeval forest the axe of the sturdy pioneer has led the way. The virgin prairies, wakened from their eons of repose, repay the efforts of patient husbandry with the richest gifts of garnered sheaves. From the golden hearts of our mountains has been brought to light the countless billions of their hoarded wealth. The ingenuity of man has chained the rivulet and the river, the cataract and the waterfall, to turn the wheel that toils for him. From orient to occident, over the great steel highways, thunders the commerce of the world. Grand and thriving cities rise along the way, their apparent growth of centuries wrought by the magic of a few short years. Wonderful labor-saving machines have multiplied the power of human hands, while the inventive Yankee has fathomed the miracle of electric force and compelled the lightning to perform the will of man.

In every valley nestles the cottage of contented labor; in every hamlet stands the temple of free education; on every hillside rises the church spire of a God-given faith. This is the only land where man is truly free; the only land in which there is no rank, no caste, no aristocracy of blood, of birth, of wealth, of place. It is the only country where labor is fairly paid; where the industrious working man, out of the accumulated savings of his daily toil, can pay for the pleasant home in which he lives and send his children to the public schools. It is the only place where the peasant is a prince and the plowboy may become the President.

Yes, thank God for it, in the United States the sweat of honest toil is honorable and honored, and the dinner pail, in the hands of an American mechanic, is the badge of America's truest nobility. We offer to confer upon every man who will understandingly and in good faith accept the sacred trust the priceless rights and franchises of American citizenship; but no man must be permitted to profane the sanctuary of liberty with his unholy presence who does not subscribe with his whole heart and soul to the tenets of our Constitution and who is not ready to yield implicit obedience to the statutes of the country whose protection he invokes. The United States of America must never become the asylum for criminals nor the hotbed of conspiracies against law and order. The government of the people, made possible by the sword of a Washington, preserved by the victories of a Grant, and consecrated by the martyrdom of a Lincoln, must never be endangered by the dissemination of those monstrous theories which would overturn all government for anarchy and subvert all society to the dominion of unbridled passion and brute force.

And now, as a nation, we face the sunrise of a second century. What a splendid destiny awaits our glorious Union, if its people keep the faith. And yet its pathway may be beset by many dangers, its sky obscured by many clouds. This republic can only live so long as it holds to the original purposes of its creation: to protect the lives, to insure the liberties and to promote the happiness of all its people. Its corner-stone is the consent of the governed; that consent only continuous so long as all are given equal voice in its affairs. The great crisis which this nation faced in 1861 came to it, not because of any inherent lack of constitutional power to preserve its unity. But it came because the framers of our Constitution denied to one class of their fellow-men that same measure of liberty and equality which they demanded for themselves.

The Constitution of the United States was framed and adopted as a partial compromise to an existing condition of things. The representatives of the thirteen colonies, assembled for the purpose of creating national government, felt that the necessities of union overshadowed all other considerations, and therefore they temporized upon the question of human rights. Such a compromise could not outlast the conscience of the nineteenth century. The institution of human slavery was inconsistent with the Declaration of Independence. A government which proclaimed liberty and equality as a God-given heritage and yet denied both to one class of its people could not withstand the test of time. The culmination of the irrepressible conflict between right and wrong, justice and crime, humanity and oppression, was sure to come. It was a conflict far antedating the adoption of our federal Constitution. The Puritans of New England and the cavaliers of Virginia brought to this country two irreconcilable theories of the rights of men. Both were descendants of that grand race which first successfully set up the bulwark of law against the unrestricted will of kings; their common ancestors in 1215 had wrested from unwilling royalty the great Magna Charta, that sublime declaration of the power of the people, that great constitutional landmark of human liberty. But the cavaliers brought from the Old World their inherited traditions of superiority. The Pilgrims planted on the shores of the New the great white cross of a second crusade; its mecca the shrine of equal rights. The Declaration of Independence breathed the spirit of Puritan faith. The Constitution of the United States submitted to the domination of the Cavalier.

The supreme hour of the nation came. Its life weighed in the balance as against its sin. It was demanded that one or the other should perish from the earth, and the republic lived.

The genesis of American liberty was in the Declaration of Independence, but the gospel of its new testament was written by Abraham Lincoln in the Emancipation Proclamation, and the Magna Charta of man's real freedom and equality was secured by Ulysses S. Grant under the shadow of a Virginia apple tree. Appomattox and Plymouth Rock, the one the complement of the other, God's two footsteps marching on. Massachusetts and Virginia, commonwealth and dominion, are at last wedded at the altar of a common faith, and on this sacred Centennial of Constitutional Freedom the descendants of Roundhead and of Cavalier all unite in thanksgiving to Almighty God for the preservation of the Union on the basis of universal liberty. And the time will never come when the American people can afford to divide their joint inheritance at Mount Vernon and Bunker Hill.

This retrospection of the mighty past is pregnant with wisdom for future guidance. It is almost impossible to hope that the present unparalleled era of prosperity and peace can be continued through all future time. In the marvelous development of the United States; in the rapid accumulation of unprecedented wealth; in the amalgamation of many nationalities; in the unseemly greed for place and power; in the startling combinations of corporate capital; in the rapid growth of great cities; in the tendency toward class distinction; in the establishment of a mushroom aristocracy, and in the growing discontent of the laboring masses is there not danger to the republic?

Rome was a republic once. And "to be a Roman was greater than to be a king." Her strength was in the rugged manhood and Spartan simplicity of her citizenship, but grown over-rich and strong her people sunk their virtues in the maelstrom of luxury and vice and forfeited their liberties forever. The free states of Greece perished in the same way and from the same cause.

It would be useless to deny the fact that in the United States there is a growing tendency to subordinate abstract right to concrete gain. The worshipers of mammon are on the increase and the man of money too often takes undue precedence in social and political life over the man of brains. This unjust aggrandizement of the rich is the temptation of the struggling poor. It breeds that spirit of restlessness and discontent which sometimes incites to lawlessness and crime. It may well be feared that on some not impossible to-morrow of financial distress the ostentatious extravagance and unwarranted arrogance of the few may drive the struggling masses to desperate measures. Do not misunderstand me. I would not sanction any resort to violence for the redress of real or imaginary wrongs. The law must be respected and enforced or liberty is impossible. The rights of property must remain inviolate and justice will not tolerate illegal acts. Mobs are a menace to free government and should be dispersed by the iron hand of power. But I would make a mob impossible by the observance of that equality and the dispensation of that fellowship which recognizes the common brotherhood of the human race.

There is no danger that any law will hereafter disgrace the statutes of our country which, by declaration or effect, refuses to any American citizen equal participation in the rights and privileges of citizenship. But it is at least possible that public sentiment, either locally or throughout the country, may become so strong in favor of the especial rights and privileges of some particular class as to permit injustice to go unpunished. This should never be. If we are worthy the freedom we enjoy, if we are fit to participate in the blessings of popular government, if we are a God-fearing, law-abiding, patriotic people, then we should see to it that every American citizen, high or low, rich or poor, at home or abroad, on land or sea, is protected in his right to live, to labor, and to vote, not only by legislative enactment, not only by administrative power, but by the ready sympathy of every American heart and the loyal assistance of every American hand. Thus will we realize the prophecy of our Lincoln that "this government of the people, by the people, for the people, shall not perish from the earth."

It is worthy of solemn reflection that upon the morning of the day which was to witness the inauguration of our first President, the people were summoned to assemble in their several places of divine worship and return thanks to Almighty God for the blessings of free government; and the first act of George Washington after he took the oath of office as chief executive was to proceed on foot, attended by the witnesses of the inaugural ceremony, to the altar of the Christian faith, where the wisdom of an overruling providence was publicly proclaimed. I do not hesitate to assert that the genius of American liberty was born of the spirit of the Christian religion. It was the practical application to the affairs of men of that gospel of equality preached by the lowly Nazarene upon the shores of Galilee.

The little band of worshipers who assembled in the cabin of the Mayflower, as it rocked at peaceful anchor by the shore of the New World, drew up the first written Constitution of popular government. This agreement, signed and executed by them all, received its inspiration from the teachings of holy writ.

Jerusalem crucified Him who taught that doctrine of brotherly love which underlies all democratic institutions, but His resurrection goes on in the souls of men, and His kingdom will come on earth with the universal republic.

By the immortal memories of the heroic past we are summoned to the duties and responsibilities of the future. We pledge to the perpetuation of popular government and the maintenance of its free institutions the unwearying devotion of patriotic hearts. We pray that the blessings of Providence may attend us in the years to come, and the shield of a Father's love be over us alway.

Ethan Allen demanded the immediate surrender of old Ticonderoga "in the name of the great Jehovah and the Continental Congress;" and at the summons the sword of oppression fell from the nerveless grasp of the representative of despotic power. George Washington, as he stood before the assembled multitude and took the oath of office as our first President, touched with reverent lips the word of God. Abraham Lincoln, in His holy name, issued the mandate that set 4,000,000 people free. And Ulysses S. Grant gratefully acknowledged His supreme guidance of the armies that saved the republic. His mercy will still lead us on. On under the dearest flag that freemen ever bore. On in the broad sunshine of liberty, equality, and justice. On to the inspiring music of the union. On along the grand highway of the nation's glory to the future of our country's hope.

THE HON. JOSEPH FIFER.

AT THE EXPOSITION BUILDING.

With the inauguration of George Washington as President of the United States the career of this government was actually begun. We have met to commemorate that event and to celebrate the achievements of a century. The lessons taught by the heroic example of the founders of this government cannot be too well understood.

The difficulties and dangers which beset our forefathers after landing on these shores developed a physical and an intellectual manhood that has never been surpassed, and, in fact, rarely equaled in the history of the race. In the severe school of poverty and adversity they were taught those lessons of wisdom and courage which enabled them successfully to resist all encroachments upon their liberties by the greatest and most aggressive military power in the world, and led them finally to throw off the British yoke and lay the foundations of the American Republic—a republic that has been for a hundred years the hope, the admiration and the wonder of mankind, the foundations of which now rest securely on the virtue, courage and patriotism of sixty millions of happy, prosperous and contented people.

We feel justly proud of our military achievements in the eight years' struggle for national independence. The courage and fortitude displayed by our fathers during those long and terrible years of war and devastation will forever challenge the respect and admiration of mankind. I would like to see a monument erected to their memory, not only at Bunker Hill, but likewise on all the battle fields of the Revolution, on which I would inscribe this epitaph, a paraphrase of that written to commemorate the courage of the three hundred who fell at Thermopylæ: " Go, traveler, and tell at the capitol of the republic that we died here in defense of human rights." But, my fellow-citizens, their title to fame rests not so much upon their triumphs in the field, great though they were, as it does upon that wise statesmanship displayed in the Cabinet, which led to a more perfect union of the states under one federal Constitution.

The revolutionary period produced many soldiers and statesmen, the memory of whom will live so long as this government shall endure; but far above them all rises serenely the majestic figure of Washington, to whose greatness the genius of men has never yet paid a fitting tribute.

From the past we turn to the future. Whither are we tending, and to what end is our political, social and moral life leading us? Are we traveling over the same road leading to the same end that has been so often trod by the nations now dead?

These are the questions about which we are deeply concerned, and which are disturbing the minds of our most thoughtful statesmen. I prefer that each individual answer these questions for himself.

I venture this much: Our desire for riches, for material prosperity, is too great! Wealth is not an end, but only a means to an end; the real object in life being the moral, social and intellectual development of our fellow-men. The ability and desire to accumulate great wealth do not necessarily indicate the highest type of manhood. I am almost persuaded that we are growing rich too rapidly, and that our ability to accumulate should not be emphasized too strongly as a national virtue. It has been truly said that popular forms of government are possible only when individual men can govern their own lives on moral principles, and when duty is of more importance than pleasure and justice than material expediency.

Of this I feel sure. A nation is approaching dissolution and decay when patriotism is of the lips and not of the heart—when religion is used as a cloak to cover hypocrisy and crime, and when avarice clutches the poor man's earnings and robs him of his meager sustenance.

> "Ill fares the land, to hastening ills a prey,
> Where wealth accumulates and men decay.
> Princes and lords may flourish or may fade ;
> A breath can make them as a breath has made.
> But a bold peasantry, their country's pride,
> When once destroyed can never be supplied."

Let us, my countrymen, look into the future with hope and confidence; let us do what we can to perpetuate the institutions under which we have so happily lived and prospered for a hundred years; for when we are in our graves and our children meet to celebrate the achievements of two centuries instead of one, they will praise or condemn us according as we deserve.

Of the revolutions that may sweep over our fair land, or the great and good who may rise up to bless it between now and that far-off day, I know nothing, but of this I feel certain: Posterity will forever associate the name of Washington, the founder, with those of Lincoln, the preserver, and Grant, the defender of the federal Union—the three greatest Americans, who gave to our people nationality, liberty, equality and fraternity.

THE HON. J. R. DOOLITTLE.

AT THE EXPOSITION BUILDING.

On the 4th day of July, 1776, the "Thirteen United States of America," in Congress, at Philadelphia, made a unanimous Declaration of Independence from Great Britain. For the support of that declaration, with a firm reliance on the protecion of Divine Providence, they mutually pledged to each other their lives, their fortunes, and their sacred honor. The War of the Revolution, under that divine protection and under the lead of George Washington, made that declaration good.

The 4th of July, therefore, the day on which that declaration was made, has always been celebrated, and always ought to be, as the birthday of our national independence.   Besides, the ideas contained in that declaration brought into the world a new political dispensation.   It declared: the rights of all men are equal and inalienable; governments derive all their just powers from the consent of the governed.   On these two ideas hang all the law and the prophets in this new gospel of man's political redemption. This is another great reason why the 4th of July ought to be, and I trust will be celebrated, not only in this republic, but in all the republics of civilized man, throughout the world, and to the end of time.

Yet neither the Declaration of Independence, nor the War of the Revolution, nor the Articles of Confederation adopted by the delegates in Congress during that war (July 9, 1778) can be regarded as the establishment of constitutional government for the United States.   It is true that Confederation styled itself "The United States of America," and it looked toward a perpetual Union; but, "each state expressly retained its sovereignty, freedom and independence, and every right, power and jurisdiction not expressly delegated" to Congress.   But very little power to govern was delegated to the Congress.   It was composed of not less than two nor more than seven delegates from each state; and in determining all questions each state had only one vote.

The Confederacy had no executive department at all.   During the recess of Congress a committee of one from each of the thirteen states, called the "Committee of States," had power to act; but only in cases where the Congress by a vote of nine of the thirteen states had expressly authorized their action.

The Confederacy had no judicial department whatever.   In certain cases provision was made that the "United States, in Congress assembled, should be the last resort on appeal" in disputes between two or more states.   But they were more like arbitrators than a court clothed with power to enforce its decisions.

The Confederacy had no taxing power.   No money could be raised except by requisitions on the several states in proportion to the value of the lands of each, with their buildings and improvements, to be estimated under such rules as Congress should direct, but all taxes were to be levied and collected by the legislatures of the several states.

As we now look back upon a Confederacy clothed with so little power for peace or for war, it seems almost a miracle that our forefathers achieved their independence.   But for their almost superhuman courage, patience, patriotism and endurance; but for their intense love of country and of liberty, which seems almost inspired; and, above all, but for their abiding faith in that Almighty Being who raised up for that period such great men as George Washington, Benjamin Franklin, Thomas Jefferson and others, they would certainly have failed. Of one thing we are certain, with the experience of the late Civil War before us, all of us, who bore any of its responsibilities, can affirm with perfect assurance, that if the government of the United States had been clothed with no more power than the old Confederacy, we never could have put down the Rebellion and saved the Union and the republic as we did. But, thanks be to Almighty God! the Constitution of the United States, under which George Washington was made President one hundred years ago to-day, proved to be no rope of sand. It is a government, established by the people of all the states, to stand forever. The Constitution makes the Union perpetual and indestructible; and, at the same time, it makes the states themselves perpetual and indestructible. It expressly guarantees republican institutions and equal rights to all the states in the Union. While it makes one republic, in peace and in war, one nation in all national and foreign affairs, it at the same time secures to all the states independence, sovereignty and home rule in all their domestic concerns. The Constitution of the United States is as far removed from secession on the one hand as it is from centralized despotism on the other. The United States is a federative republic. That is the only form of national government which can secure home rule to the people of all the states, and yet may become continental as a nation in its progress and development. This federative republic is the outgrowth and heir of all the ages. Under God we believe it is to stand forever.

One hundred years ago this day George Washington, that providential man—hero, patriot and sage—"first in war, first in peace and first in the hearts of his countrymen," was inaugurated first President of the United States. Fellow-citizens, we have come here upon the recommendation of the President of the United States and the Governor of the State. The citizens of Chicago in vast assemblages are now uniting with the millions of their fellow-citizens throughout the whole land to celebrate this first Centennial of that inauguration. It is worthy to be celebrated, in prayer and praise, in anthem and eulogy, in song and oration; with music, cannon and every demonstration of joy. First, because of the man who was inaugurated; and, second, because of the great event— the greatest in the history of mankind since the crucifixion. There is but one personage in all history who stands higher than Washington: and He was even more than man. I refer to Jesus of

Nazareth, the great social reformer, as well as the Redeemer of mankind. It was He who in one short sentence of seven words, "Thou shalt love thy neighbor as thyself," laid the axe at the root of all abuses and all special privileges, of all tyranny, oppression and slavery over the bodies and over the souls of men. It is that same idea of justice, equality and brotherhood which nearly eighteen centuries afterward inspired the Declaration of Independence and breathed into this republic the breath of life.

In conclusion, fellow-citizens, no event, I repeat, since the crucifixion of Jesus Christ has done so much to elevate mankind as the establishment under God of this great republic upon the cornerstone of equal rights and human brotherhood, which are but other forms of expression for "Love thy neighbor as thyself." This abiding faith has sustained me on many trying occasions. Once, in the Senate of the United States, in the darkest hour of the Civil War, I did not hesitate to declare my firm belief that the United States is that great political power which the greatest of the prophets foretold, twenty-five hundred years ago, was to come upon the earth. That, after the golden kingdom of Assyria, and the silver kingdom of the Medes and Persians should be destroyed; after the brazen kingdom of the Greeks and the iron kingdom of the Romans should decline and fall, a new political dispensation—a higher, better and diviner power was to come. It was to come when the Roman Empire should be subdivided into the ten lesser kingdoms of modern Europe. And it did come.

In this country it has come.

There was no room for it in the Old World. This New World was reserved under God for that very purpose, and here there is room. Here, aye! here, the God of heaven has set up that new political power which shall never be destroyed; wherein the governing power, to quote the words of the inspired volume, "shall not be left to other people;" which simply means the people shall govern themselves; in the beautiful language of Abraham Lincoln: "a government of the people, by the people, and for the people." And the promise is, that, not by war or conquest, but by the light of its example, it shall break in pieces and consume all other forms of tyrannical, monarchical and aristocratic governments for civilized man. That promise it is fulfilling every hour. Just in proportion as man becomes civilized and Christianized, he becomes republicanized—in one word, Americanized.

Yes, fellow-citizens, as I believe, the divine promise is that the great republic of the United States, whose Constitution and government was inaugurated by Washington one hundred years ago to-day, with a population of less than four million, and which at the end of its first century has nearly sixty million, if true to itself, shall stand forever.

THE HON. C. C. ALBERTSON.

AT THE EXPOSITION BUILDING.

In the secret council chambers of a Masonic lodge in the State of New York, resting upon an antique oaken table, time-stained, dusty and well worn, is a book. That book should be sacred to the truthseeker of every land, because it is a Bible. It should be particularly sacred to the patriotic citizen of this republic, because upon its cover is inscribed these words: "On the 30th day of April, 1789, upon this volume was the oath administered to George Washington to support the Constitution of the United States." That book should be preserved forever; that book should be enshrined in gold; that book should be shown with reverence to the pilgrim of every land who comes hither seeking civil or religious liberty.

We are met to-day in the dawning of the spring time season, in this crowded city by the lake, to commemorate that occasion. We are met to take a retrospective view of the last century of our nation's history. Says Mr. Emerson: "Ours is an age of retrospection." Whether or not this is true, comrades and friends, this is a day of retrospection; therefore let us look back over a century of progress and gather inspiration from the past for the future. Not only have we met to look back and review the past and thank God for it, but we have met to-day to do honor to that man who is the patron saint of the order the uniforms of which I am proud to see before me.

From ages immemorial men have delighted to visit the graves of heroes, but not on that stately mausoleum in Paris, where rests the remains of the Corsican General, nor in the abbey where the Iron Duke was laid to rest, nor to the stately monument which marks the resting place of the Bard of Avon, does the freedom-loving and truth-seeking pilgrim of earth come with half the devotion he feels who bows at the tomb under the willows which grow by the side of the rolling Potomac. And in ages to come men shall delight to do honor to his memory, and under the inspiration of his deeds and of his character they shall unite in saying with his eulogist: "Hail, thou uncrowned king of the republic!" Uncrowned and crownless, yet as true a king as ever ruled, and as true a king as ever wielded scepter over submissive millions.

We are a proud nation. It is right that we should be. We have something to be proud of. We have a history, and thank God for it. We have a history of Providence. I would that upon the white stripes of that banner might be inscribed this sentiment, for it is the truth! "God's providence is our inheritance."

Before I close I beg you in your retrospection remember that that flag is not a mere piece of muslin. Remember that that flag is not so much bunting only. That flag is a synonym of liberty. That flag is a synonym of union. That flag is a synonym of opportunity, for under that flag, and under that flag alone, can we say to the young man starting out in life's career, however poor he be, however humble and obscure origin, you are a king; you are a free man; you may aspire to the highest honors. Under that flag alone is the son of the woodchopper equal to the son of the millionaire. Thank God that under that flag no brainless fop can stand up and claim the signs of a noble young man simply because he happened to have a decent parentage. Because a calf is born in a stable it is no sign it is a colt. The only aristocracy in this country is the aristocracy of worth, not of birth. The only royalty in this country is the royalty of character. The only sovereigns in this country are those who are sovereigns not by virtue of what rests upon their heads, nor by virtue of what is over their breasts, but sovereigns by virtue of what is in their heads and within their breasts. That flag stands for something else: It stands for fraternity of patriotic citizens, who, joining them together hand to hand, heart to heart, shoulder to shoulder, victory to victory, conquest to conquest, jubilee to jubilee, impulse to impulse, and inspiration to inspiration, have sworn to see that flag remain forever in the heavens. And against the insidious influences of foreign pauper criminal immigration, and against the insidious influences of Anarchists, Socialists, Nihilists, Communists, and such men, who, coming to our shores, seek to bring hither the institutions of other lands—to these men we say, Palsied be the hand and palsied the tongue that would do aught to rob that flag of one single star.

I will close by the repetition of those matchless lines written by our own American:

> "Sail on, O Ship of State!
> Sail on, O Union, strong and great!
> Our hearts, our hopes are all with thee,
> Our hearts, our hopes, our prayers, our tears,
> Our faith triumphant o'er our fears,
> Are all with thee—are all with thee!"

THE HON. RICHARD PRENDERGAST.

AT THE MEETING IN TENT A.

It is well to rejoice and to celebrate the toils, the sufferings and the wisdom of our fathers. While we praise their efforts let us not forget to draw proper lessons from their example.

What is the Constitution? Not a messenger of law and order appearing suddenly in the skies and descending to bless men for all time. It is the written expression of a nation for the guidance and control of its members. It was the last act in the great chain of events that resulted in the eternal union of liberty and law—in the establishment of a system of government that has for its cornerstone the recognition of the people as the sole depositories of power. Our government is not the child of chance. An orderly procession of causes, operating from the discovery of the continent until the present hour, have made the Constitution not only the instrument the fathers left it but the ever-broadening charter of a people's imperial power.

On the southern half of the continent the ambition of the conquerors was to seize the wealth the natives had amassed, and the blighting effects of that course are felt in those latitudes even to this time. Different purposes animated those who conquered the wilderness of the North—with them industry and virtue were the sources of material progress—and built up colonies capable, though few in number and scantily supplied with the materials of warfare, to repel the assaults of the savage on the one hand, and on the other to overcome the strength and the armies of Great Britain.

The centuries before the Revolution were given, in the providence of God, to the formation of a people strong in their reliance upon Him. The colonists not only beheld the evils of tyranny manifested in distant lands, but their fathers had fled from tyranny, and they themselves were sought to be made the victims of its exactions. The light that in Europe began to beat upon the ancient claims of privilege spread to America, and the colonists became diligent inquirers into the nature of government, its origin, functions, and its end, and from their experience, their studies, and their needs, they evolved this principle: That government is the means for the preservation of order among great bodies of men, and of resisting external and internal violence. They believed that all the powers of government were of right derived from the people, and from them alone, and they rightly judged that this doctrine so well approved by their own reason was the decree of heaven itself.

The contest between the monarchical principle and the popular principle was inevitable. The rights of kingship if not upon the decline had reached their highest point. The rights of manhood had been gathering force for ages, and had entered upon their upward movement. The contest between these forces, though fated to be waged in America, was a struggle most momentous in its consequences to the human race and for all time. To establish the right of self-government upon this continent would be to set the beacon of liberty so high that its light would penetrate the farthest domains of arbitrary power. Monopoly of government reigned every where, and it was fortunate for human rights that the vanguard of liberty consisted of men so fitted to be her champions as were the fathers of our republic. Their struggle may rightly be regarded as the instrument in the hands of Providence to establish the new evangel. They were the children of a high destiny, without, perhaps, comprehending the full measure of their dignity and importance as factors in human history. The work they set themselves to do grew beyond their highest expectations, but they grew equal to all its needs. Perhaps they thought but of resistance to taxation without representation, and as time went on it may be they grew to desire the independence of the several colonies; but the power that they resisted was one, the effects of which, though manifested in special instances, had general operation. Resistance to be effective had to be resistance of united colonies. The words "Join or die" became a watchword of liberty. Resistance was impossible without unity, and unity made resistance successful.

Great Britain attacked Massachusetts when she shed the blood of the patriots at Lexington, but that blow struck such fires of patriotic anger throughout all the colonies as fused them into one people. Lexington, Concord and Bunker Hill are the sacred precincts from which a nation came to life. Throughout the revolutionary struggle American arms were glorified by the cause they were used to vindicate. War, always dreadful, sufferings unsurpassed in severity were sanctified, because they were the means used by God to promote His great designs. Out of that struggle came the Declaration of Independence, a harbinger of victory, that epic of man's redemption from political thralldom, whose effects have not ceased to thrill the nations yet.

When at last the united colonies were received into the family of independent nations as an equal new difficulties arose; new dangers threatened. The revolution against concentrated power had a tendency to recommend forms of government filled with elements of disintegration, and the articles of confederation adopted under the influence of revulsion from centralized authority soon demonstrated that, even though free, man was still human, and that order could not prevail without the existence of organized authority.

Prior to the Revolution there was no visible bond of connection between the colonies sanctioned by law. They were communities distinct from each other. Their foundations had been somewhat dissimilar, and in the development of each there had grown up interests, sentiments, laws peculiar to itself. The common belief was that on the accomplishment of the Revolution each colony became sovereign and independent of all other powers and communities. This view took but small account of the part that necessity has in the formation of states; of that necessity which is the result of all of the conditions that exist at a given time and place, and whose power is as imperative as it is oftentimes invisible. It soon became apparent that the plan of a league of independent states was insufficient both for the preservation of internal peace between the colonies themselves and for the purpose of asserting the power of the American people upon the theatre of international affairs. The statesmen of the time and the people divided on these questions. Some of the most fervent patriots of the Revolution opposed the adoption of the present Constitution. Patrick Henry, who will live forever in the annals of patriotic eloquence, was among the number who believed they saw in the new Constitution the grave of liberty. But Washington, Jefferson, Hamilton, Adams and Madison proved themselves to be as ripe in statesmanship as they had been patriotic in the days that tried their souls.

For months and years the burning question was: What form shall the government of the country take? What shall be the measure of the authority that must be vested in a general government? What portion of the sovereign powers of the states shall they part with for the common weal? And, as the result of all, there was formed that instrument, bold, yet conservative, an innovation, yet replete with the elements of conservative strength, the Constitution of the United States. This instrument was the solemn act of the whole people of the United States—not a compact or a league entered into by sovereigns and from which as interest or whim dictated each was at liberty to withdraw. It is the definition by the people of the boundaries of their agents' power; it is the organic law on which the national government rests, and at the same time it is a pledge on the part of the whole people to each state and community that the substance of republican government shall exist in every state forever; it is the pledge of the nation that self-government shall prevail in all grades of governmental being; it is based upon universal manhood suffrage, and, to judge it aright, it is to be construed together with those great occurrences that were practically contemporaneous with it and from which it emerged. The spirit of the Declaration of Independence, with all its sublime truths, is as truly a part of the Constitution as any word written in its text.

And we celebrate to-day, not merely the complete formation of government, as provided for in the Constitution, but beyond this we celebrate the consummation of that great movement which transformed dependent colonies into an independent nation, a movement which found the individual dependent upon acts of parliament and royal decrees, in the formation of which he took no part, and left the individual the unit of sovereignty, and the people the source of all power.

And what a heritage is American liberty. Under its benign spirit education has ceased to be the patrimony of the few and has become the heritage and the birthright of all. The spirit of Thomas Jefferson breathing the purest of democracy, most generous in its recognition of the rights of all men, permeates all our institutions. The very first amendment to our Constitution is a guaranty of absolute and perpetual religious equality before the law. The fairest countries of the world had been from time to time, and even for ages, plunged into strife and fratricidal war, because, failing to understand that the conscience of man is beyond the domain of human control, man sought to usurp a power over his brother which even divine authority has never exercised—the power to interfere with man's free will, the most exalted faculty the Creator has bestowed upon His children. The colonists themselves had not been free from acrimonious contests upon this question; but, blessed be the Giver of all good, to whose love we owe this boon, that question is at rest with us forever.

According to the spirit of our laws every man is free to pursue happiness—to seek his own welfare in such way as his own judgment approves. In other lands labor is not honorable; with us in all its varied forms it is the only source of honor. The hand, the heart, and the intellect accomplishing some rightful purpose are the best titles to esteem and favor. Elsewhere man is doomed to labor as a curse; with us he seeks it as a blessing. Upon this continent labor first breathed the breath of life, first came to its high estate, and with uplifted eye looked upon the earth, and sea, and sky, its dominion, and felt that it, too, was fit for empire. True, slavery, that remnant of the ancient curse that had existed in so many lands and in so many forms, had unfortunately struck its roots deep in the social, industrial and political conditions of our country. While desiring its extirpation, the fathers were compelled—accepting immediate non-interference as a lesser evil—to leave its amelioration and extinction to future times. For this they should not be condemned. The circumstances confronting them forbade any other course. But who shall declare that their act was even an error? The subject of slavery sustained the high debate, which for generations made the Constitution, its limitations and its extent, the boundaries of state and of national authority, its subject. The right of dismemberment of the Union and the claim of perpetual union ranged their supporters upon such lines that war alone could, as it did, determine the controversy. Perhaps it is well that this question arose and was settled with slavery as the provocation for difference of opinion. Had other questions and other times ranged the people of the country into hostile forces, who may picture what the result might be?

We are so accustomed to universal suffrage that it is scarce conceivable that civilized governments at any time sought the true sources of their power anywhere but in the consent of the governed. And yet, in the United States for the first time universal manhood suffrage was made the foundation of government and the arbiter of every public question. Growing out of this idea was the proposition that the place of man's birth was of no consequence in determining his right to vote. The republic sent its invitation to all lands that the oppressed might come, that they would be welcome, not only to take part with us in the ordinary affairs of life, but that upon every individual who came with heart loyal to the principles of the republic she would place the crown of citizenship. Native or foreign-born, do we realize the dignity that is ours, we who are the ministers in the temple of the law?—more than this, the creators of law itself? From time to time a half-panic has possessed the faint-hearted, and a timid cry has been raised to restrict immigration. Our nation is an empire of emigrants. Columbus and the missionaries, the Puritans and the Cavaliers, Lord Baltimore and William Penn, Jackson and Phil Sheridan—all were emigrants. The republic was not founded by natives. The republic was not founded for natives. The republic was founded for man, for every man who was born upon this continent or who would come to these shores willing to assume and to discharge the duties of citizenship. As heroic deeds as glorified our country's history were achieved by the foreign-born. Nor in civil life are they less in loyalty and worth than those so fortunate as to be born here. The highest boast of our revolutionary fathers was that the light of liberty was to shine so brightly that its influence was to be felt in all lands, so that the heavy-laden of all climes might be attracted by its beauty and come to share in its benefi-cence. Let us still be friendly to the millions who have come. Let us tender great welcome to the millions who are coming, who are coming even now, with sturdy frames and honest hearts, to cast their lot with ours. Let the only condition be that they will do their duties by the republic even as we are bound to do ourselves.

Do they need education? Let us not give them effusive plati-tudes. The best way to transform the foreigner into an American is for every citizen to put conscience into all his public duties. Let us teach by the great force of example. How can he who was born a subject perhaps of arbitrary power be tractable under authority where, misinformed, he perhaps dreamt of unrestrained freedom, when he beholds the prize of citizenship lightly esteemed and its duties even neglected by those who should excel, and when he sees the actual government of affairs all too often in the hands of the unworthy? Do we all appreciate our power? More still, do we all realize the responsibilities arising from our power? Do we discharge the duties that are inseparable from our rights? The right of self-government was worth a war, and the price of liberty—the sufferings of those who struggled and the lives of those who died—was not too great. What does duty to the republic demand of us? Not life, not liberty, not property, not sufferings, not privations; but in these, our peaceful days, simply that we watch and guard and rightly use the treasure so hardly won, so wisely preserved and so happily transmitted to us by the fathers, the full fruition of whose courage and wisdom we celebrate to-day.

The ballot is the freeman's arm. Before its force every wrong must fall; but if we permit its abuse, its power can be used with deadly effect against us and against posterity. Ordinary crimes against the elective franchise violate the integrity of the ballot, it is true; but there is a more insidious way by which its vigor is sapped, its essence poisoned, its power destroyed. That is by bribery of public servants, by illicit interference at the sources of law and in all departments where the law is administered. The coarse forms of offense attach to the externals. These are very easily seen, quickly discovered, and susceptible of prompt punish-ment. But the sinister corruptionist sends his agents where the people's servants are placed to do the people's will, and plays foul with delegated power. These are the arch enemies of liberty, whose misdeeds make or tend to make self-government a by-word and a thing of scorn.

The great and the good of other times took part in public affairs. They were politicians. But with them place was a post of duty. So should it be with us. What nobler task than to be the guardians of the republic, even though it be in the obscure post of sentinel? In our times no sacrifice of material interests is involved in the performance of our duty. But it can not be performed merely by voting the day of election and abstaining the remainder of the year from all public afiairs. How true it is that eternal vigilance is the price of liberty! Let us revive the good old New England town meetings so far as our conditions will permit, and they do permit a revival of the spirit of those town meetings. Let our elections be contests between principles and on occasions between men, and not a blind contest of partisan cohorts. Let good citizens regard it as an honor to have served upon a jury—to have been the dispensers of justice. A careful, prompt, cheerful and honorable discharge of public duties should exalt a man in the opinion of his neighbors. Public opinion is the general conscience finding voice. Let us all join in creating it. Let its power be such that the briber, the gift-giver, the violator of the ballot, the wrong-doer of every kind shall be broken and bowed and sent his way in shame. What resistance would be evoked by an attempt on the part of a legislature to deprive us of the right to take part in any one or all of the duties of citizenship! And yet that which we would fight to prevent we too often do ourselves.

Every generation has its own duty to perform; its own legacy to leave to posterity. May I submit that our duty is at least to transmit unimpaired to those who shall succeed us the priceless blessings of civil liberty? Shall it be said by the historian that our strength proved our weakness; that because there was no external foe we gave no heed to the corroding influences that were at work upon the pillars of the state? The fathers struggled with monopoly and overcame its power. Are we unable to cope with it when it assumes another form and has somewhat different designs? The tyrant of those days denied the equal protection of the laws—denied the right to take part in the making of the laws. We have to deal with agencies that would leave the form of self-government to us, but at the same time use their powers for undue and selfish advancement. Those who at the foundation of the government foretold danger based their prophecies upon the history of other nations. They said that wealth would increase mightily, and when it did that corruption would prevail, and that the people would lose the zest for liberty. Let it be our task to prove that a nation may be wealthy, yet its public functions not corrupt, its people not forgetful of their duties. Let us remember that the republic was founded not for the purpose of amassing wealth, but for the purpose of elevating manhood and making liberty something more than a name, making freedom a great reality to all men.

No man has the right to be a private citizen in the sense that he takes no interest, or but slight interest, in public affairs. This nation and all its powers, general, state and local, constitute our household. Let it be our earnest study and our continuing labor to see that its affairs are ordered well, and that our voice shall give the orders. After all, the highest work of man is not to become so that he may have no care for the morrow. Providence has deigned to give to us power that can be the means of bettering the conditions of the millions of the human race here and elsewhere. Let us begin at home, and, as we help to brighten the outlook for those who toil, whose bone and sinew and muscle is the staff by which the banner of our country is sustained and from which it floats, there will go out from our borders such moral energies as will break the bonds of privilege everywhere, such lessons of practical brotherhood that the lot of the unnumbered poor will be bettered, and such reverence for the nature which God has given to man that government by the law and by the conscience and for the welfare of man will prevail in all lands and in all times; such great conceptions of right and duty that the whole race will be elevated to higher levels of existence than earth has witnessed yet.

The genius of the day will be my apologist for offering some verses that the hour inspires. Name them, if you will, a "Centennial Hymn:"

> Great spirit, through the universe,
>   Though myriad forms Thy powers proclaim,
> What race, as ours, is bound with love
>   To praise and magnify Thy name?
>
> Thy word bade both the oceans part
>   And raised this continent on high;
> Thou filledst it from unmeasured stores
>   And blessed it with great destiny.
>
> And lo! when time was all fulfilled
>   Thy wondrous purpose to declare,
> Thou gavest to man another world
>   That he might found free empire there.

Thou taughtst him once again Thy truth,
   That force is evil, love divine—
And rule alone is just that flows
   Below, yet parallel, with Thine.

Thou chastenedst him; but, purified
   By deep communion—yea, with Thee—
He learned and builded on this rock,
   Thy word—"the mind of man is free."

Thy counsels guided while were wrought
   The nation and the nation's laws;
We thank Thee, bless Thee, bow in praise—
   Thou art, O God, the Sovereign Cause.

My friends, let us be animated by the principles of the sages and the heroes whose work we commemorate; let us hope that the breath of a newer life will stir the breasts of men, that the horizon of human sympathy will broaden so as to embrace them all, and that the Constitution will be to those afar and to those who abide beneath its fostering care, indeed the temple in which the fathers of the republic enshrined Liberty, so that her spirit would abide among the sons of men forever.

BISHOP SPALDING.

AT THE MEETING IN TENT A.

A great people needs not praise; and the millions who to-day assemble in all their cities and towns, in their public edifices of religion, of government, and of education, are gathered, not in a frivolous spirit of vanity, not in a spirit of boastfulness, but in the spirit of true joy and deep thankfulness. Indeed, if we look at what has been accomplished within a hundred years here in America, it is easy to grow boastful. Yet a dispassionate view of the subject forces us to recognize that much of what has been achieved is due rather to fortunate circumstances than to the character and energy of the people.

America was discovered at a time when Europe was merging from the darkness of mediæval barbarism, from its confusion, its lawlessness, and its ignorance. Thus already the populations of the Old World were prepared to some extent to begin a freer and higher kind of life here in the New World. And when North America was colonized, monarchy in Europe was everywhere degenerating into despotism. The disruption of the church had ushered in a century and more of religious wars and fanaticism. Thus the lovers of liberty and the lovers of peace were more than others attracted to these shores. Again, when we declared our independence, when finally after years of struggle our independence was recognized by the world, the era of steam and electricity was about to begin in the world. Thus the nineteenth century dawned as the century of inventions, the century of enlightenment, the century of the diffusion of knowledge, and of the growth and assertion of the principle of liberty. Our ancestors brought with them to America the greatest political principle that has ever been applied to the government of states, the principle of representation. Again, here they found a country rich in all mineral and vegetable productions; they found an invigorating and wholesome air, and a climate stimulating to every kind of human energy. Thus, my friends, we perceive at a glance that God's providence in every way prepared for us a field wherein men might labor with a hope of bringing forth the best fruits.

Yet, after all has been said of the circumstances of the age, of the character of the early colonists, of the political and religious principles by which they were animated, of the climate and soil, yet we must say that a great sum of achievements still remain for which the people alone must be given credit. Why has this country become the most attractive on the whole earth? Why is it from every part of the world men turn their faces toward us and seek here higher blessings than they have hope of finding elsewhere? We offer them better opportunities; we offer them facilities for leading brighter and higher and nobler and richer life than can be found anywhere else on the earth. Why to the north of us, in Canada, has there not been the same development? Why to the south of us, in Mexico and in the islands, why nowhere in the New World has there been a development which can be compared with ours. Those regions have climates in some respects superior to ours; they also were colonized by Europeans, and yet we have so far outstripped them that we alone are Americans. We are Americans!

The great achievement of the American people is the establishment of a federal government on republican and democratic principles, an achievement which gives us a place and a part in human history, for there is nothing else like it. We have a country almost as vast as the whole of Europe. Yet this country, by the power of its federal government, makes headway and keeps on its specific course without a standing army, without any obstructions, simply by the intelligence and the good sense of the people. The rest of the civilized world supports standing armies. The life of the people is drained to support them, and they stand there as enemies facing one another. My friends, this would have been our fate; we here would have formed a multitude of nations, and these nations would have come into conflict with one another, and, as a result, they would have created standing armies, would have brought aristocracies and privileges, and all those forces that are inimical to the people and a democratic rule. It was because our ancestors created a federal government, leaving the states independent, creating a higher unity in the nation; it was because of this that our immense prosperity, our immense increase in numbers and wealth and power have come to us.

We celebrate to-day not the inauguration of George Washington as President. George Washington and any other man sinks into utter insignificance in the presence of this day. We celebrate here the putting into action the Constitution of the United States, the organization of our federal government. George Washington had some share in creating this Constitution, but only a minor share. When this Constitution was framed there was not a statesman in all Europe, probably there was not a statesman in all America, who believed that it would work. The attempt was sneered at as visionary. The very men who sat in the convention in Philadelphia accepted compromise after compromise, and finally agreed upon the Constitution because they were afraid to go home without having done something. These very men did not believe in the stability of their work, not one of them. It was from the menace of anarchy, from the menace of utter lawlessness, from the inability to pay the debts of the old Congress, from a thousand evils that were pressing upon them, that they were driven to adopt some experiment; and this experiment, made up of patchwork of different enactments, probably against every one of which there was a majority in the convention, this experiment of government was launched upon the world, and it has worked as though God Himself had given it to us.

All the men of the South feel that it was God's mercy that kept them from winning in the late unhappy war. I am a Southern man myself, and such is my opinion, also. It was God's providence for the future of the human race that kept them from victory.

We have such a power on this continent that no nation will dare to interfere with us.

In South America, in Central America, in North America, no nation will ever attempt to interfere with us; therefore we need no army. Therefore war here is out of the question. Europe will not attack us, for Europe is too disunited; the European states are too much in dread of one another, too much threatened by the awful power of Russia. In all America none can harm us. We are left to grow and prosper. War has been the great curse of the human race. War has been the bane of nations and of civilization. More and more is the idea gaining that war is barbarous, is criminal.

What shall we do? Certainly the American people are not foolish enough to think they have no problem yet to solve. Mark you, my brethren, in a hundred years from to-day there will certainly be 300,000,000 of people in the present territory of the United States. But we are not aiming at that. If we were hogs we might count ourselves by the million. We are not aiming to become the wealthiest nation on earth; we are bound to become the wealthiest nation. Our wealth will make all former riches look like poverty. We are not aiming to give all men as much personal liberty as order will permit. Already we have done this. We must keep up this liberty. What is our aim to be? It is to lift up the people, to make nobler men and women, wiser men, more enlightened, more moral, braver and truer. We want the highest race here, not the most populous, not the richest, but the highest. What do we do with our animals? We seek for the best breed of animals, and shall we not have in this country the best breed of men? We want the best blood of the earth. We come from the very flower of the Aryan races, and we come from the best blood of them, from the peasant and farming populations; not from the scrofulous aristocrats and kings of earth. We want Americans to be a higher race of men than have ever existed.

I will tell you, my friends, I myself believe that the people of the United States to-day are the highest people on earth. I would not boast at all. I would not say a word boastfully about this, but I have traveled in various countries, and I am old enough to observe, and I am convinced that there is no nation on God's earth that can bring forward the same number of men and women of the high average that we can here in the United States. Again, no other people in the world are so eager to make headway, to learn, make new inventions. We do not want to conquer any nation. The idea of conquest was an old, barbarous idea. We could conquer Canada, could not we? God knows we could take all America, but we don't want to do it; the American people do not want to do it; they have outgrown that barbarous era.

What will we do? We will help Canada and Mexico and Cuba. I believe the American people look upon these countries as countries in which they are interested. They want to do them good. I was down in Cuba a few weeks ago. I found the people there all looking to the United States. They say: "Would to God we did belong to you!" In Mexico, I found the intelligent people delighted that the railroads had been built, that our machinery is coming to Mexico, that our enterprising men were going there to open the mines and to establish factories. We want to help them. Mexico is a republic. Canada will be a republic. Let them be federal with us. Our interests are one. Let us help them, encourage them, enlighten them, stimulate them. That is our mission.

It is our mission, beyond doubt, gentlemen, to do good in the world. First of all, to begin at home here. There are children now living who will see Chicago with 5,000,000 of people. In a country like this the great danger is from ignorance, from immorality, from low-mindedness. If anything is going to do us harm it will be having in our cities and towns thousands of ignorant paupers, idle criminals, of low-minded men and women. We must work against this.

There is practically no difference between the two parties now. There is the tariff and free trade, and they both lie about it. It really does not matter to a man of principle which party wins. There is bound to grow up a new party.

It may be a slow growth. These organizations are tenacious, the Republican and Democratic. But one of them is bound to give way, and we are going to more and more identify politics with morality. Americans know that righteousness is life. We know the worldly temporal blessings of sobriety, of honesty, of thrift, of prudence, and economy. Now, since we are to create a state of affairs beneficial to all men, we are going to identify more and more politics and morality, because we are going to look more and more to men rather than to things. We are going to look at our machinery, our crops, and our hogs, and we are going to look at our men, and we are going to understand more and more that not only private persuasion, not only the teaching of the churches, but the power of political influence must also be brought to bear upon public morality. In fact, one great question that is going to be forced into politics—we can sneer at it now, but it is going to come—is the question of prohibition. Mark my words, the saloon in America has become a public nuisance. The liquor traffic, by meddling with politics and corrupting politics, has become a menace and a danger.

Those who think and those who love America and those who

love liberty are going to bring this moral question into politics more and more; also this question of bribery, this question of lobbying, this question of getting measures through state and national legislatures by corrupt means; they are going to take hold of our press, which has done so much to enlighten our people, which represents so much that is good in our civilization, must also be reformed. It must cease to pander to such an extent to the low and sensual appetites of man. My God, man is animal enough! You do not want to pander to his pruriency. You don't want to pander to the beast that is in him. Do not publish filth. Respect the people; respect the mothers and daughters and the sweet innocence of children. Publish that which will enlighten and stimulate noble aims, but leave out what is fit for brothels only. Our rich men are numerous, their wealth is great. Their numbers and their wealth will increase. But our rich men must do their duty or perish. I tell you in America we will not tolerate vast wealth in the hands of men who do nothing for the people. Rich men must establish universities, must create museums of art, and they must beautify our cities and make their wealth an instrument for the general good. Then they will become our leaders and those to whom we will point with pride.

There also comes before us the question of education. The state must maintain education. It is not possible to educate the whole mass of people except with the help of the state. We must more and more discuss this question of education in an impartial mood. We must look at it calmly. It is not a question for fanaticism. It is not a question for religious bigotry. It is a question to be looked at with a philosophic mind. And that man is an enemy of the people, is not an American, is an apostate, who would view it otherwise; but, for God's sake, study the best methods of education. Study all the philosophy of education. Let us get a right and not a false education. Let us more and more see that the conscience is educated, that the whole man is educated. To be sharp of wit, to have a keen mind, is not to be educated. The man must be a full-grown individual, in mind, in conscience, in imagination. We must seek to educate our people to love higher pleasures, to take life a little more at ease; not to work themselves to death. We must teach our people to love education. The mass of the people seem afraid of high education and are talking against high schools, colleges and universities. My brethren it is stupid talk; it is unworthy of Americans. We want all men as far as possible to have the best and the highest training. Look at those men who framed the Constitution! There were fifty-five of them, and twenty-nine of the fifty-five were university and college men. I tell you we want it as an honor, as a source of wisdom; we want them as models of thinking, of style and of action. Let us then in God's name provide the highest education for those who are willing to take it. I, myself, am convinced that the national government ought to establish in Washington a national university, the greatest, the most richly endowed, the most thoroughly equipped on earth; we ought to have it. It would be a God-send for Congressmen and Senators to be near such men.

Though we have inaugurated the era of peace through the intelligence of the people, yet there are many problems before us. Greatest of all problems, there is the task of raising hundreds of millions of the most enlightened, the most moral, the most religious, the most helpful men and women that exist on God's earth. Here, in the New World, let there be a new humanity, and let science lead charity by the hand. Here, in the New World, let each man work for all and all work for each, and then a hundred years hence man will think less of his material achievements and more of his moral, religious and intellectual conquests.

THE REV. DR. E. G. HIRSCH.

AT FARWELL HALL.

I wish I were eloquent to-day that I might lend words that would suggest the thoughts that come from the flags before me and from the men that fought for and bled for those flags. If I am to-day patriotic, who is it that breathes the air of this our free country on a day like this who can resist the inspiration and not be carried along by the current? We of the present are at one to-day with those that lived a hundred years before us. Space is to-day naught. Ever since the earliest rays of the rising sun touched the eastern shore of our broad land, in the early hour of this morning, the bells have been ringing out, and, following the path of the sun, that carries all joy, has been swelling as it rolled along, from the East to the West, from the Atlantic to the Pacific, the one sentiment of liberty.

The sentiment which is quick within the heart of us all to-day obliterates all distinctions of position and of birth. He whose cradle stood under the protection of the Stars and Stripes feels that the citizen who was born in another country, and who has come to pledge his loyalty to our flag, is in patriotism his peer; that native and foreign-born citizens are twain to-day. And the distinctions that actual life works—the distinctions of the accidents in life to-day—have no weight for us. The poor laborer is to-day under the inspiration of the sentiment that is active all over our land, and feels his equality with the more favored child of fortune.

Where is the tongue that can do justice to the suggestions and inspirations of this hour? This day is like the child of the sun. There is no one eye that can bear the brilliancy of the king of day. We must dissolve the solar ray into the beauteous color of the rainbow before we can study its nature. And it is the brilliancy of the American idea which must be carved into an arch of different colors and different lines ere the human mind is able to grasp it in its full comprehension and take in the full depth of its beauty and the full glory of its splendor.

Those beauteous lines all come to us, but I can examine but one idea which suggests itself to me as important to be considered in an hour so full of inspiration as this. One hundred years ago, thirteen colonial states were confined to a narrow line of coast on the Atlantic Ocean. To-day we have bridged this Western continent. We have reclaimed the swamps, we have cleared the forests, we have builded cities. The hand that wielded the pioneer's ax was too stiff to thrill into music the thin harp strings, and the arm grown muscular by swinging the mighty hammer found the chisel too light to fashion into marble the beautiful ideas of the poet. What we needed, and what our civilization produced, was men that dreamed but little, philosophized but little, but who were men that acted, were proud to act, and eager to act. But under this intense life of activity there runs a golden thread of the truest idealism. It is not true that we are slaves to mammon as a nation. Wherever the American pioneer pitches his tent, there he has uplifted the schoolhouse and the temple. Wherever the American home is planted there flowers out into beauty and blossoms into perfume the true virtues of a pure domestic life.

The sun has its spots; we expose our shortcomings to the gaze of the world. We have not yet learned the vice of national hypocrisy as they have learned it and practice it in Europe. But we know that public exposure of our shortcomings is the surest and safest road to ultimate redress.

A people's character can be measured by the men whom it worships. We worship not those alone around whose brow the god of war has wreathed a laurel crown. We are indeed a nation that will defend to the last drop of blood its honor, and in wars for our defense we have challenged the world's admiration for our bravery and for generals that are the peers of the greatest masters of strategy whom history names. But it is not as the general alone that we remember Washington and Grant and Sheridan and Jackson and Scott. It is because "first in war," Washington was also "first in peace." The religion of the American people is devotion to liberty, and the realm of the empire of liberty is widened on every page of our national history. Our great men show the heights to which we may rise; and it is by these Americans—Washington and Adams and Jefferson and Monroe, by Lincoln, Grant and Garfield —that we wish to be judged, and we have a right to the judgment of the world.

Great possessions entail always the duty of great performances and great responsibilities. If we revere the name of Washington, in this reverence we take upon ourselves the duty of emulating the example of the Father of his Country. The Constitution which he and those that lived and worked with him adopted, drafted, planned and put into practical execution, is the most conservative document that ever was devised for the government of nations. Our Constitution is conservative because it stands like a rock against the easily-swayed, frenzied, waving ocean of popular passion and popular prejudice. France was a good friend to us in our hour of need. Next Sunday in France they will celebrate also a centennial day. What is the difference between American liberty and French liberty? America has a Constitution that is conservative, while France, to her misfortune, never drafted a constitution that had this tendency, and thus when feeling runs riot in France but a word or a hasty syllable is all that is needed to set off the powder of public passion, and then comes the explosion; then comes destruction; then comes disorder.

The American Constitution is a divine commandment of liberty; but liberty according to the American idea is always wedded to law and to responsibility. And this is the sense, the beauty of this our celebration. We must to-day, of all years—native and adopted citizens—renew our oaths of allegiance to the Constitution. We must all of us again learn what was exemplified in the life of Washington—that where there is a right there is a corresponding responsibility. There are great burdens upon our age. There are great problems staring us in the face. There are dangerous shoals and rocks that threaten shipwreck, unless we be sturdy, faithful pilots and steer the ship of our national government free of the shoals and free of the eddies, and free of the dangerous rocks in the line of our national life. What our age most needs is men that are imbued with the principles of Washington and Jefferson, with the principles, and the loyalty, and the unswerving devotion to duty exemplified and illustrated in the lives of those great founders, the first President and the first councillor of our beloved American republic. Our time calls out for men with that love of liberty and devotion to duty which immortalized Washington and his associates. We must resolve to be men as they were men. Then the future has no danger that we cannot meet; then the rocks and the shoals will be passed triumphantly, and our ship of state, our National Union, our national prosperity will be carried forward on the ocean of future greatness. Then those that come after us will say that the men of 1889 were worthy of those of 1789.

In the harbor of New York stands the statue of Liberty enlightening the world—a gift from our sister republic, France—a gift of the countrymen of Lafayette, the friend and ally of our beloved land. That statue of Liberty sends out the first greeting to the visitor from foreign shores, and speaks the voice of welcome to those who have escaped from the oppressing governments of the ancient world and come to make their home with us. That statue also bids godspeed to the ships that leave the great harbor of New York to carry our produce to the Old World. Look upon that statue on this day of celebration. It gives a parting salute to the age that closes; it brings a greeting to us that now take sail out on to the mighty ocean of a new century, and thus this day seems to me to speak most eloquently the prayer which we must realize through our government and which has been voiced so beautifully by that American poet:

> " Sail on, O ship of state!
> Sail on, O Union, strong and great!
> Humanity, with all its fears,
> With all the hopes of future years,
> Is hanging breathless on thy fate. . . .
> Our hearts, our hopes, all with thee;
> Our hearts, our hopes, our prayers, our tears,
> Our faith triumphant o'er our fears,
> Are all with thee—are all with thee."

Long may she wave, the flag of the Stars and Stripes—the Red, the White, and the Blue—the emblem of liberty wedded to law, to responsibility and duty. May never one single star be eclipsed, one single stripe fail. In the night of slavery may the stars shine out and the golden rays of daylight, like the streamers of red, bring joy to all those that love liberty, and thus insure us what the white typifies—peace and prosperity under the benign worship of our constitutional, national, united life.

THE HON. L. D. THOMAN.

AT FARWELL HALL.

The greatest test of excellence is success. Whatever may have been the doubts and misgivings of the delegates who placed the keystone in the arch of free government, time has demonstrated the wisdom of their conclusions.

A celebration at the close of the first century of a government founded on a written Constitution, is an occasion which admits of the most extravagant demonstrations of thanksgiving. As the Magna Charta, the Petition of Right and the Bill of Rights have been styled the bulwarks of English liberty, so the Declaration of Independence, the Articles of Confederation and the Constitution of the United States have been the safeguards of the American Republic. The revolutionary sentiment of Independence, of representative and free sovereignty of the people, was given imperishable expression in those documents. An idea of freedom, triumphant in battle, inspired the American scheme of government. It reflects the best thought of ages. It is simple in construction, yet novel in the minuteness of detail; expansive in its purposes, yet limited in its powers; charitable in its considerations, yet jealous of its interests.

Constitutional government was not evolved without a struggle. Every word bears the evidence of patriotism. And while some of the delegates in that memorable convention may have been influenced, in approving or dissenting, by political motives, yet the result of their deliberations has been to the republic a sacred heritage. Having suffered the hardships of a proscriptive government, they worked as patriots and not as partisans, submitting a method of government which made every man a sovereign, yet charged him with the responsibilities of aiding in the proper administration of free institutions.

It is a great privilege to be a plain American citizen. It is a distinction greater than to be a king, prince or potentate. It is freedom; and,

> "Freedom has a thousand charms to show,
> That slaves howe'er contented never know."

Who should enjoy this privilege? This is one of the important problems of the time which must be solved.

The morning of the second century of our national life dawns with a threatening which omens danger to our free institutions unless met with an earnest resistance.

In the wonderful symmetry of our organic law popular sovereignty is the omnipresent spirit, and in the most generous manner have the benefits of a free republic been dispensed. The obligation demanded in full payment for these considerations is obedience to law. It is important, therefore, that the privileges and benefits of American citizenship be withheld from those who do not know and will not learn the law. If the early years of this republic made it desirable to confer citizenship indiscriminately there is no reason for it now. The republic has passed its infancy and is now powerful in its manhood. The end of time alone will destroy it, unless the spirit of patriotism surrenders to the influence of the dangerously ambitious politician. The American heart is quickly touched by an appeal for the distressed of other lands, but the American republic should no longer confer citizenship without some evidence that the honor is being worthily bestowed. The American Congress should have long since enacted better legislation than we now have upon the subject of naturalization, and it possibly would have done so except for its effect upon party organization. It is, at this hour in our history, a sad commentary on our system of conferring citizenship to see the candidate with an uplifted hand, and hear him take the oath to support a law which he never read, and, in many instances, never heard of. This pitiful exhibition of our trifling requirements to give full citizenship to an alien is almost forgotten when we remember that an equally ignorant native-born citizen is given, and is quick to enjoy, the political privileges of this American republic. I believe the time has come when no man should be granted the privileges of American citizenship, whether alien or native-born, until he has read understandingly the Declaration of Independence and the Constitution of the United States. It may be possible to be a good American without reading these documents of faith, but he who does read them will be a better American.

Another danger to our national life, which was anticipated by the convention which framed the Constitution, is the attempt to displace the shield—Democracy—and supplant it with the crown—Aristocracy. "No title of nobility shall be granted by the United States," says the Constitution. This is a forcible declaration. It shows the character of the framers of our organic law. It is a check upon the parvenu who is a servile to the manners and customs of undemocratic governments. The disposition of some American citizens to crave distinction, by assuming the character of nobility, is a dangerous infraction of our organic law, and cannot be tolerated with safety to the permanent stability of a

Democratic government. Our history will not be unlike the history of other governments, which attempted Republican form, if we depart from the character we assumed one hundred years ago. The conspicuous and enviable place which we now occupy in the eyes of all nations will be lost to us and we will become the mere remnant of a once great national independence. The success of this republic, in its life and national prosperity, is attributable to the fact that we have not departed very far from the path of the simple, plain and earnest democracy of our fathers. There must be no titles of nobility. There should be no attempt toward aristocracy. The blood from the veins of the peasant is as rich on the altar of this republic, as that from the viens of the millionaire; the humble citizen from his home of poverty, who offers his tribute in support of the Constitution and the law, is as deserving of a seat at the feast of rejoicing on this festive day, as he who comes from his palace, the walls of which may be covered with a coat of arms.

The greater study of the American Constitution and its powers, will add strength to our national life. The growing youth should be impressed with the importance of the preservation of this sacred document. Its lines and precepts, well observed, make citizenship noble. Our devotion to it is the best test of our right to be protected by it. It is the freeman's shield, staff and comforter.

How persistent, how stable have been the forms of our government! For sixty-one years intervening between 1804 and 1865, not an amendment was proposed to the Constitution. Who, glancing down the vista of the future, can now foresee any great national episode which would demand additions to the present charter? Here is a conservatism as cautious, as hesitant and sluggish as that which is crudely assigned to the effete dynasties of other continents.

The efficiency of the American Constitution is due to its easy interpretation, its close union of the coördinate branches of government, and its positive separation of the powers of the executive and legislative authorities. The line which separates the duties of these two branches of government is marked and should be maintained. Yet there is a danger which besets us and which demands an earnest consideration, and that is the encroachment of the legislative branch, in attempting the control of the executive department in the selection of public servants. While this usurpation is the growth of more than half a century, yet its influences are daily becoming more dangerous by reason of the greater number of rewards to bestow. Are we in fact a free representative government, when the servants of the people are slaves to party politics?

In the civil departments of administration, during the first forty years of our government's existence, not to exceed one hundred removals were made, except for cause, while to-day it requires but forty minutes to accomplish the same work, and the cause need be only political. Can it be said that this is an advancement in the science of government? The spoils system of politics is condemned by the history it has made. It has attempted to break down the line of demarkation between the executive and legislative branches of our government; it has made politicians instead of patriots, and partisans in the place of statesmen; it has caused the sacrifice of manly independence and of womanly virtue, and its curse is written in the pages of our nation's history with the blood of the lamented Garfield.

> "O, that estates, degrees and offices,
> Were not derived corruptly;
> And that clear honor
> Were purchased by the merit of the wearer."

The spoils system of politics is a most unfortunate departure from the ideas of administration entertained by the fathers, and practiced by them from Washington to Jackson. The exhibition of partisan zeal witnessed in some of the contests in American politics warns us of our danger, and unless the patriotic spirit which impelled our forefathers to strike for freedom asserts itself in support of a non-partisan subordinate civil service, our independence will be subverted to the base uses of political masters, our institutions will be corrupted, our liberty destroyed, and we will suffer the penalty of all governments where offices have been sold to the highest bidder. This problem is not insignificant. It affects the well-being of the nation. Official honor, national economy, the welfare, peace and prosperity of the people depend upon it. The growing youth of the land must be taught that good government demands pure and unselfish politics, and that merit is the first and best test for preferment in all employments.

Let this anniversary be marked by pledging anew our devotion to constitutional government. Let the promise be kept, that the laws of this free republic shall not be a sealed book, but a living letter; not be the heritage of the rich, but the birthright of the poor; not be the two-edged sword of craft and oppression, but the staff of honesty and the shield of innocence.

THE REV. JOHN HENRY BARROWS.

AT THE CAVALRY ARMORY.

This is the patriot's holy day. We celebrate with reverent rejoicing the birth of a nation in its organized life. We recall and revere the greatest name in modern history, which has won the eloquent eulogies of all mankind, a man of whom Mr. Gladstone has written: "He has been to me for more than forty years a light upon the path of life," a man in whose honor, when the news came of his death, the flags even of a British fleet were placed at half-mast, and whose monument, overtopping all other marble ever reared on the earth, is yet not whiter than his moral splendor. Surely, this is a day on which to recall the words attributed to Benjamin Franklin, when minister of our young republic at the court of France. At a great banquet which was given in Paris, the British Ambassador proposed the following toast: "Great Britain, the golden sun whose beams enlighten all the nations." He was followed by a French minister, who, not to be outdone, proposed the following: "France, the silver moon whose radiance illumines and cheers the darkness of the world." And then Franklin arose and offered this sentiment: "George Washington, the Joshua who commanded the sun and the moon to stand still, and they both obeyed him."

There has risen on this side of the sea a national power governed by a new sentiment, inspired by a new principle, which more and more checks, guides, or disturbs the nationalities of Europe. Samuel Adams once prophesied that America would be in a condition to give laws to the Old World. When our nation emerged triumphant from the recent civil conflict, a low growl of hate and fear passed round the council table of the kings. But that America has such a commanding position to-day is due primarily to the fact that by the sword of Washington the tie which bound us to Great Britain was broken, and that under his leadership the thirteen colonies were brought into a federal union.

I know that Prof. Goldwin Smith has said that the American Revolution was a mistake. If we had only remained loyal to Great Britain, he says, we would have ultimately become self-governing and free, like Canada and Australia! Why did he not add like New Zealand, South Africa, or the Bermudas? Do we not feel at once that these British colonies have comparatively little significance to mankind matched with America? But who knows that these distant colonies would to-day be free and self-governing had it not been for the successful resistance of our fathers to the schemes of George the Third, and the maintenance of our independent nationality? England seems to have needed the lesson which we gave in order to learn how to govern her distant dependencies. But who does not feel that America, which represents the "sentiment and future of mankind," that America, which has given to science, invention and literature such a galaxy of genius, and to statesmanship such names as those of Washington and Hamilton and Webster and Lincoln; America, the anchor and the pole-star of freedom, whose record is so splendid with heroes and martyrs, means far more to the world than such dependencies —however worthy and prosperous—as I have named? A recent ambassador to England tells us that "America is in the air," that is, that the great fact of an independent and prosperous republic this side the sea is continually thwarting the plans of the European monarchies, and stimulating the hopes of the people. America has had severe critics who have told us many wholesome truths and have offered some serious misjudgments. They have declared that we have no literature any more than Canada or Australia. But they have not thought of reproaching Canada or Australia for such imagined deficiencies. A nation which in one century has had such writers as Hamilton, Franklin, Irving, Bryant, Prescott, Emerson, Motley, Bancroft, Lowell, Whittier, Holmes, Hawthorne and Longfellow; such orators as Fisher, Ames, Clay, Webster, Everett, Beecher, Phillips and Sumner, may still retain some slight self-respect in reviewing its intellectual history. But the very fact that we have been so savagely criticised, and also that such elaborate works as those of Bryce and De Tocqueville have been written about us, indicates how important is deemed the phenomenon of the American republic.

Perhaps providence is as wise as the ex-Oxford professor who thinks we ought to have remained a part of Great Britain. Since the nation is not the work of chance, since it had its origin in God, and like God has continuance, authority and a moral being; since He who has made of one blood all nations of men has determined the times before appointed and the bounds of their habitation, I cannot believe that God ever meant that this nation, rapidly becoming the foremost of peoples; that this land, "enthroned between her subject seas," whose unity and independence have been engraved by the hand of the Almighty on the courses of the rivers, the trend of the mountains and the coast lines; that this continent, which within a hundred years, as Mr. Gladstone prophecies, is to be the home of 500,000,000 of people, speaking the language of John Milton and Edmund Burke, and living under the institutions of Anglo-Saxon freedom, should remain the dependency even of so wondrous an island as that which Shakspeare saw and loved, set like a jewel in the silver circlet of the German Ocean, and God never called this nation to so commanding a destiny without requiring of all its citizens a supreme allegiance to the flag which represents the imperial commonwealth of time.

On the pediment of Story's noble statue of John Marshall, at the foot of the National Capitol at Washington, is a beautiful bas-relief representing Victory leading Young America to swear eternal fidelity to the altar of that Union which Washington founded, which Webster championed, and which has been cemented by the heart's blood of a million patriot martyrs. That sculptured allegory represents the scenes in thousands of schools and churches and vast assemblies throughout our land to-day, where, amid a forest of flags, and with hearts made jubilant with patriotic song, American youth are pledging their young fidelity and enthusiasm to that nation which was born when Washington was inaugurated.

> "Bright on the banner of lily and rose,
> Lo, the last sun of our century sets."

And now this memorable day finds the new century blossoming throughout the continent with unnumbered celebrations and brilliant with such exhibitions of national joy as that which gladdens us within these walls.

When the Father of his Country had taken the oath of office, there came from the assembled multitude in New York the deafening shout: "Long live George Washington, President of the United States." And to-day, if the American people could express in one exclamation the deepest convictions of their hearts, they would cry out: "God save the American Republic, which Washington founded, and make it worthy of him who consolidated thirteen commonwealths into one nationality." The hundred years which are passed have witnessed not only the enlargement of the empire of liberty in other lands, not only an unexampled prosperity in America, but also the most destructive civil strife that reddens the pages of time, in the midst of which the nation was threatened with disruption. With what sad memories we should meet to-day had that strife ended in dismemberment! Gathered in this throng are some of the victorious veterans of the war, and therefore I feel that the air we breathe is vital with brave and cheerful prophecies. Looking into the coffin of Garrison, his great friend and companion said: "He has made it certain that whether one flag or two floats over our soil, this continent can never again be trodden by a slave." Looking to-day upon these rejoicing banners and the faces of this jubilant assembly, and seeing the forms of men who fought at Donelson and Vicksburg and Atlanta, let me express the conviction that so long as the rivers flow into the lakes, the oceans, and the Gulf; so long as the Alleghanies, over which the young Washington carried the flag of England, and the Rocky Mountains, on which the youthful Fremont placed the flag of the republic, lift their green or snowy peaks toward the stars; so long as civilized men tread the streets of great American capitals and a worthy yeomanry tills the Valley of the Mississippi; so long as there abides in our children's hearts the spirit of those men who, in the thick of battle, plunging into the "fire-lined jaws of hell," clung to the standard with a grip which only death could unbind, so long will one flag, the flag of Yorktown as well as Gettysburg, the flag which fell at Sumter and rose again to lift with it a race into liberty and a nation into triumph, so long will that flag float over the republic's undivided and imperial domain.

In the last twenty-five years there has been a hopeful expansion and deepening of our national consciousness. The attempt to divide our national unity developed its strength and insured its perpetuation. When the blow was struck in the august face of our American nationality, we discovered that in spite of long indoctrination in the error of state sovereignty, in spite of the eclipse which slavery had brought to many minds over the consciousness of a supreme national life, and in spite of acts of secession, not the deliberate work of the people but the hasty work of desperate leaders, the nation still lived. The flag had divisions, but the flag was one. The Constitution was the work of the people of the United States, and the people was one people. The government under the Constitution had all the elements of universality and supremacy, and the government was one. Hence, when the blow fell, the nation, slow to believe in danger, and proudly conscious of strength, rose like a giant startled out of sleep, equipped 2,000,000 of men, guarded 4,000 miles of coast line with battle ships, carrying on its military movements at points as far removed as Liverpool from Damascus and Lisbon from St. Petersburg, until the bubble, which Lord John Russell said had burst, had crystallized and shone resplendent, as what John Bright always believed it, the crown jewel on the brow of freedom.

The great history which we review to-day had a great and noble origin. Our nationality has had many builders and rebuilders. Washington may be taken as the greatest type of the men who fashioned our national beginnings, and Abraham Lincoln as the leading representative of the men who solidified and expanded the American state. And in the development of the nation, as new communities have sprung into power, while civilization has rolled toward the sunset, the men who have helped in building the great fabric of Western life on the old foundations of the Christian church, the Christian school, and the Christian family, men who crossed the prairies as their fathers crossed the sea, upbearing the Bible in their van, deserve to be ranked with those ancient worthies who brought the institutions of political and Christian liberty to our shores in the seventeenth century. Reverting to that earlier genetic period, we find ourselves in the midst of great spiritual conflicts in England, Scotland, Holland, Germany, Sweden and France. The men who carried empires in their brains surpassing that of Alexander, men like Carver, Bradford, Winthrop, Hooker, Cotton, Davenport and Roger Williams, were largely men who believed themselves the agents of Divine Providence. They were men whose character made New England as Mr. Gladstone has written, "the centre of those commanding moral influences which gave to the country as a whole its political and moral atmosphere." They were men who found in the Bible the truth and inspiration which made them the enemies of human tyranny.

At about the time when our Constitution went into effect, a company of men having the same spirit with the fathers of America became, on the banks of the Ohio, the founders of the Northwest. Under the strong favoring aid of Washington the first great settlements were made at Marietta after the Ordinance of 1787—the second great charter of our freedom—had been passed by the Continental Congress. Without this ordinance, as Senator Hoar has said, "the Constitution of the United States itself would have lost half of its value." And he adds that the American youth who visits the Capitol of his country, and "admires there the evidences of its grandeur and the monuments of its historic glory," will find there nothing which will so stir his heart as two fading and time-soiled papers whose characters were traced by the fathers a hundred years ago. They are original records of the act which devoted this nation forever to equality, to education, to religion and to liberty. One is the Declaration of Independence, and the other the Ordinance of 1787.

The inquiry has been frequently made in recent years: "When was it that we became a nation?" Shall we answer by saying: "Not until Lee surrendered his sword to Grant at the Appomattox Court-house?" There, certainly, our unity was forever assured. But go back thirty-five years. Webster has finished his answer to the heresy of South Carolina, and the Senate Chamber echoes with the immortal words: "Liberty and the Union, now and forever, one and inseparable." Was it from the waters of that memorable debate that the American nation emerged resplendent, "like Venus rising from the sea?" I believe that there and then was furnished the ammunition back of the bullets which slew the Rebellion. But for more than forty years the nation has been developing under a Constitution which opened with the words: "We, the people of the United States." But was the nation born in 1789 when it hailed Washington as its first President? Undoubtedly, so far as its present organic life is concerned. But there were elements of nationality anterior to the event which we this day celebrate. That Constitution, which has been called "the most sacred political document in the whole world," was the wise expression of the organizing will of the people back of it. The nation, weary of sailing the sea of democratic liberty in that leaky and perilous craft called the Articles of Confederation, embarked in a new and nobler ship, named the Constitution, built strongly with ribs of the British oak. The vessel was the creation of the people, and the people made no provision for its destruction by admitting into it any right of secession. To have done this "would have brought on board," as one has said, "a case of dynamite with a clock-work adjusted to explode it and blow up the ship of state within a number of days." The preamble to the Constitution formed at Montgomery in 1861 confesses to the wisdom of our fathers by the words, not "we, the people," but "we the deputies of the sovereign and independent states."

Nations are not manufactured suddenly and to order like cotton cloths. If this were so, they would soon be torn to rags. Nations are historic growths, rooted in the soil of earth and bathed in the dews and sunbeams of heaven. Go back of our present Constitution and you find the nation there, impoverished by war, tumultuous and discordant, but capable of emerging from chaos into order and power. Without a stronger government than the Articles of the Confederation provided, Washington said: "I do not see how we can long exist as a nation," thereby confessing the national existence. Go back to the American Revolution. It was directed by a Continental Congress. It was fought by a Continental army, led by one who never tired of speaking of "My country." It has been described as the act of the whole people in the endeavor to realize the nation. But you ask if America was not born when the Declaration of Independence was sent out on the Fourth of July, 1776. No. The Declaration announced formally one element of national life not even then assured. I mean independent sovereignty. But, mind you, it was a declaration, not a creation. It set forth or declared what already was. The consciousness of nationality had already in some little measure stirred the American heart. It made itself felt and feared eleven years before in a Continental Congress in New York, assuming the functions of a sovereign and separate authority in treating with Great Britain. It had brought the American colonies together in denying the right of England to inflict upon them the taxation schemes of George the Third. It had become intenser since the farmers of Concord had fired "the shot heard round the world," and the raw militia had fought the English on Bunker Hill. It is significant that, after learning that these minute men had quietly taken the fire of the British troops, Washington said: "The liberties of the country are safe." Thus the national consciousness had been quickened, and it found expression in the pen of Jefferson, writing, "When in the course of human events it becomes necessary for one people to dissolve the political bands which have connected them with another." The great Declaration was signed in the name and by the authority of the good people of these colonies, which, united and not separate, assumed a distinct national existence among the governments of the earth.

Do we not begin to understand what John Adams meant in affirming that the American Revolution was completed before the war began? In the colonial mind and heart, in the convictions, habits, aspirations and purposes of the men who occupied this territory, there existed the sentiment, confused but finally potential, of an American nationality. To develop and crystalize this sentiment, one man, the father of the American Revolution, Samuel Adams of Boston, gave the toil of his life; and to construct out of the colonies, which, loosely united, had achieved their independence, one homogeneous and mighty nation, George Washington consecrated the energies of his patriotic spirit and the commanding influence of his unequalled character.

Thus our celebration to-day brings us into contact with a long and inspiring history. It is right to say that the American nationality is a growth into whose majestic strength new forces have been added from time to time, and that it stands to-day, like the California pine, with a trunk broad enough to be the shade of an army, while it waves its top in the sunlight of God, higher than any other of the majestic growths of the past. And yet to find its germ we must go back of constitutions and revolutions to the Christian purposes of those men who fled from the corruptions and tyrannies of the Old World and battled with the savage and the soil, the winter and the wilderness, in the New.   One student of our history traces the origin of our nationality to the pastor of the Pilgrims, John Robinson of Leyden.   Bancroft found it in the cabin of the May-flower.   Rufus Choate tracked it to Geneva.   Others have followed it to the teachings of John Knox in Edinburgh, or the soil of Naseby and Marston Moore.   Lowell thinks that the "red dint on Charles's block marked one in our era."   Prof. Rogers of Oxford, believes that American independence was one of the glorious results of Holland's successful resistance to Spain.   Another declares that we must go back to Martin Luther to find the moral force which made America possible.   It is certain that some of the chief impulses which led to the colonizing of these shores and the found-ing and development of an independent nation sprang from the Word of God.   It was an echo of the Scriptures which Jefferson sounded in the great Declaration.   "We rummaged everywhere," he wrote, "to find the Biblical formulas of the old Puritans."   One of the most eloquent voices that championed the Declaration on the floor of Congress was that of Dr. Witherspoon.   "The Inde-pendent divines of England," says Sir James McIntosh, "were the teachers of John Locke," and John Locke was the chief teacher of that "last of the Puritans," whose constant prayer was that Boston might become a Christian Sparta, the chief organizer of the Ameri-can Revolution, moulding the popular sentiment of which Wash-ington was the executive, a man who was deemed by friends and foes alike the pioneer of independence, whom President Garfield declared to have been "the greatest embodiment of the Revolu-tionary ideas," and whom Senator Hoar calls the greatest of Ameri-can statesmen in the soundness and sureness of his opinions and in the strength of original argument by which he persuaded the peo-ple to its good; I mean that half-forgotten figure, Samuel Adams. And every student knows with what constant and heartfelt trust in God the first President of the American commonwealth began, continued and finished his unequalled public career.

Lord Beaconsfield has said that "America has prospered, because she has remembered Zion."   Even Benjamin Franklin, at the crisis of the convention which framed the Constitution, declared his firm belief that without the Divine aid we shall "suc-ceed in this political building no better than the builders of Babel." To account for the American nationality, either its origin, its ideas, its development or its destiny, without recognizing its vital con-nection with the Word of God, is like attempting to account for the growth of the palm-tree without the sun in the heavens.   All the great formative and reformative periods of our history have been intensely religious. Even Emerson wrote: "Our helm is given up to a better guidance than our own. The course of events is quite too strong for any helmsman, and our little wherry is taken in tow by the ship of the Great Admiral, which knows the way and which has the force to draw men and states and planets to their goal." And surely, they who believe in a moral order administered by infinite love and wisdom, manifest in a nationality now so splendid and various, which was not planned as a warehouse or a glittering exchange, but rather as a temple wherein God should abide, a dwelling-place for the Invisible, more resplendent than "the Mount of Alabasta topped with golden spires" which once blazed on the summit of Moriah, may find their faith and expectation worthily expressed by the most patriotic of our poets:

"God of our fathers, Thou who wast,
Art, and shalt be when those eye-wise who flout
Thy secret presence shall be lost
In the great light that dazzles them to doubt,
We, sprung from loins of stalwart men
Whose strength was in their trust
That Thou wouldst make Thy dwelling in their dust
And walk with them a fellow-citizen,
Who build a city of the just,
We, who believe life's bases rest
Beyond the probe of chemic test,
Still, like our fathers, feel Thee near,
Sure that, while lasts the immutable decree,
The land to human nature dear
Shall not be unbeloved of Thee."

And since our nationality has had a heavenly birth, it is right to expect of it a notable addition to the political, intellectual and moral achievements of mankind. A grim English critic once sneered at America by saying it had never done a greatly noble thing. Is there nothing greatly noble in covering a continent vaster than Cæsar's empire with the arts of civilization? Is there nothing greatly noble in the colossal achievement of incorporating 8,000,000 of foreign and somewhat alien population, unused to self-government, and by means of the common school and the exercise of liberty largely Americanizing the prodigious immigration? Is there nothing greatly noble in the sudden and marvelous growth of science, invention and literature on this side of the sea? Is there nothing greatly noble in the working of our National Constitution in times of peril, the government continuing without a jar after the assassination of two Presidents, events that would have shaken many a European throne? Is there nothing to draw out one word of cheerful augury in our successful encountering of such a peril as slavery, which England and George the Third fastened upon us; of such dangers as rebellion and inflated currency and a disputed Presidential election? Is there nothing greatly noble in a population delivered from the measureless misery which is the lot of millions in the Old World? Is there nothing greatly noble in the valor and self-sacrifice with which both armies contended in the late Civil War? Why shall not Gettysburg take rank with Marathon in the history of human liberty? Are not the waters of Hampton Roads, covering "the soft ooze where the Cumberland lies," as sacred as Athenian Salamis? I know we have many occasions for humility and for solemn concern when we think of the perils besetting us to-day, especially from the despotic liquor power and a vicious spoils system of government. But we have so many occasions for rejoicing and gratitude that we should not keep company with despondency for an hour, nor with despair for an instant.

It has been the teaching of our greatest statesmen that the maintenance and spread of religion were essential to our safety and prosperity. De Tocqueville said that despotism may govern without Faith, but liberty cannot. Ours is the only great nation where religion has had a fair field unencumbered by state alliances. A hundred years ago the Methodist Churches had only a handful of congregations. They now number more communicants than there were then people in the country. The Baptists, who were then mildly persecuted North and South, have to-day nearly three millions of members. The Congregational Churches in New England were not then entirely disestablished, and when their severance from the state occurred it proved a blessing and not a curse. The Episcopal Church in Virginia, whose parsons were discredited on account of their Tory leanings, and who had become so dissolute that the Legislature found it needful to pass special laws prohibiting them from drunkenness, was disestablished in 1785, and thenceforward, under the great leadership of Bishop Meade and others, the church of Madison and Washington began its better life, and to-day numbers more communicants than were in all the American churches at the opening of the century. A hundred years ago the Presbyterian Churches were often built with funds raised by means of lotteries, while drunkenness prevailed in all ranks among clergy and people to an almost incredible extent. The temperance reform is one of the brightest pages of the past century, and we ought to thank God that in a hundred years most of the liquor has gone out of the veins of the American church, although it must be sadly confessed the political power of the liquor interest was never more despotic and destructive.

At the beginning of this century French infidelity ruled the educated classes of America and Christianity was thought to be speedily doomed. But what has been the outcome? In 1800 there were 350,000 church members in a population of 5,000,000, while to-day out of a population of 65,000,000 there are 17,000,000 church members, including a Roman Catholic population of 6,000,000. When we reflect that the numerical strength of the church has augmented three times as rapidly as the population, when we note the rise and progress of Sunday-schools which this century has witnessed, when we recall the fact that nearly all the great missionary, philanthropic and reformatory societies are less than a hundred years old, when we contemplate the vast sums that are given for Christian education and watch the troops of colleges, which, as Mr. Beecher once said, "go lowing over our Western plains like Jacob's kine," and as we joyfully remember that on every day seven new church buildings are erected on the soil covered by the national flag, and that on every Lord's day 10,000 new confessors of the Divine Man of Nazareth are enrolled beneath the standard of the cross, we surely have good reason for believing that Washington's hope expressed in his first inaugural has been realized, and that our people still render their dutiful homage to the Great Author of every public and private good. And besides all this, there has been a great sifting and simplifying of doctrines, a happy dying out of sectarian animosities, a growth of mutual love and confidence among the Christian denominations, a magnifying of likenesses and minifying of differences, a decay of theological system building, an increased devotion to Biblical study and a growing willingness to combine in works of charity and reform. And surely these are signs of hopeful progress worthy to take rank with any of the marvels of invention or with the growth of our national area and the expansion of our national power.

The perils already passed and the precious things already gained ought never to be forgotten when our eager minds are fastened on the new things which seem so desirable. There are but few blessings which the nation now covets, which are worth mentioning compared with the blessings already secured; compared with the peace of our homes, the safety from violence, which in the name of law plunders a man's pocket as in Turkey, or takes his life, as in Russia; compared with the right to choose one's occupation, which more than one-half our race do not yet possess; compared with liberty of travel, of speech, of worship, of assembly; compared with all those circumstances which in this country beckon us with friendly hands and cheer us with kindly voices, and do not crush down our aspiring manhood, as in so many lands.

The rights and opportunities possessed by us have been won by the tears and toils of sixty centuries, the best of which is just ended, by the labors of men of whom the world was not worthy, prophets, dying without the sight of the Canaan into which we have entered.   What if Stephen, stoned at the gate of Jerusalem, could have seen Christianity enthroned in the Roman Empire?   What if Athanasius, holding out alone against the world, could have seen modern Christendom embracing the leading nationalities, England carrying the Bible in every ship that wakes the "countless laughter of the sea," and America with church bells echoing from spire to spire, from the shores of hundred-harbored Maine to the soft flowing waves of the Pacific!   what if Socrates, dying a martyr to intellectual liberty; what if Milton, writing his noble plea for unlicensed printing; what if the martyrs of Holland and Scotland, dying for civil freedom, could have witnessed the spectacle of a free state enshrining and defending a free church, which is the glory of our nation!   What if Samuel Adams, declaiming in his young manhood before the royal Governor on the right of resisting the supreme magistrate, or Joseph Warren, closing his eyes in death beneath the flag of Bunker Hill, could have seen Cornwallis surrendering the British army at Yorktown!   What if Washington, assuming the Presidency of 4,000,000 impoverished Americans, could have foreseen this Continental Republic with 65,000,000 of the most prosperous and progressive people on the globe!   What if Lovejoy, shot down at Alton for defending a fundamental principle of liberty, or Garrison, dragged through the streets of Boston with a halter around his neck, could then have seen the last fetter broken from the last American slave!   What if Ellsworth, dying at Alexandria in the darkened dawn of the mighty struggle, could have seen the victorious armies of Sherman and Logan and Sheridan and Grant march over the long bridge into the streets of Washington, and pour their flashing columns and carry their tattered standards in battalions majestic as the oncoming waves of the sea under the eyes of an assembled nation!   By a hundred bloody steps on

> "The world's great altar-stairs.
> That slope through darkness up to God,"

humanity has ascended to the heights on which we breathe, and let us not in our thanklessness and folly forget the great things which the Lord has done for us. This is a day for grateful memory and triumphant hope. There are multitudes here who passed through the struggle, which, settling the question whether our nation can long endure, settled also in effect every other mighty moral question which confronts us.

God grant that this golden Centennial day may deepen in all our hearts a reverent, hopeful and Christian patriotism, a profounder regard for those elements of individual and national character which make the just renown and lasting glory of states, or, in other words, a firmer devotion to the ideals which were made real and lustrous for all time in the inflexible rectitude, the matchless fortitude and Christian faith of George Washington!

When the news came of the Whisky Rebellion in Pennsylvania, Washington and Hamilton were resolute to put it down. There is a Whisky Rebellion in America to-day more desperate and dangerous, and it behooves every man who has any reverence for the memory of Washington to lend his utmost influence to crush it. Let us not pile our eulogies on the grave of the Father of his Country and build his monument to the skies; let us not quote approvingly his words regarding the worship of God and reverence for his day; let us not point to his example as "the defender of the mothers and the protector of the daughters" of America and as the embodiment of reverence for law and justice, and then do absolutely nothing to crush the home-blasting, heaven-defying, earth-polluting conspiracy against our liberties and our laws which the greedy, grasping, corrupting liquor-conspiracy has become in our land. I have no doubt about the result—the saloon must go. It is a breeding-place of vice, a public nuisance, defiant of law, merciless to its victims, a corrupter of the youth, an ally of all that is basest in our politics, and long before we celebrate another Centennial it will be as much of an outlaw as is piracy to-day on the high seas of the world.

And then, how can we remain content after such a celebration as this, with the general tone of our public life, with offices still the spoil of partisan success, with politicians stumbling along with their lanterns, taking the place of statesmen guided by the stars? Coming into fresh communion with the spirits of such men as framed our Constitution and guided our national beginnings, are we not touched to the quick to hear Prof. Bryce saying that the "true faults of American democracy are a certain commonness of mind, a want of elevation in the conduct of public affairs, an apathy among the luxurious classes with regard to public duty, a great laxity in the management of public business?" Are we not getting tired and ashamed of the despotism of the ring and the political boss? Are we not sick of that system which has made the opening days of the present administration in Washington a prolonged vexation? Are we not utterly weary of permitting the lower class of political workers to determine who shall be our rulers? Says an honored American: "*The people of the Northern States thought four years of war not too dear a price to prevent half their country from being taken from them. But the practices of which I have been speaking are slowly filching from us the whole of our country— all, at least, that made it the best to live in and the easiest to die for.*"

Surely, it should be the purpose of every Christian patriot to carry into public duty a faithfulness in some measure like his beneath whose peerless splendor the American people began their uncertain life. The resolve should be recorded on this Centennial day that this nation shall have not only a new birth of freedom, but a new birth of political decency and dignity. Then may we hope to see more brains and less "boodle" in the United States Senate, more patriotism and less partisanship in the civil service, more conscience and less corruption in municipal and state affairs, more Scriptural politics everywhere, and ultimately no saloon politics anywhere.

Let us resolve anew that this "land to human nature dear," which represents to the world the sacredness of humanity; that this land made holy by the tombs of the Pilgrims, by the sacrifices of the Revolution, by the character of our great national hero, and by the blood which stained the wheat-fields of Antietam, the tawny tide of the Rappahannock and the turbid flood of the Mississippi, shall rise up from the devout and thankful services of this great Centennial day purified, resplendent with new hope, and bathed with new moral glory. Let us resolve that the growing power which America holds among the nations shall be the growing power of freedom and righteousness. Let us resolve that the spirit of Washington and the fathers shall be carried into the moral struggles which await us now, that justice shall be done to the lowly, that safeguards shall be placed about the tempted, that enlightenment shall come to the ignorant, and that punishment shall not fail the guilty hand that strikes or desecrates the flag of orderly freedom for America, and of life-giving hope for mankind. And may God save the republic!

THE HON. E. A. OTIS.

AT THE CAVALRY ARMORY.

Throughout all this broad land the American people have assembled to-day to commemorate the greatest event in the history of our nation. One hundred years ago to-day the government of the United States was established and George Washington, its first President, entered upon the discharge of the delicate and responsible duties of his office. We have been accustomed to date the birth of our nation from the declaration of its independence in 1776. That event marked but one era, and was preliminary only to the forming of that more perfect union which we now enjoy. That declaration from the master hand of Jefferson announced the great principle that all men were created equal and endowed by their creator with certain inalienable rights, to the maintenance of which our fathers pledged their lives and fortunes; but it was only the first step, the beginning of that marvelous growth and development in free government which has since become the admiration of the world.

When the war for independence was successfully accomplished and peace restored, the greater problems still remained to construct a system of government which should preserve for future generations those privileges which had been so dearly won. No graver question was ever presented to any nation, and upon its success or failure depended, in large measure, the existence of free institutions everywhere. The old articles of confederation of the colonies soon proved to be a complete failure. There was neither power or responsibility. Instead of creating a single united people they were a mere association of thirteen separate states, with but little in common to bind them together. To the student of history the era from 1783, when peace was declared with Great Britain, to 1789, when the government was inaugurated, will always appear the most unsatisfactory and fraught with danger to our further existence of any in our whole career. It lacked cohesion. There was no central power and no means provided to enforce measures for common defense and general welfare. The interests of Massachusetts and Virginia were as diverse and different as the characteristics of the Puritan and the Cavalier, by whom they were first settled. It was fortunate for the infant republic that those distinguished statesmen who had supported their country through the war for independence still survived to assist in preserving what had already been achieved. The subject of a more perfect union forced itself upon the attention of Washington and Adams and

Jefferson and Hamilton and their associates very shortly after the War of the Revolution was ended.

As early as 1784 Washington writes to the Governor of Virginia: "The prospect before us is fair. I believe all things will come right at last, but the disinclination of the states to yield competent powers to Congress for the federal government will, if there is not a change in the system, be our downfall as a nation. An extension of federal powers would make us one of the most wealthy, happy, respectable and powerful nations that ever inhabited this terrestrial sphere. Without them we shall soon be everything which is the direct reverse."

Similar views were shared by others, and the general feeling was expressed that the old articles of confederation must give way to a more powerful government or we would lose all that had been gained by the War of the Revolution. The country had been relieved from the direct pressure of that struggle and was now looking forward to material growth and development. The army which Washington had so long commanded had been disbanded and its members absorbed into the ranks of civil life. They had received neither pay for their services nor other suitable acknowledgment, but without a murmur, following the advice and example of their illustrious leader, they surrendered the power which the fortunes of war had placed in their hands, and, like the followers of Cromwell, became as distinguished in peace as they had been in war. It was fortunate for our country that this powerful element was in a position where its influence could be felt and appreciated. The great and controlling need was the establishment of one nation in the place of the many commonwealths. We required a government strong enough to enforce its laws and provide for its own preservation; free enough to protect the humblest citizen in all his inalienable rights. No nation was better equipped for such an object. The people were intelligent, trained to self-denial and removed from the influences of Europe; they had learned the lessons of self-government from the date of the earliest settlement. No nation was ever so well supplied with wise and patriotic statesmen. The men who framed our government were the peers of any body of legislators of which we have any record in history. It is perhaps sufficient to say that the result of their deliberations in the system of government which they founded has challenged the admiration of the civilized world. The Constitution which was then formed, with slight amendments adapted to our growing wants and changing circumstances, is that under which we now live to-day. The student of history who compares it with all other forms of government of which we have any knowledge, will be lost in wonder and admiration. Our forefathers, indeed, while they did not "build better than they knew," were far in advance of their time, and no more perfect system of popular government was ever created by the ingenuity of man. One hundred years ago England was ruled by one of its most arbitrary kings, France was still a monarchy, and nowhere else on the civilized globe was there a system of government in existence "of the people, by the people and for the people."

It is almost incredible that in that era a Constitution should be formed which for one hundred years should require so few changes or amendments. In other countries systems of government have arisen and passed away, but ours, in all essential particulars, is to-day as our fathers left it. This has been the cause, in a large measure, of our marvelous material growth and development, which has no parallel in the history of the world. The entire population of the United States at the Revolution did not exceed in the aggregate that of the State of Illinois to-day, while the original thirteen states have grown to thirty-eight, with the certainty of an early increase in their number. We have become a nation in fact as well as in name, and the title of an American citizen confers dignity and receives a respect which the Roman citizen never enjoyed. There has never existed a government so powerful, and yet so free, where the checks and balances are so admirably adjusted, where Federal, State and Municipal powers worked together in such harmony, and where complete equality before the law is so absolutely the foundation and corner-stone. It is a significant fact that never before in the world's history has any nation attracted to itself so large an immigration from other countries. Every nationality in Europe is represented in our own city, where their labor and industry and prudence have largely contributed to our material prosperity. If this country did not offer these exceptional advantages, no such tide of immigration would possibly have reached our shores.

It would be difficult to estimate the effect of our system of government over the civilized world. That France is to-day a republic, and that England itself is practically governed by its people instead of its queen, is owing in large measure to the results of free government founded by our fathers and maintained by their successors. For much of this we are indebted to the patriotism and virtue of our Revolutionary hero, but most of all to one man, George Washington of Virginia, whose name will go down in history as a type of pure, lofty and unselfish patriotism. A government which he helped to establish one hundred years ago has since successfully withstood the strongest tests. Its powers were taxed to the utmost when in 1861 the effort was made to destroy it by secession. That doctrine, after four years of war, was settled forever, and it is now universally conceded that these United States constitute a nation strong and powerful enough to protect it from all enemies, foreign or domestic. That this great crisis in our history was safely passed is due under Divine Providence in large measure to the lofty patriotism and virtue of that most distinguished son of Illinois—Abraham Lincoln. The Union was the great object for which he contended. He labored to preserve that government which Washington had founded.

The names of Washington and Lincoln will go down side by side as the two great men which America has given the world's history. Washington founded a government and Lincoln saved it from destruction. Their names will ever be held in grateful remembrance so long as free institutions shall endure or virtue and patriotism be honored among men.

THE HON. WILLIAM E. MASON.

AT THE MEETING IN TENT B.

I have had the great pleasure of addressing in three different schools to-day the children of our city, and as I looked into their bright young faces I was proud of my city, proud of my country, proud of the past and present, and hopeful, aye, certain, of the future I told them of one circumstance which I would like to repeat to you older children. The last time I visited the tomb of Washington, standing upon the deck of the steamer, I engaged in conversation with an ex-soldier, who told me the following story:

"During the war we were stationed near here part of the time, and the Confederates were stationed over there, and Mount Vernon was between us. I used often to visit the tomb of Washington, and on many of those occasions I would meet some of the Rebel soldiers and we would sit and talk together. We always used to leave our arms outside of the inclosure, and not take them up again until after we had left the tomb of Washington."

How pleasant it is to think that in those times of bloodshed and carnage there was one sacred spot where men, sons of a common country who were at war with one another, whether from the North, the South, the East, or the West, could meet as brothers and for a short season forget the bitterness of the strife in which they were engaged.

Mistakes are the easiest things in the world to make. Our country has made some mistakes, and, sad as it may seem, history proves that there is no vicarious atonement for a political sin. On this great day of rejoicing it is well for us to boast of our glorious past, but in the spirit of humility to better prepare for the future should we confess the errors of the past. We boasted of the wealth piled up for us by the slave, but the first touch of his unsandaled foot was a curse to American soil. The harmony of the national music was destroyed for a hundred years by the plaintive song of the slave. No picture could be painted of the genius of America in which the whipping-post and the slave-pen did not rear their ugly heads. We boasted of our freedom, but the world pointed its finger at our slaves and proved us a nation of liars. It was a violation of the law of nature; it was America's great mistake. The law of compensation demanded settlement. The slave-pens will not furnish fences for our cemeteries, nor the whipping-posts material for headboards to our graves. The prophecy of Lincoln was fulfilled. Every drop of blood drawn by the lash was repaid with one drawn by the sword, and every dollar accumulated by the unrequited toil of the slave was scattered like chaff before the wind to the four corners of the earth.

The highest and most dignified office in the whole world is that of American citizenship, and he is best fitted for it who appreciates and understands the law of compensation; that no wrong, no crime can be committed, either against a foreign nation, the savages upon our frontier, or the humblest citizen, in the name of our country, that will not at the present or the future demand a settlement and recompense in full. The watchword of our forefathers was "Liberty and Self-Government."

The chairman spoke, and I approve of all he said, of the wonderful progress which we have made in a hundred years. If you should ask me to-day, with the inspiration of the moment, what I thought was the surest sign of progress, I should say: Not this iron horse that draws its load along the iron pathway of commerce; not these great ships which come and go with sails belied with the breeze of prosperity; not the telegraph which sparkles from continent to continent; not the telephone, whereby we speak to friends, who are miles away, as face to face; not the mysterious phonograph which locks our words in deadly silence, and at our command gives them forth again as from the grave. None of these are the surest evidence of progress. I will tell you what it is. It is the churches that set their steeples against the sky, the schoolhouses which dot this great country of ours, the schoolhouses which fill the streets of our great city and which are spread all over our wonderful land, teaching our children, the coming generation, to make this country better and better every year; the institutions of learning; the institutions of charity, wherein we shelter and teach the deaf, the blind, the lame, the halt and the insane. These, fellow-citizens, are the great evidences of a greater America lying yet in the future than has ever been known in the past.

Fellow-citizens, we want more music to-day and less talking. Look at this wonderful past of ours. I have been something of a student of the history of my country and I am surprised every time I turn to the future; my eyes are dazzled with the prospect. There is no imagination, I believe, to-day that can comprehend the magnificence of what is to come. We are standing upon the great threshold of our beginning. Why, we are only a hundred years old. Did you ever stop to think that a country never grows old? Did you ever stop to think that eternal youth wreathes the brow of that nation which is true to itself? If we are true to our children who flock about us, and if they are true to their opportunities, the nation can never grow old. If we do justice to the coming generation, and if they do justice to themselves, we have the spring of eternal youth forever within our grasp.

But why should we speculate upon the future? I say no man can describe it. Did you ever in your life attempt to describe something that was too grand for you? Did you feel the poverty of human language? Did you ever think to yourself how poor words are to express your feelings? That is the feeling that comes over me when I think of the future of this wonderful country. I must say in the language of another:

> "Far out on the sea there are billows
> That never will break on the beach;
> And I have heard songs in the silence
> That never will float into speech;
> And I have dreamed dreams in the valley
> Too lofty for language to reach."

THE HON. J. M. LANGSTON.

AT BATTERY D ARMORY.

One hundred years have passed since the fathers of our republic gave to the world a new form of government, one conceived, as Lincoln said, "in liberty, dedicated to the proposition of equal rights, and founded upon the consent of the governed "—"a government asking nothing but what it concedes, and conceding nothing but what it demands; destructive of despotism, it is the sole conservator of liberty, labor and property;" reflecting and illustrating in the harmony and exactness of its action, as well as its justness, the law of nature as it pervades the law of the land.

The inauguration of such a government with its century of magnificent achievements, in the spirit always of dependence upon our Heavenly Father, we celebrate this day in genuine American sentiment, purpose and aspiration. The animating principle of our government, its inspiring and controlling spirit, is defined in the immortal words of the Declaration: "We hold these truths to be self-evident: that all men are created equal, and endowed by their Creator with certain inalienable rights, among which are life, liberty and the pursuit of happiness; to secure these ends governments are instituted among men, deriving their just powers from the consent of the governed."

The century of our national life now closing, in all that pertains to our progress, wealth, power and name, the stability and glory of our free institutions, offers abundant, incontestable proof of the wisdom, the inspiration of our fathers in building our government upon the rock itself of political truth. The millions of our population of every kindred and tongue, dwelling together in peace and good neighborhood; the vast states and territories, each an immense commonwealth, which compose our Union, which may not and which shall not be broken; the innumerable appliances which constitute the irresistible physical and moral forces, which combined have worked out in matchless order under our Constitution, through the government, the greatness and the glory of the nation, the fruits of the first hundred years of our existence, testify in certain, positive terms to the wisdom and divine sagacity of our fathers in this work.

Our experience, under the Articles of Confederation, had taught us that a more perfect union was needed among the states and a larger measure of power in the national government; and the great worthies of the republic—wise, sagacious and patriotic as they were—showed themselves indeed equal to the task which Providence imposed upon them. At once, guided largely by the wisdom of their remarkable experience, and directed even more largely, as we may justly believe, by the God of nations, they framed and adopted our Constitution, which, in view of its blessings, shall be forever known and regarded as the masterpiece of all written state papers. What the Ten Commandments, the Sermon on the Mount are, to all great utterances of their kind and class, our Constitution is to all documents of its sort. So, too, the government which it defines, and for which it provides, surpasses all others in view of the admirable and wonderful results accomplished by and under it, and will outlive any at present, or ever known among men.

Inaugurated on the 30th day of April, 1789, whether tried by the necessities of peace or the exigencies of war, it has proved in either case, in every respect, under every circumstance, equal to every just demand. Even when for four bloody years a Rebellion such as the world never before knew, marshalled the loyal hosts against the disloyal in solemn, terrible defense of the union of these states and the authority of the government, its powers and resources were found ample for every requirement; and upon the overthrow of the Rebellion it proved itself competent to the duty of restoring order, in peace, with every state held in its proper place in the Union, its authority supreme throughout the land, with every human being free therein and the equal of all others before the law. In its conception, in its aim, in the results thus far gained under it, in the precision and firmness with which it has defined and fixed the powers of the general government, our Constitution demonstrates and justifies the wisdom and determination of the people to preserve and perpetuate it as the source, through the agency of the government, of all our rights, privileges and immunities.

This day's demonstration, the manifestation of admiration, love and veneration for the Constitution and the government, shown by the people of all classes and of every section, is prophetic of the eternity of their existence. From every heart, from every lip, in every voice of gladness and joy, the sentiment this day borne high in popular aspiration and purposes is—let our Constitution and Government stand forever. On a memorable occasion Daniel Webster, in referring to the origin of the Constitution, used these words: "Mr. President, I am a Northern man. I am attached to one of the states of the North by the ties of birth and parentage, education and the associations of early life, and by sincere gratitude for proofs of public confidence, early bestowed, I am bound to another Northern state by adoption, by long residence, by all the chords of social and domestic life, and by an attachment and regard springing from her manifestation of approbation and favor which grapple me to her with hooks of steel. And yet, sir, with the same sincerity of respect, the same deep gratitude, the same reverence and hearty good will with which I will pay a similar tribute to either of these states, do I here acknowledge the commonwealth of

Virginia to be entitled to the honor of commencing the work of establishing this Constitution. The honor is hers; let her enjoy it; let her forever wear it proudly; there is not a brighter jewel in the tiara that adorns her brow." But if to Virginia belongs the proud honor so happily ascribed to her by the great New England Senator, were he permitted to witness this day's doings in this land, from North to South, from East to West, he would conclude that it matters little now to what state belongs the honor of originating the Constitution, or what special cause contributed thereto, since every state now vies with every other, and every loyal and faithful citizen with every other in devotion and fidelity to its provisions.

Every citizen faithful and true, this day in the secret chambers of his own soul, makes solemn vow to his God that he will hold in sacred pledge to the government his life, his property and his honor. Nothing less pays our debt of allegiance; nothing less meets our solemn duty. Indeed, the loftiest aspiration of the American citizen can reach no point in patriotic purpose, in moral sublimity and beauty which realizes his true ideal but such resolve. Let such spirit, then, enter and possess, control and move every genuine heart, and, stirred by such influence as by a baptism of fire on this day, which may prove to be our national Pentecost, let us go forth to duty, sacrifice and reward. Then the second century of our national life under our Constitution and our government shall be distinguished for even greater and more important results than any which mark the past. Then far above all material progress, however great, far beyond all growth in population, territory and physical prowess and strength, however great these may be, our intellectual, moral and religious development, culture and power, will, under the benign influence of our improving Christian civilization, especially mark our progress and distinguish the coming century of our nation. The closing day, then, of our second century under the Constitution and the government shall find the nation far advanced—it may be it shall have reached the earlier days of the millenium of liberty, learning, labor and law—when we shall be even more than fellow-citizens to our neighbors—when we shall be brothers, indeed—while God shall be Father of us all.

But how shall this glorious end be gained? It can only be accomplished as our individual and national purpose shall be continually inspired and sustained by the good spirit to which appeal is made by Washington himself in the last paragraph of his first inaugural. His words are:

"Having thus imparted to you my sentiments as they have been awakened by the occasion which brings us together, I shall take my present leave; but not without resorting once more to the benign parent of the human race in humble supplication, that since He has been pleased to favor the American with opportunities for deliberating in perfect tranquility and dispositions for deciding with unparalleled unanimity on a form of government for the security of their union and the advancement of their happiness, so His Divine blessing may be equally conspicuous in the enlarged views, the temperate consultations and the wise measures on which the success of this government must depend."

THE HON. PETER HENDRICKSON.

AT BATTERY D ARMORY.

We stand to-day upon the summit of the centuries; we look back over the past and we look forward into the future, and on this auspicious day we would reason together and give an account of the faith we have in the future of the republic. Your presence here, the look of gladness and devotion which is pictured on the thousands of faces in this vast assembly, and the festal feeling with which the whole atmosphere of the day seems charged, bear testimony to the fact that the day is one of joy and not of grief.

It is the conditions and the circumstances of to-day that pronounce judgment upon the century that is past, and the century makes us look with reverence upon the intellects and characters of the men who have shaped it. Reverence is the noblest activity of the human mind. In this reverence there is an element of fear which guards our minds from presumption and our lips from uttering rash speech. In this reverence there is hope which gives buoyancy to the whole being. In this reverence there is affection, which is the power that moves the world and makes men invincible.

These feelings gathered into one by the rays of light from a hundred years of history, and finding their focus in this day and this hour, we sum up in one word, Patriotism. And if this day has any significance any more than a mere merry-making, it is to find the ground and basis for this feeling of patriotic devotion and give it expression in grand unison of heart and voice.

Patriotism! What is it? Is it a myth invented by some enthusiast? Patriotism may be called localized philanthropy, but it is more than this—something that eludes definition, something that we are cognizant of when we sing, "I love thy rocks and rills, thy woods and templed hills." Patriotism is both a principle and a

passion, harmonized and controlled by intelligence. Its foundation is knowledge, its active principle is love of man, and its scope
is our country. Patriotism is not a plant of accidental growth;
like all virtues it must be cultivated and nurtured to become
strong. Of this, too, there is a spurious article as well as a genuine. There is a cultured plant and there is a weed. That patriotism which consists merely in upholding and defending your country
and its institutions because they are yours, may have its uses, but
it is based on false principles and degenerates into mere passion,
The imitation is rooted in selfishness, the genuine in self-sacrifice.
The weed is luxuriant in foliage but meager in fruitage. How to
nurture this plant of patriotism so that it may be at once fragrant
in the bloom and abundant in fruit should be the first aim and the
persistent effort of the citizens who understand the responsibility
imposed by free institutions.

You will pardon me, I trust, Mr. Chairman, if I should have
misapprehended the true purpose of this great national anniversary. We are to-day dropping wreaths upon the graves of the
heroes of a hundred years ago, but we are doing this not to add
luster to their fame only; our minds are more in the present and
the future than in the past, and what we do to-day should be a
testimony to future generations of the sense of duty and responsibility with which we accept the inheritance of the century that is
past, and of the solemn care with which we transmit the treasure
into the hands of the centuries yet to come. We therefore in
mind take the present and the future generations by the hand and
lead them back over the hundred years that are past, and while we
learn we would also teach a lesson from the fountain and source of
our liberties and our laws.

George Washington and the Federal Constitution! The two
are inseparable. When the lips have named the one, the thought
has embraced the other. Wherever liberty is considered a boon
and order is thought better than anarchy, the name of Washington
is revered and the Federal Constitution respected. Washington was
not an angel. Washington was not a demon. George Washington was a man. No angel has ever governed a state; no demon
has founded a dynasty or an empire. These are the works of men,
and in our day it has come to pass that men are judged by their
works and not by the adulations of enthusiasts or the railleries of
irreverent fault-finders.

Nothing but a weak mind and a small soul can ever approach
the character of Washington without reverence. No name or fame
in history stands less in need of being surrounded by the halo of

sainthood, and no character can be less harmed by the scrutiny of impartial criticism.   No American patriot will ever be humbled by the necessity of drawing the veil of charity over the life or the record of the Father of his Country.   These are facts, the contemplation of which should fill our minds with humility and our hearts with gratitude.

The Federal Constitution is, in the words of Gladstone, "the most wonderful work ever struck off at a given time by the brain and purpose of man."   It is the greatest work of constructive statesmanship known to the race.   The homage which is to-day everywhere accorded to this Constitution is not due to its age, but to its adaptability and power.   The ideal republic of Plato is hoary with age; its ingenious structure has been the delight of scholars and poets for many centuries, but it has never commanded the loyalty and homage of a people.   The symmetrical system of Locke is twice as old as our Constitution, but it has never enjoyed a celebration or an anniversary.   These were babes born out of due season, founded on fancy and elaborated by the imagination. The progress of mankind is tentative; step by step we find our way through the tangles of history.   No invention and no system that has not sprung from present needs and solved pressing difficulties have ever been useful to man.   Washington was great because he filled a great place, the Constitution is great because it has solved a great problem.   It was the product, not of speculation, but of experience.   It is for their services that we love and cherish both Washington and the fundamental law of the republic.

There is that in man which forbids his full appreciation of any gift unless he knows its cost.   If you would inculcate the lessons of patriotism, if you want the citizen of the future to love the institutions under which he lives, if you want him to appreciate the value and the responsibility of citizenship, you must show him what it has cost.   You must teach him the agonies of its birth, you must conduct him to its cradle and show him the perils that surrounded its infancy and point out to him the calamities from which he has been rescued.   No lesson in patriotism, no instruction in statesmanship can be better than a study of the history of the five years from the conclusion of peace to the adoption of the Federal Constitution.

Never have the destinies of a great future hung more tremblingly in the balance than when that memorable assembly gathered at Philadelphia in the month of May, 1787, to begin the work which should secure a more perfect union between these states.   The magnitude of the task and its beneficent fruits will be seen when we reflect that a union between these thirteen feeble states was as much dreaded and feared then as is disunion to-day. Massachusetts and Rhode Island were as jealous of their neighbors and more unwilling to give up their sovereignty to a general government than were South Carolina or Louisiana in the days of nullification and rebellion.

The five years from 1783 to 1788 are the saddest and darkest in our history. Anything approaching to that now would be called anarchy, and with fear and trembling it was so recognized then. The Continental Congress was despised and discredited, had been driven out of Philadelphia by a handful of riotous soldiers whom neither state nor city authorities could control. There were no funds with which to pay the defenders of our liberties or provide for any common need. We were ridiculed and mocked at by all the powers of Europe; even France was ashamed of having aided us to achieve an independence which we were incapable of enjoying. There were men who had struggled to sever the bond which united them with England, who now in the face of this future regretted their vain sacrifices and toil, and wished themselves back under the sheltering wings of the mother country. These little states who had learned to sing the songs of freedom and of self-government were yet ignorant of the sentiment of union which to-day is the pride of every American and the only guaranty of the future of the republic. I am not drawing a fancy picture. I am not exalting the present at the expense of the past when I say that you can raise more funds for a common object in the city of Chicago to-day than you could in the thirteen states one hundred years ago yesterday.

Now what is it that has secured to us this contrast? What is it that has harmonized 60,000,000 people from all quarters of the globe and made them one in spirit and hope under a union that is loved and respected by all? It is this charter of our liberties, this pillar of our national temple, and this rock on which we rest—the Federal Constitution. And who gave us this Constitution? I answer: it was not the people of the states, it was not the Continental Congress. Next after the "divinity that shapes our ends," it was George Washington. So much did these liberty-loving thirteen states fear a union, that it was not till it became known that George Washington was chosen delegate that many of the states would have anything to do with the Constitutional Convention. So great was the power of his fame even then that it created confidence and courage all over the country. Where Washington would take the lead it was safe to follow. Does any one say Washington was not a statesman as well as a soldier? I answer: there is one element without which no amount of learning and genius can make a statesman, and that is courage and moral conviction. This it is which made the Constitution what it is and has kept it where it is, and that element in it is due to Washington more than to any other man. Washington presided over the convention, and his character was its foundation and defense. Listen to his words when delegates began to propose half measures because they feared that the people would accept nothing else. In that solemn and decisive moment he rose from his seat and pointed out the only course of safety. "It is too probable," he said, "that no plan we propose will be adopted. Perhaps another dreadful conflict is to be sustained. If, to please the people, we offer what we ourselves disapprove, how can we afterward defend our work? Let us raise a standard to which the wise and honest can repair; the event is in the hand of God." Is there no statesmanship in this? Is there a man in this assembly who would be afraid to trust his destiny to a convention presided over by such a man? Washington was first in peace as well as in war. This is no idle phrase. Let it never pass our lips unless our hearts give it its full meaning and our voice its due emphasis.

But Washington, though chief, was not alone. We should do injustice to the memories of the past and to our sense of right if we did not to-day remember with gratitude the names of Benjamin Franklin, James Madison, Alexander Hamilton, Thomas Jefferson, John Jay and the Adamses and the Pinckneys, and other immortal men who, both in and out of the convention, did so much to erect this noble structure, and prepare the minds of the people for its acceptance.

But we should also do injustice to the people of these colonies if we did not recognize the fact that what in the outset proved the greatest obstacle to the Union was in the end its safety, its rock of defense. Intense love of self-government, rooted in experience and cherished by patriotic devotion, was the first characteristic of the people of the colonies. The obstacle which this presented was the fact that each man's patriotism was centered in his own state, his loyalty wholly absorbed by his own local government. An unseen, unlocalized and indefinable union presented no image to them but that of a foreign tyrant. The great work of the Constitution was to create a new centre for this strong affection and transfer it from the government of the colonies to the government of the Union. It was to enlarge the mind and expand the affection. To create the conviction that my colony was not my country, but only a part of it. It was to get the inhabitant of Massachusetts, of Delaware, of Virginia, to rise to the grand conception that his Fatherland was not a colony, but a continent. That he was not first and foremost a Virginian or a New Yorker, but an American. That the colonies had fled from common troubles, had sought a common refuge and had freed themselves from a common oppressor in order to gather under the ægis of a common government and become not many small but one great empire. How grand was this thought and how all-important was the change!

And here, too, let us remember that the great power which alone could make such transformation was the fame and name of Washington. As the presiding genius of the convention he created confidence. As the first head of the new government, as the common centre of the new and larger Fatherland, he drew the hearts of the people from the old allegiance to the new. Here let us behold the greatest work ever performed by mortal man, here let us realize the true significance of this solemn day, and humbly uncover our heads in the presence of the sublime spirit and character of Washington, which even to-day presides over the destiny of the republic.

But while the Federal Constitution is the central pillar of this noble temple whose first century of life terminates to-day, there are other forces without whose support it may be doubted whether the structure would have withstood the storms. It was the vastness of the territory which made it so difficult for the colonies to conceive of the Union in the sense in which it presents itself to our view. The Constitution could not unite and harmonize material interests so different and so diverse. Without a material bond to unite and hold them together the unity of mere law would be inefficient. This material bond was at this moment in the throes of birth. At the very time when the Constitutional Convention was seated at Philadelphia, the first steamer was launched on the Delaware River. The Federal Constitution and the steam engine are the great twin products of Anglo-Saxon intelligence and enterprise. It may well be doubted whether either, without the aid of the other, would be active forces in Chicago to-day. The Constitution was born in the nick of time. The planets were in the right conjunction, and the twins were born under the star of hope. If it were not for the steam engine you and I might not be here, and wherever we might be and whatever we might be doing we should not be celebrating the adoption of the Constitution. It was by this marvelous coincidence that the bond of law was supplemented by a bond of intercourse to which we are indebted for what we are to-day.

But there is a third pillar in the structure, without which political and material bonds would be torn asunder. That pillar is the public school. I would not say one word here that on this day of harmony and common joy should arouse any prejudice or the slightest murmur of dissent, but I should do violence to my most settled conviction if I did not say that the public school, a common education for the young, under the same teachers, on the same benches and in the same classes for all children and youth, not of the laborers only, but of rich and poor, the native and the foreign, of all creeds and of all colors, is as essential, is as vital to the stability of this nation and to the lasting happiness of the people as the Constitution and the steam engine combined. It was possible to unite the colonies into one because they were young and pliable and devoted to a common teacher and master. It will only be possible to melt so diverse a population together into common love and devotion to the same institutions by accustoming them to live and play and act together without prejudice and distinction in the tender years of childhood and youth. These are the gifts of the century that is gone, and these are the pillars of the Union and the guaranty of fraternal friendship through centuries to come. The Constitution will change in the course of the future as it has changed in the past, for it is not a dead carcass or a fossil, but a living law, and this change will be a growth, not in the direction of curtailing popular government, but of expanding it; not by taking power from the people, but by giving larger power to the people. But remember this, that larger power will never be safe in the hands of the people without a large intelligence and a common intelligence, and this intelligence for all without distinction and without exception.

There are weak and ignorant men who even to-day affect to believe that this Constitution is an experiment, and the perpetuity of the Union an unsolved problem. Let them not desecrate the sacred precincts of the second century of our national existence with this malady of doubt. Has not this Constitution and this Union borne its test? Has it not grown strong by adversity? Has it not conquered not only the arms, but the hearts of doubters and foes?

Classic fable tells us that when Hercules was born he, too, inherited the hate of the divinity of doubt and opposition. When the infant giant lay in his cradle the malignant goddess sent two serpents to press their deadly venom into the breast of the sleeping infant. But the infant was not asleep. He stretched forth his right hand and his left, and in his giant clutches he choked the vile reptiles in the dust and returned to placid repose. So has the Constitution triumphed over the divinity of hate. Her reptiles came to his infant cradle. The black serpent of slavery on the one hand and the green serpent of disunion on the other, and the youthful giant arose and in one hand he seized the black serpent and in the other the green serpent, and he bruised their heads against the rock, and buried their vile bodies in the dust forever. Is there any one here that doubts?

And this Constitution is ours and in joyous echo I hear the word "ours" coming from every state, from every county, from every hamlet and from every fireside to-day in this goodly land. It fills the American heart everywhere from Maine to the farthest point of Florida, and from the Golden Gate to the Atlantic, and in every breast there is forgiveness, fraternity and affection. If this Constitution has borne the strain of the century that is past, may we not to-day, in joyful assurance, hand it down to the centuries that are to come and bid them guard it with the same jealous care and the same intelligent devotion which has attended it in the past? We have faith that the future will not be found wanting. Washington was a hopeful man, for he was sound and healthy in body and mind. The Constitution was born of this hope, and with faith it is handed down to the future. We know full well that the whole brood of hateful serpents is not dead. The divinity of discord is still sending forth her progeny to perplex the children of men. Some of them are even now pointing their venomous fangs at the young state and its Constitution. We can see their slimy heads in the grass. There is the serpent of corruption and fraud, the serpents of spoil and plunder, the serpent of monopoly, the serpent of sectional jealousies, the serpent of anarchy, the serpent of strife between the rich and the poor, and, more than all, the old serpent with its hundred heads and its thousand fangs, the snake that destroys the heart and the conscience and the home, the old dragon of strong drink. We are not blind to their dangers, but we stand here calm in the faith that the same giant will stretch forth his hand and one by one crush their heads under his heel, and when the next great centennial of this day shall dawn the joyful shouts will rise from the lips of hundreds of millions "We have performed the task which you set us one hundred years ago."

THE HON. CARTER H. HARRISON.

AT THE "OVERFLOW MEETING" IN DEARBORN PARK.

It has generally been accepted as a fact that on the 4th day of July, 1776, at Independence Hall, in Philadelphia, a nation was born. This is not a historical truth. On that memorable day freedom had its birth—that freedom which seems to have been conceived on this continent, which was brought forth when Thomas Jefferson, in the immortal Declaration of Independence, declared that "all men were born free and equal"—a declaration up to that moment unheard and unuttered since history had begun. This solemn assertion was signed by men who knew that the wage of battle was by them thrown down, which was to give to the signers the right to live as freemen or the penalty of dying as traitors.

Freedom, that day born, was afterward, during a long war which tried men's souls, again and again on many a battle-field baptized in blood. After nearly eight years of privations, such as only earnest patriots would have endured, the world acknowledged the United States of America independent. These states felt themselves each sovereign and independent and bound together only by a solemn, but yet voluntary agreement, severable .at the will of each or of any of them. It was soon found that this bond was but a rope of sand which had not and could not create a nation. The men who fought for freedom and independence saw that their labors and privations were likely to prove to have been done and suffered in vain. A demand went up from the wiser people of the several states for something more enduring than a mere severable agreement. This demand was uttered continuously by the one man, who all Americans agreed had been singled out by Providence as the Father of his Country. His earnest warnings were heard and heeded and in September, 1787, a convention over which he presided framed the Constitution of the United States. This Constitution was not immediately ratified by the states, but a majority finally agreeing to it, on this day one hundred years ago, the nation which had been lying in embryo was vivified at New York—the nation which is to-day the grandest and really the most powerful the world ever knew, for it is a nation of sovereigns, each sovereign in his individual freedom, and each ready to support the integrity of his country. On that day, whose Centennial we celebrate, the nation was fixed and baptized, and its machinery put in motion with George Washington at its head.

Fellow-citizens—Our immortal first President, in his address when taking the helm of the Ship of State, solemnly and reverently asked the blessing upon his country of the Almighty God. Following his lofty example, let us, too, ask the favors of the same ever-living God to bless the country, now that it commemorates the birth of our nation.

PROF. A. C. GEYER.

AT THE DEARBORN PARK "OVERFLOW MEETING."

A striking and most interesting part of the open-air meeting was the eloquent speech by Prof. A. C. Geyer of Indiana. His subject was "The Test of a Century of National Life," in which he vigorously and eloquently followed our political development from the time that the great purposes of the fathers were embodied in the Federal Constitution to the present, when those purposes are an accomplished fact, and when our mighty and grand country stands before the world as the only perfect embodiment of regulated and law-ordered *liberty*. The fathers had made the moral sentiment of the whole people the foundation on which the superstructure was reared, and had intrusted government to the hearts of the governed. On this continent was established the complete reversal of theories and policies which had hitherto been in the ascendency. Instead of centralizing power and making special grants of political sway; instead of making a mighty standing army, wielded by a monarch's will, the defense of government, American statesmen had given birth to a government in which the people are the only source of supreme power, and whose fortress of defense is the people's devotion. A century of political vicissitude had demonstrated the triumph of these principles. The American people had published to the world by their achievements a confirmation of their character and strength. They had verified their capability of self-government and their worthiness of liberty. They had proved that power can exist silently and potently in the hearts of the people, ready to be called into exercise at the moment of command, etc.

It is impossible to do justice to the speech without printing it in full, and no stenographer was present to take it. It was patriotic, vigorous and eloquent to the end, and in spite of the cold atmosphere in which it was delivered the speaker held his vast audience as in a spell, and now and then evoked storms of applause. No halting, no wearying, but a continuous, easy and rapid flow of genuine eloquence and beauty of thought and language, and a fearlessness and force of utterance which drive conviction to the heart.

V

THE BANQUET

THE BANQUET

The events of the day concluded with a banquet at the Union League Club, at which the gentlemen who had come from other cities to assist in the celebration were the guests of the evening. About two hundred representative citizens participated. The Hon. Walter Q. Gresham presided.

For two hours the guests lingered over the feast. Then cigars were lighted, glasses replenished and the rest of the evening given to toasts and responses.

"WASHINGTON AND THE CONSTITUTION."

BY THE HON. JOHN M. HARLAN.

"I am glad I am in Chicago," said Justice Harlan as a preface to his response. "I like to be in Chicago and whenever I get away from Chicago I want to get back. The country is beginning to appreciate Chicago. When the last administration was hunting for a Chief Justice of the United States Supreme Court, it had to come to Chicago to find him. When the present administration wanted a Minister Plenipotentiary and Ambassador Extraordinary to Great Britain it came to Chicago to get him. And it is not improbable—you cannot tell what a nation will do—that soon enough they will come to Chicago for a man to occupy the White House." Complimenting the city thus and bowing to Judge Gresham, Justice Harlan, amid cheers, began the following address:

It is the concurring judgment of political thinkers that no event in all the history of the Anglo-Saxon race has been more far-reaching in its consequences than the organization of the present government of the United States. And at this Centennial celebration of that event it is in every sense appropriate to connect the name of Washington with the Constitution which brought that government into existence. It is appropriate because his splendid leadership of the Revolutionary armies made it possible to establish upon this continent a government resting upon the consent of the governed, yet strong enough to maintain its existence and authority whenever assailed. But it is especially appropriate for the reason that he was among the first of the great men of the Revolutionary period to discern the inherent defects in the articles of confederation; and but for his efforts to bring about a more perfect union of the people, the existing Constitution, it is believed, would not have been accepted by the requisite number of states. He was, indeed, the pioneer of the union established by that Constitution. Of the accuracy of these statements there is abundant evidence.

As early as the 4th of March, 1783, in a letter addressed to Gov. Harrison of Virginia, he expressed the opinion, based upon his observation during the war and his intercourse with the people of the states, that if the powers of Congress were not made competent to all general purposes the blood that had been spilt, the expense incurred and the distress felt would avail nothing, and the bond which held the country together, already too weak, would soon be broken, when anarchy and confusion would prevail. It is a fact, not without some interest, that the Revolutionary patriot to whom that letter was addressed was the great-grandfather of our honored fellow-citizen now holding the exalted position of President of the United States. In the same month in which Washington communicated these views to the Governor of Virginia, he wrote to Hamilton: "My wish to see the union of the states established upon liberal and permanent principles, and inclination to contribute my mite in pointing out the defects of the present Constitution, are equally great. All my private letters have teemed with these sentiments, and whenever this topic has been the subject of conversation I have endeavored to diffuse and enforce them." To Lafayette, who never lost his interest in the people whose liberties he aided to secure, he said that "to form a new Constitution that will give consistency, stability and dignity to the Union and sufficient powers to the great council of the nation for general purposes is a duty incumbent upon every man who wishes well to his country." In the same year, as the time approached to surrender his authority as Commander-in-Chief of the army, he addressed a circular letter to the Governors of the states declaring that "according to the system of policy the states shall adopt at this moment, it is to be decided whether the Revolution must ultimately be considered as a blessing or a curse; a blessing or a curse, not to the present age alone, for with our fate will the destiny of unborn millions be involved." He, therefore, expressed the deep conviction that "an indissoluble union of the states under one Federal head" was essential to "the existence of the United States as an independent power"; that it was "indispensable to the happiness of the individual states that there should be lodged somewhere a supreme power to regulate and govern the general concerns of the confedcrated republic, without which the Union cannot be of long duration"; and that "it is only in our united character as an empire that our independence is acknowledged, that our power can be regarded, or our credit supported among foreign nations."

Shortly after this magnificent letter was issued and when about to disband the army he had led to victory, he addressed these words of farewell to his comrades: "Although the General has so frequently given it as his opinion in the most public and explicit manner, that unless the principles of the federal government were properly supported and the powers of the Union increased, the honor, dignity and justice of the nation would be lost forever, yet he cannot help leaving it as his last injunction to every officer and every soldier who may view the subject in the same serious light to add his best endeavors, with those of his worthy fellow-citizens, toward effecting those great and valuable purposes on which our existence as a nation so materially depends." Thus did the great commander sheathe his sword. Under the influence of the purest patriotism the soldier expanded into the statesman. With a foresight and breadth of vision that was extraordinary he saw that upon the recognition of our independence by the mother country the crisis in the struggle for republican institutions was only beginning, and so his purpose was to send forth every soldier in his army as an apostle of constitutional government. And what he said to the army was repeated in letters to the molders of public opinion. To John Jay he wrote that we could not long exist as a nation "without having lodged somewhere a power which will pervade the whole Union in as energetic a manner as the authority of the state governments extends over the several states." To Madison: "Thirteen sovereignties pulling against each other, and all tugging at the federal head, will soon bring ruin on the whole."

Entertaining these views, Washington entered the convention of 1787, which Jefferson described as "an assembly of demigods." It does not appear from the record of those times that he participated to any extent in the discussions of that remarkable assembly.

I say remarkable, because, in the recent words of the foremost Englishman of this generation, "the statesmen of the American Revolution have taken their place once for all amongst the greatest political instructors of the world." But such was the grandeur and nobility of his nature, so entirely free was he from mere partisanship, so awful was the reverence for his character, that Washington's influence upon the deliberations of the convention was far greater than that exercised by any other delegate. From the beginning of the struggle between the advocates of a more perfect union and those who dreaded, or professed to dread, any diminution whatever of the powers of the states, he deemed it "impracticable, in the federal government of these states, to secure all rights of independent sovereignty to each, and yet provide for the welfare and safety of all." And that was the general view by which the convention was guided. Indeed, it is not too much to say that every vital principle of the Constitution, as originally adopted, was in harmony with the views he had avowed and urged upon the leading statesmen of the country for years before the convention met. But when its work was submitted to the people of the states, it became apparent that the enemies of a national government, such as was to be created by that Constitution, were neither few in number nor insignificant in ability and influence. To the grief of Washington it was disclosed that many statesmen, who were conspicuous in the struggle for independence, were opposed to the adoption of the proposed Constitution; some, in the mistaken belief that it would altogether subvert the authority of the states; others, because it did not contain a bill of rights, recognizing the fundamental principles of life, liberty and property that were brought by our ancestors from the mother country. But the soul of Washington was undaunted. Conscious that the people were looking to him for counsel and guidance, he proved himself equal to the perilous crisis through which the country was then passing. From his quiet home at Mount Vernon he conducted a campaign in behalf of the proposed Constitution that was as important and effective as the victories he had won upon the battle fields of the Revolution. He felt, what all now believe to be true, that upon the result of that agitation depended the consolidation of the Union, and, in all human probability, the fate of republican government upon this continent. To Patrick Henry he transmitted a copy of the Constitution, confessing that while it did not contain all that he desired, its adoption was of the last consequence. "From a variety of concurring events," he wrote, "it appears to me that the political concerns of this country are in a manner suspended by a thread," and that if nothing had been agreed upon by the convention, "anarchy would soon have ensued, the seeds being deeply sowed in every soil." To Edmund Randolph he declared that the proposed Constitution "or a dissolution of the Union, awaits our choice, and is the only alternative before us." To Lafayette he wrote: "There is no alternative, no hope of alteration, no immediate resting place, between the adoption of this Constitution and a recurrence to an unqualified state of anarchy, with all its deplorable consequences." Such was the language he employed in personal interviews and in an extended correspondence with the leaders of thought in all the states. His efforts to rally the people in behalf of the Constitution, which was to transform the helpless confederation into a strong and permanent union, were crowned with success, and although he took no part in the Federal debates, and wrote nothing like the masterly papers in the *Federalist*, the country acknowledged him as the real leader in the struggle for constitutional government. "His influence," said Monroe to Jefferson, "carried this government." "Were it not for one great character," said Grayson, "so many men would not be for this government." Over all the discussions in the states as to the adoption of the Constitution, says the historian Bancroft, there hovered "the idea that Washington was to lead the country safely along the untrodden path." Many who thought that the Constitution should contain a bill of rights, advocated its acceptance in the expectation, which was fulfilled, that he would be the first President, and that, under his administration of the government, all the necessary guarantees of life, liberty and property would be secured by amendment of the fundamental law. This silent soldier, so modest yet so masterful, was, in truth, the keystone of the combination of patriots; and, as we look from this distance, we can but feel that if he had died at that juncture the strong, symmetrical arch of the Union would never have been erected.

I have preferred, Mr. President, upon an occasion like this, to give these proofs of the patriotism and wisdom of Washington, rather than employ any terms of general eulogy. It is stated in his diary that the evening of the day when the convention of 1787 concluded its labors, he retired at an early hour "to meditate on the momentous work which had been executed"—an eloquent picture of himself, unconsciously drawn for us with his own hand. We may well believe that the deep, calm nature of this man of "massive mold" was profoundly stirred when, at the close of that memorable day, he looked forward into the future and attempted to forecast the destiny of his beloved country under the form of government proposed for its adoption. If the work of that day appeared to him to be momentous in its character and in its probable results, how much more so does it appear to us, at the close of the first century of our constitutional existence, as we look back over the wonderful history of this nation? We are only in the spring-time of our national life, and yet we have realized all that Washington could possibly have anticipated from the creation of the present government. What more could be desired in a system of government than is secured in the existing organizations of the general and state governments with their respective powers so admirably adjusted and distributed as to draw from Gladstone the remark that the American Constitution was "the most wonderful work ever struck off at one time by the brain and purpose of man?" Despite the fears of many patriotic statesmen, at the time of the adoption of the Constitution, that that instrument would destroy the liberties of the people, every genuine American rejoices, in the fullness of a grateful heart, that we have a government under which the humblest person in our midst has a feeling of safety and repose not vouchsafed to the citizen or subject of any other country; with powers ample for the protection of the life of the nation and adequate for all purposes of a general nature, yet so restricted by the law of its creation in the exercise of its powers that it cannot rightfully intrench upon those reserved to the states or to the people. I will not here allude to or discuss particular theories of constitutional construction. But I may say, and I am glad that it can be truthfully said, that the mass of the people concur in holding that only by maintaining the just powers of both the national and state governments can we preserve, in their integrity, the fundamental principles of American liberty. But while renewing this day our allegiance to the Constitution of Washington, let us not, my countrymen, forget that the liberty for which our fathers fought is liberty secured and regulated by law, not the liberty of mere license. There is no place in our American system for the unrestrained freedom that respects not the essential rights of life, liberty and property, but regards a government of law as inimical to the rights of man. The true American, whether native or naturalized, stands under all circumstances for the law and for the rights of his fellowmen as recognized and defined by law. Those who hold otherwise are enemies of our free institutions, and should be treated as such. These observations are not inappropriate to this occasion. They find some warrant in our history and in the actual circumstances of some portions of the country. This country opens wide its doors for the reception of honest, industrious immigrants who desire to enjoy the blessings of our institutions, and who assimi-late with our people. But we cannot close our eyes to the fact that foreign governments are throwing upon our shores and crowd-ing our great cities with vast hordes of men who have no proper conception of the philosophy or spirit of American liberty. Recent investigations under the authority of Congress show the coming to our land in startling numbers of worthless characters gathered from the highways and by-ways of other countries, as well as crim-inals from foreign jails and penitentiaries, all of whom will in time be invested with the privilege, at the ballot box, of sharing in the control not only of states but of the nation. In view of these facts thoughtful, patriotic citizens, native and naturalized, may well ask whether the safety of our government and the integrity of our civilization are not seriously menaced by the presence here of so many that place no value upon the inestimable right of suf-frage and have little sympathy with, or knowledge of, our institu-tions. We can perform no better service to our country than to see to it that the right to shape its destiny shall not be bestowed upon those who are unworthy of it. Let us raise our voices in favor of such further enactments, constitutional and statutory, as may be necessary to guard our American civilization and keep this country for all time under American control.

"JAMES MADISON."

BY BISHOP SPALDING OF PEORIA.

After the applause elicited by Justice Harlan's speech had died away, Judge Gresham introduced Bishop Spalding, who responded to the toast, "James Madison." He spoke briefly but pointedly, and his words were well received. He said:

The debt which we owe to the framers of the Constitution is greater than it is easy for us or any man to realize. The day the Declaration of Independence was made was our great day, but the Constitution saved it from becoming dangerous. The Federal Con-stitution saved the work of Washington from being in vain. The names of our greatest benefactors are frequently unknown. James Madison is not fully appreciated. It was a small thing in his life that he was President of the United States. That was his failure. His life was greater. He was the father of the Federal Constitu-tion. Modest and retiring, he was nevertheless the type of a true man. He owed his education entirely to himself. Though not in any sense a genius he was endowed with that common sense which is of more use to man than genius. We should not give credit to Madison or Washington for what we possess. But deep adversity taught our American fathers what they could not have learned from their own resources. The colonies were not thirteen independent governments, but independent states, having no joint being. The Federal Congress had no supremacy or powers over the states, and riots and disturbances were bringing the states into disrepute and threatening discord and destruction.

It was James Madison who first introduced a motion in the Legislature in Virginia for a convention to regulate commerce on the rivers, first between Virginia and Maryland, then the other colonies were taken in, and so the plan grew. Madison was at the bottom of all this.

The Federal Congress falling more and more into disrepute, the Constitutional Convention was finally called. It was called on the Virginia plan, as suggested by Madison. It was his idea that the people and not the states should be represented in the Congress. The present Congress represents the individual American citizens. That was Madison's idea. It is from James Madison that we know the history of the Constitutional Convention. Washington was not an orator or a leader of an assembly of men. Hamilton was an aristocrat and wanted a constitutional monarchy. Madison was the soul of the convention. New York did not vote for Washington, although they celebrate him to-day. The religious liberty guaranteed by the Constitution is one of the most important accomplishments of it and is producing the best men and women.

Perhaps it was unfortunate that a compromise was made with slavery. It is true our fathers had not the faintest idea of such a nation as we have to-day. They were Massachusetts men, Virginia men, and so on. They are not to blame. We are all the creatures of circumstances. No statesman in Europe but who thought the Federal Constitution would be a failure. Not one of the signers believed the Federal Constitution would work.

We owe everything to the Federal Constitution. It has made us to-day the most united and best organized and strongest nation on the earth. Madison had the largest conception of things. He was an abolitionist. He did not believe in slavery. He said the contest would not be between the big states and the little states but between the slave-holders and their opponents. Madison, who failed as a President, forced us into a war because he did not know anything about war. He was a man of peace. He was a thorough American in that. We do not believe in the mediæval ideas of conquest, of annexing Canada or anything like it.

The European powers will see that their only salvation is to dismiss their armies and look to a federal arrangement like ours to settle their differences. We have abolished the duel; we have abolished private warfare—we will abolish public warfare. Utopian at present, gentlemen, but it will come.

James Madison believed in this. I propose to you James Madison.

"THOMAS JEFFERSON."

BY THE HON. L. D. THOMAN.

Mr. L. D. Thoman responded in the same succinct and happy way to the toast on "Thomas Jefferson." Following is his address:

It is not only a privilege but rather a duty to eulogize the deeds and preserve the memories of those who either in peace or war have conferred benefits or lustre on their country. It inspires ambitions to emulate their example. The American youth is strengthened in his love for popular government by learning well the sacrifices required to obtain it. The human mind is so constituted that it is not only interested, it is aroused and stimulated, by lofty ideas of excellence. A conception of what has been done is an important factor in achieving eminence in any profession or any enterprise.

Few characters in the history of governments and their administration command more attention than Thomas Jefferson. His extraordinary abilities, his devotion to the cause of liberty and his unbounded faith in the intelligence, character and strength of the people for self-government, make him one of the most conspicuous characters in history.

Jefferson was a republican in the broadest sense of the term as applied to citizenship. I believe that his untiring devotion to the cause of a plain and simple interpretation of the Constitution gives to us the privilege of celebrating the 100th anniversary of the inauguration of the first President of the United States. One hundred years of an undisturbed popular government and free sovereignty! What a reflection!

Public men of merit in all times have been the subjects of severe criticism; but whatever else may be said of him, all must admit that Thomas Jefferson was devoted to the cause of liberty.

It would be supererogation to review his whole life to justify this assertion. One reference will suffice. In the administration of public affairs he followed clearly the policy defined in his first inaugural address, a state paper which for simplicity, fullness and force has never been equaled in political literature. He dealt with public questions in the interest of good administration. He was a party man, but not a partisan. He was a politician, and yet he did not permit his politics to dwarf his patriotism or to warp his judgment. The criticism that Jefferson was a Virginian and not a Nationalist is not justified by the history of his public life. He was jealous of his achievements; and when a majority of his countrymen rallied to his standard and became the advocates of his beliefs he called this organization his party. It must be conceded that his abilities as an organizer were masterly when we consider that he was able to marshal the forces and succeed in the victory of 1801, when Hamilton, Marshall, Henry, Ames, the Lees, the Adamses, Otis, Livingston, the Pinckneys and Luther Martin were the leaders of the opposition.

It is but fair to say that the first twelve years of government under the Constitution were years of experiments. Officers were naturally timid in their assertion of prerogatives, while yet intensely jealous of right and reputation. Keen, observant and politic, Jefferson easily saw their mistakes and knew the necessity for their correction. It is not, therefore, strangely wonderful that an immediate change in the administrative affairs occurred upon his inauguration. The policy announced by him met with popular favor; the man and the hour had arrived for the interpretation of the principles of the free Constitution in accordance with the designs of its framers; and such an interpretation was given to its provisions as at once aroused the approval, the admiration and the patriotic ardor of the people.

In giving shape to our politics the Jeffersonian age also gave direction to our intellectual and material progress by an impetus which will be felt and acknowledged through all time. Our Constitution to him was the law of the land.

The responsibility for the preservation of this corner-stone of civil liberty is upon us. To discharge the duties of citizenship in a conscientious manner is our highest duty. As Cæsar was stimulated in his passion for military glory by seeing the statue of Alexander the Great; as the Athenian youth drew inspiration for patriotic devotion from the cold marble statutes of Solon, the law-giver; Conon, the Admiral; Pericles, the mightiest of their statesmen, and Demosthenes, the prince of their orators, so we will be inspired to more fervent patriotic duty by a closer study of the greatness of the fathers who gave us this heritage. We may be Republicans, or we may be Democrats, but when it comes to supporting the Constitution, Liberty and the Union, we should know no party.

"JOHN MARSHALL."

BY THE HON. ROBERT T. LINCOLN.

"John Marshall" was the next toast proposed, and the Hon. Robert T. Lincoln responded. Said he:

In a commemoration like this, in which the first thought of all is the contrast between our country now and as it was a century ago, it is impossible that time can be given to notice many of the causes which have made its greatness or to speak of many of the men whose names stand out in the pages of its history as having been the leaders, or, perhaps I should say, the representatives of the popular sentiments which have been the impulses of our national progress. In making a choice among the names of our great citizens of those who are to be the subject of special encomium on an occasion like this, when only a few of those worthy of it can possibly receive it, the choice will most naturally fall on some of those who have conducted the affairs of the nation in its chief office, and among them almost inevitably the thrill of admiration is most excited in every patriotic breast by the memory of those who have done their country service by leading its armies to glorious victories. But I am asked to speak of one who had just reached his full manhood when the Declaration of Independence was proclaimed, whose military service was honorable but short, and nothing but that of a subaltern; of one who not only was never President, but who, save for a few months, never held an administrative public office. While he was a man who omitted no occasion to impress on his fellow-citizens, with unsurpassed logic and earnestness, what he thought was best for their common welfare, and at times consented to serve in the Legislature of his state and once in Congress, so that he might be enabled to act as well as to counsel, he was primarily a lawyer and again and again refused public offices of honor which would have taken him from his professional work. At last, however, there came to him a summons which withdrew him forever from his private pursuits, but which he could not refuse to obey.

The Department of Public Service to which he was called by President Adams, and for which he seems to have been specially created by Divine Providence, is in our republic and was peculiarly so in its young days of the most transcendent importance. If his duties had not been done as they were it is easy to believe that so far as our nationality is concerned we could not be enjoying as we now do the full fruits of Washington's generalship and civil administration and of the work of the framers of our Constitution.

He was made the Chief Justice of the Supreme Court of the United States—a court which had come into existence only twelve years before, with powers at the first view so extraordinary that those not familiar with our complex system of government can hardly be made to understand the possibility of the co-existence of Congress and the court. In England, from which we mainly derive our legal system, there is no written constitution, and there is, since the disuse of the royal veto, hardly an imaginable restriction upon the power of Parliament in making laws for the kingdom, and the highest court can do no more than interpret and then enforce any of its statutes. If the judicial interpretation is unsatisfactory to Parliament it is promptly met by a new enactment. Educated and trained in a busy legal life of a quarter of a century in the traditions of centuries of the absolute supremacy of the ordinary Legislature, the professional mind even of Marshall must have had a struggle before he came to realize fully that it was the foremost of the duties of himself and his judicial associates to apply a standard of validity to the enactments of the national Legislature and the Legislatures of all the states, and not to shrink from declaring any one of them a nullity if in the opinion of the court, in a case properly brought before them, it failed to keep within the limitations of that wonderful and novel instrument, the written Constitution of the United States.

It has often been said that no other court with such powers was ever created before or since—that no other court could in any case nullify the supreme legislative will of a nation as well as that of the sovereign states composing it. The fallacy of such a statement lies, of course, in ignoring the fact that the supreme legislative will of our nation is embodied, not in the acts of the Congress, but in the Constitution adopted by the whole people, by which the Congress was itself created and its powers defined and limited; and in ignoring the other fact that all attributes of sovereignty inconsistent with the provisions of the Constitution were voluntarily surrendered to the nation by each state as it entered the Union—so that in fact when the Supreme Court declares an act of Congress

invalid—as being contrary to the Constitution—it is only interpret-
ing the supreme law and enforcing conformity in the inferior, just
as is done by a state court when it declares a municipal ordinance
unwarranted by the general law under which the municipality is
created.

All this, after years of national education, seems simple enough,
but when Marshall assumed his seat if it was clear to his great
intellect it was not to a large part of the people. A few years
before the jurisdiction of the court had been sustained in a suit
brought by a citizen against the State of Georgia, and, with much
excitement, there was at once adopted the eleventh amendment to
the Constitution, preventing for the future any suit by any individual against a state. The jealousies of the states toward the
national government, which had made the formation of the Union
so difficult, were thoroughly aroused, and it must have been with
great anxiety as to the future that Marshall entered upon the
grave duties which he was to perform for nearly thirty-five years.
But his judicial genius, his legal ability and training, and the work
he had done in urging the adoption of the Constitution, made him
thoroughly fitted for the work before him. When all his judicial
laborers are considered he is alone to be ranked with the great
Lord Mansfield; but on this occasion we can only advert to that
fundamental characteristic of his which guided his legal genius in
settling, in many diverse cases, the absolute supremacy of the
national government in those things committed to it by the people
through the Constitution, and made him well called its Great
Expounder.

In his own state the conflict between those who wished the
establishment of a national government with such strength as to
avoid the evils of the frail Confederation, and those who wished to
retain undiminished the principle of sovereignty for each of the
states was so ardent that it lasted for years, and at the end the
Constitution was adopted by the Virginia Convention by a majority
of only ten votes, and then not until after it had been adopted by nine
out of the other twelve states. In procuring this result Marshall was
the ablest supporter of Madison, to whom the chief glory must be
given. In his work he was inspired by an ardent longing to have
a country greater than his native state. He wrote of himself that
in the army, when he found himself associated with brave men
from different states hazarding their all in a precious common
cause, he was confirmed in the habit of considering America as his
country and Congress as his government. For him the adoption
of the Constitution—the creation of the United States as a nation—

was the highest public good. His devotion to the national government so created was at the foundation of all his public acts, and over and over again did he sway the vast power of his court to the preservation of its sovereignty. In deciding the case of Cohens against the State of Virginia, when the state denied the power of the court to review the decision of a state court against a right claimed under an act of Congress, he said:

"If it could be doubted whether from its nature the Constitution were not supreme in all cases where it is empowered to act, that doubt would be removed by the declaration that 'this Constitution and the laws of the United States which shall be made in pursuance thereof, and all treaties made or which shall be made under the authority of the United States, shall be the supreme law of the land; and the Judges in every state shall be bound thereby, anything in the Constitution or laws of any state to the contrary notwithstanding.'

"This is the authoritative language of the American people; and, if the gentlemen please, of the American states. It marks with lines too strong to be mistaken the characteristic distinction between the government of the Union and those of the states. The general government, though limited as to its objects, is supreme with respect to those objects. This principle is a part of the Constitution; and if there be any who deny its necessity none can deny its authority.

"To this supreme government ample powers are confided; and if it were possible to doubt the great purposes for which they were so confided, the people of the United States have declared that they are given 'in order to form a more perfect union, establish justice, insure domestic tranquility, provide for the common defense, promote the general welfare and secure the blessings of liberty to themselves and their posterity.'"

This was but one of his many decisions, but in this language is the cardinal rule which guided him in doing his part to establish our nation as a sovereign power. In this he never faltered, and in this, even were it his only claim to the veneration of posterity, he is a noble and never to be forgotten example to all Americans.

"BENJAMIN FRANKLIN."

BY THE HON. C. C. ALBERTSON.

The toast, "Benjamin Franklin," called forth the following speech from the Hon. C. C. Albertson:

Somewhere between the covers of a peculiar book, which some of us are simple enough to believe is the revelation of the Infinite Father to His children on earth, I have read the words: "There were giants in the earth in those days." Though referring primarily to the epoch when the race was in the cradle of its infancy, there has never been an age since the first-born century took up the reins of Time and started on the track of Eternity concerning which its historians cannot truthfully say: "There were giants in the earth in those days." Mr. Chairman, I have been to some extent a student of history—ancient, mediæval and modern—and I have never yet read the record of any era in any land or under any sky of which it could be more appropriately said than of the Revolutionary period in our history: "There were giants in the earth in those days."

Benjamin Franklin was a colossal character. He was not so by reason of the paucity of great men in the age in which he lived. Some men may appear great on account of the smallness of their associates. It doesn't take an extraordinary man to seem a giant among pigmies. Franklin was a giant among giants. He had his birth in an heroic age—an age which saw a Patrick Henry, a Jefferson, a Jay, a Morris, a Pinckney, an Adams, a Madison, a Washington—yet the brilliance of their fame dims not the lustre of his glory. He lived and moved within a circle of illustrious men whose names we honor, and whose memories, though their ashes have long since mingled with the soil, and though their lips have long since taken the sacrament of the dust—whose memories are still as green as the foliage that buds in the spring time. Some of them were statesmen, some were orators, some diplomatists, some philosophers—all patriots and heroes; yet among them Benjamin Franklin made his mark and stood with unsurpassed distinction. Mr. Chairman, some characters are like the sunlight and air in this respect. They belong to the world at large, and not to any one party, nation, or age, or time. Think you that any particular party can claim such names as Cicero or Pericles or Charles Martel or Mirabeau or Washington or Madison or Lincoln or Grant? They are the property of the world. Think you that any partienlar sect or creed can claim such names as St. Paul or St. Augustine or Hildebrand or Savonarola or Fenélon or Luther or Lovejoy or Beecher? They belong to the church catholic—the communion universal.

I have the pleasure, sirs, to night to respond to a name that belongs to the "parliament of nations, the federation of the world." We delight to honor the heroes of our history. Whether they won their laurels in the pulpit righting the wrongs, lightening the yoke, and brightening the skies of earth by the proclamation of eternal truth, within legislative halls enacting wise and beneficial laws for the government of citizens, or in the temple of justice defending the liberty of individuals or communities, or in the Courts of foreign powers demanding recognition as an independent nation, or in the laboratory of science solving the mysteries and translating the hidden language of nature, or on the battlefield to the sound of martial melody vanquishing with swords and bullets the country's foes, their deeds are immortal and their lives become atoms in the slowly rising but imperishable monument of a land redeemed and happy.

Benjamin Franklin is such a man. So long as Columbia has a place among the nations of the earth, so long as philosophy has a temple among men, to use another's words: "So long as human tongues anywhere plead, or human hearts anywhere pant for liberty, those tongues shall prolong and those hearts enshrine the memory of Franklin." In the darkest days of our colonial history, when the twilight shadows lingered along our seacoast, and across our mountains and our valleys, so that our fathers' prayers swung like a pendulum between alternate hope and fear, hopes that the twilight was the gray mist of the sunrise, fear lest the shadows were those of the evening sunset, here was a man who dared predict, yea, confidently foretold at home and in the palaces of kings across the sea, that the twilight was the breaking of the day, the dawning of the morning. And when the morning came, and for the first time in the ages the eyes of men saw the light, and the ears of men were banqueted with the songs of unfettered freedom, there was not one who could more justly claim a share in the victory than he whose name I present to night.

Sir, I yield to no man in my appreciation of the worth of the character of Washington, "triumphant on the field, illustrious in council and dignified in the chair of state," but I would remind you that he was born of parents well-to-do and able to afford their son the benefits of education and good companionship. Here is a man whose parentage was humble and obscure. Cradled in poverty, battling with starvation, walking the streets of Philadelphia on a cold October day, his only roof the sky above him, his only raiment what he carried with him, his only food a dinner of dry bread, his only wealth a Dutch dollar and a shilling's worth of coppers, his only friends a good constitution and a healthy conscience. Yet step by step he trod with lion heart the path of penury. Stage by stage he mounted up until he took his place among the kings of history—kings uncrowned and stainless, but kings as true as ever wielded sceptre over submissive millions. A king by virtue, not of earth, but of worth; not of what he wore upon his head nor over his breast, but by virtue of what was within his head and under his breast. In this brief time cannot be told his efforts in establishing the postoffice system, of which he was for years the chief; his influence in establishing the public press, which presaged the popular education of the masses; his value as the author of precepts calculated to develop and foster honesty, industry and economy; his views in natural philosophy, in which he reached up into the cloud-land and brought down the lightning and tamed it for our future use in correspondence, locomotion and illumination; his labors as a liberal and refined humanitarian, and leader and president of laudable and well organized societies designed to alleviate the miseries of public prisons and to promote the abolition of negro slavery; his practical philanthropy, which is continued until this day in well directed channels by which worthy young laboring men in Boston who need financial aid are assisted; his power in constitutional conventions, giving greater energy to the government of the Union by revising and amending the articles of confederation; his skillful diplomacy at the Court of France by which that nation reinforced our arms and recognized us as an independent government; his influence at the English Court by the aid of which at length even that reluctant king acknowledged our governmental sovereignty; his long career without reproach or stain as an example and incentive to the aspiring youth in after years; the nobility of his character in which he added to the lofty endowments of the mind the kinder affections.

There is only time to remember these without dilating upon them, but I will say that among all the Revolutionary heroes whose genius has defended and whose lives have adorned that period of our nation's history, you cannot point to one whose intellect was brighter, whose patriotism was purer, whose acts were more potential than those of him to whose memory I pay this tribute of respect. He was a scholar without being a pedant, a specialist without being a hobbyist, a statesman without being an office-seeker, a patriot without being a politician. A many-sided man, a man whose character was like the city which the angel measured with a golden rod, its length and breadth and height equal. Grateful to his God, for he was not an infidel, faithful to his country, and fraternal to his fellow-man he lived, and at the age of eighty-four, in the land he loved so well, he fell to sleep. "Peace to his ashes; green grow the grass above his grave." A beautiful epitaph is his:

" The Body
of
Benjamin Franklin,
Printer,
Like the Cover of an Old Book,
Its Contents Torn,
Stripped of Its Leaves and Guilding, Lies Here the Food for Worms. Yet the Work Itself Shall Not Be Lost, for It Will (as he believed) Appear Once More in a New and More Beautiful Edition Connected and Amended
by
The Author."

I propose, sir, as a toast, the immortal memory of Poor Richard.

"ALEXANDER HAMILTON."

BY THE HON. J. S. RUNNELLS.

The Hon. J. S. Runnells was heartily cheered for his response to the toast "Alexander Hamilton." He said:

It is not alone because a President was inaugurated a hundred years ago that this day is memorable. It is not alone because a century has passed since Washington took the oath of office that the hands of labor are at rest and the streets are filled with music. If there were no other significance to the day than the beginning of an administration—even that of the Father of his Country—we could fill the measure of its importance with much less of emotion, much less of gratitude, than inspires our hearts to-day.

It is a memorable day because it marks the commencement of the operation of constitutional government in this country. It is a fitting time, surrounded as we are by the blessings that government has conferred, to recall with reverent gratitude the services of its founders. We have not, like the Hebrews of old, the feasts of commemoration upon which they recalled the mighty deeds of their fathers in the conquest of the Promised land. We have not, like the pious Mohammedans, the annual pilgrimages to the holy city in commemoration of the triumphs of the prophet. We have not, like the Romans, the feast days or the mythology in which to deify the great who by valor or by wisdom have deserved well of the republic. Our festivals are the days when our hearts are led back by some recurring anniversary to the times when independence was won, when liberty protected by law was established, or when the Union was preserved. Our national temple is filled with the presence of those who at Bunker Hill and Yorktown, in Congress and convention, by sword and by debate, wrought out for us and those who are to come after us a form of government which has been fittingly described as the "embodied wisdom of ages."

In this great work Alexander Hamilton bore a most prominent part. Save of Washington alone, I think it may be said of him as it could be said of none other of the great galaxy of statesmen of his period, that he was indispensable to the work. I know of no other man's part in that work for whom Providence had not provided some possible substitute who could have performed it. I know of no other man who could have performed the work that was done by Hamilton. In that mighty exigency his mission was as personal and peculiar as was that of Peter the Hermit, who avowed he was ordered of heaven to awake a slumbering world from infidelity. In his boyhood he roused a public meeting to patriotic fervor where men of mature years had failed. At a time when college youths are struggling with their Homer he was stirring the community with essays upon the science of government. At an age when young men are usually receiving the honors of graduation, he was the trusted aid of the great commander and conducting desperate enterprises. At a time when men are usually trying their first case at the bar, or just embarking upon business life, he had led the forces upon the redoubt at Yorktown and written the farewell address. At an age when men are just laying the foundations of their success he was Secretary of the Treasury, had founded the financial policy of the country, established the public credit, created a party which under various names has survived a hundred years, and established the prosperity of his country upon firm foundations.

I look in vain for a parallel to his career. I know that history is replete with examples of men like Alexander, like Hannibal, like Charles XII., who achieved fame in their youth. I recall the history of William Pitt, who was Prime Minister at twenty-four, and

died of a broken heart at forty-seven upon hearing of Austerlitz;
but I know of no one in the whole range of history who at a similar age could compare with him in the variety of his powers and
the extent of his achievements. He lived in a generation of master
minds. Washington, Jefferson, Adams and Jay were his compeers
at home. Pitt and Fox and Burke and Grattan were his contemporaries in England. Mirabeau and Napoleon and Carnot and
Talleyrand were making the history of France. Hardenbergh and
Stein and William von Humboldt were the leaders of thought in
Germany. It was an age of genius, of great deeds, of master
minds. Yet Talleyrand—whose heart never clouded his judgment
—said, after reviewing all the famous men of his time, that Napoleon and Charles James Fox were Hamilton's only intellectual
equals.

The Constitution of the United States is his monument.
Whatever he claimed for the other great minds who assisted in
its formation, whatever he conceded to those who labored for
its adoption, to him belongs the greatest praise, both for its
conception and its establishment as the organic law. It was his
hand that laid its foundation deep in the soil of order and
strength, and it was his understanding that, conceding much
of his preference to accomplish the purpose of National unity,
reared its shapely architecture; it was his powerful reasoning
in the *Federalist* and his eloquent utterances in convention
that crowned the stately edifice with the approval of the people.
Said Guizot: "There is not in the Constitution of the United
States an element of order, of force, or of duration which
Hamilton has not powerfully contributed to introduce into it
and to give it predominance."

The task presented to Hamilton might well have appalled
him. A meaner soul would have sought refuge from the difficulty in the delights of home and profession. A lesser mind
would have laid it down in despair. But conscious of a power
which a great Frenchman said enabled him to "divine things,"
and instinct with a purpose as clear to him as the face of the
Madonna was to Raphael, he proceeded to establish the finances
of his country upon immutable principles. Webster's words
were not mere panegyric when he said: "He smote the rock
of natural resources and abundant streams of revenue gushed
forth; he touched the dead corpse of the public credit and it
sprung upon its feet." He came to a treasury with neither money
nor credit; he provided the one and established the other. He
found the Government without means for its own sustenance;

he devised a sound system of national revenue. He found it without a currency; he established a mint, provided a coinage, and founded a national bank.

Pause for a moment to consider the magnitude of the work he accomplished.

The problem of the government in 1789 was one of ways and means. The surrender at Yorktown had left the colonies in complete exhaustion. The Confederation had not restored their strength, while it had shocked to the verge of paralysis the confidence upon which prosperity depended. The victorious colonists, triumphant over the mother country, were impatient of restraint and reluctant to assume Federal burdens. The lesson of the surrender of local power was one hard to be learned. Dreams of Athenian democracy were everywhere rife. The catch-words of liberty, equality, fraternity, were wafted from over the seas. The talk of the Paris clubs was reëchoed upon the hillsides of New Hampshire and upon the plantations of the Carolinas. Jealousy of the rights of states, so fruitful of later disaster, thus early stood by the cradle of the nation. The individual ambitions of smaller men, which had been gratified by prominence in the states and colonies, would now be checked or denied by the establishment of the central power. The leaders of the smaller communities would appear with diminished perspective upon the larger arena of national life.

Brougham says it was the boast of Augustus that he found Rome of brick and left it of marble. What might have been the boast of Hamilton? He could have said that he found his adopted country had achieved her independence only to be discordant, impoverished and threatened with dismemberment; he could have said that for more than a decade, with voice, with pen, with unceasing labor, with all the strength and all the garnered treasures of his matchless intellect he strove, to use his own words, "to justify and preserve the confidence of the friends of good government; to promote the respectability of the American name; to answer the calls of justice; to restore landed property to its due value; to furnish new resources to agriculture and commerce; to cement more closely the union of the states; to establish order upon the basis of an upright and liberal policy;" and, finally, he could have said that his great object was accomplished, and that he had so stamped his purposes upon the policy of the nation as to unite order with liberty, thus creating that "union of felicities" which makes states immortal. He could have said that he had forced upon a hesitating, reluctant people that interpretation of the Constitution by which he could foresee, in the language of Carlyle, "an immeasurable future filled with fruitfulness and a vernal shade."

"Whoso can speak well," said Martin Luther, "is a man." Hamilton's oratory placed him among the foremost of men. "Two-thirds of the convention are against me," he wrote of the New York Convention elected to determine the momentous question of the adoption or rejection of the Constitution. With the same courage with which he led the attack upon the redoubt at Yorktown he plunged into the unequal conflict. Day after day, rejoicing like a strong man to run a race, he plied the majority with argument from his well equipped storehouse. Assaulting, defending, thrusting, parrying, now appealing to the fears of his adversaries with pictures of the perils of anarchy—now regaling them with bright visions of the results of stable government—appealing to history—citing precedent—meeting invective with reason and abuse with courtesy, he at last heard the leader of the opposition confess that he had been converted by Hamilton's arguments. The vote was taken, New York was enrolled among the adopting states, and the great fight for the Constitution was over.

When some future Plutarch shall weigh the great men of that epoch he will give to Washington alone the palm of superiority over him. He will make John Adams his only possible rival as an orator, but even him he will place upon a lower plane. He will go across the seas to find in Burke alone the sharer of his sceptre. He will say that Hamilton was greater than Burke because he was lawyer and soldier as well as orator and statesman. He will say he was greater than Pitt because it is worthier to create a government than to administer it. He will say he was larger than Adams or Jefferson, great as they were, because his victories were not, like theirs, limited to the fields of statesmanship. Jefferson called him the Colossus of the Federalists. Ambrose Spencer, the distinguished jurist and a political adversary, said he "was the greatest man this country ever produced." Chancellor Kent said he "rose to the loftiest heights of professional eminence," and applied to him the praise of Papinian, that he left all others far behind. John Marshall placed him next in merit to the Father of his Country. Another contemporary declared, voicing the admiration of many of the time, that "he more than any man did the thinking of the time."

A hundred years hence others may meet as we meet to-night to celebrate this anniversary. The great names which command our reverent homage will not be dimmed by another century of national life. The Revolution, the Constitution, the Union will be watchwords no less inspiring then than now. Lexington and Bunker Hill, Saratoga and Yorktown will have the power to thrill them as now. Washington, Jefferson, Lincoln, Grant will be as fondly remembered upon that occasion as on this. In the memories of that hour I believe no name will be recalled with more grateful pride, more fervent admiration, more reverent praise than that of the mighty genius whose light was quenched, all too soon in the fatal glade of Weehawken. The coming years will only make brighter the fame and higher the appreciation of the lawyer, soldier, orator, statesman, patriot—Alexander Hamilton.

"ABRAHAM LINCOLN."

BY THE HON. JOHN M. LANGSTON.

By a very happy choice the toast on "Abraham Lincoln," the freer of the black man from bondage, was responded to by the famous colored orator, the Hon. John M. Langston. He said:

Our country has produced at least three great men. Each is himself. Each bears his distinct individuality, as each seems, under providence, to have been appointed to a special national mission. One shall ever be regarded as the Father of the Country. He gave us national independence, sovereignty, and position among the great powers of the earth. The other met with tongue and pen and deeds—manly and heroic deeds—and alas! his sacred life, the false, vulgar, treacherous public sentiment favorable to slavery, its spread under the guise of squatter sovereignty and the slave oligarchy—the full power which to accomplish its selfish ends would even disrupt the Union and destroy the government.

Lincoln shall ever be accounted our national emancipator; and prouder title no man shall ever know.

He who wielded the great sword of freedom, who commanded the marshaled loyal hosts gathered to battle for, save and perpetuate the Union, the government and our free institutions, shall ever bear the brilliant, deathless name of our national savior. This shall be in all the ages the illustrious designation of Grant.

As to the greatness of George Washington, Abraham Lincoln and Ulysses S. Grant, there can be no question now anywhere in the world. As to which was the greatest in power, heroism and deeds, there can be no need of debate; for each met in his life and

labors the full measure of his duty, and answered every requirement imposed by the severest exigency of his situation. These
men severally represented the immensity, the power and beauty of
individual character as developed and illustrated under American
institutions and influences, and as connected with high official
responsibility and duty. The biographical annals of the past—
those of no other country can furnish, all things considered, three
such names as these. The grandeur and immortality of their
respective achievements in behalf of our republic and popular liberty and equal rights, render their names as famous and as enduring as their achievements. Let these names—those of the trio of
good Americans—stand forever associated in the minds and affections, the admiration and love, of our great nation, whose power
and influence because of their lives and deeds shall reach for good
yet in some sacred and advantageous manner all the people of the
world, even those who dwell in the uttermost parts.

The name of Washington, in its associations with the triumphs
and glories of our independence and the inauguration of the
national government; the name of Lincoln, in its associations with
the victories of law and liberty in the overthrow of the late Rebellion; and the name of Grant as connected with the conduct, the
struggle, and the achievements of the Army of the Republic as
directed against those who sought the severance of the Union;
should be no less dear to us than those moral and material blessings,
precious and priceless, for which they stand.

"First in war; first in peace; first in the hearts of his countrymen"—these words declare the place accorded in popular estima-
tion to the Father of our Country. Standing around the solemn,
sacred scenes of Gettysburg the emancipator of our country.
November, 1863, employed these matchless words, which fixed forever his place in history and the affection of the people. He said:

"But in a larger sense we cannot dedicate, we cannot consecrate,
we cannot hallow, this ground. The brave men, living and dead,
who struggled here have consecrated it far above our power to add
or detract. 'The world will little note nor long remember what
we say here, but it can never forget what they did here.' It is for us,
the living, rather to be dedicated to the great task remaining before
us—that from these honored dead we take increased devotion to
the cause for which they here gave the last full measure of devotion; that we here highly resolve that the dead shall not have died
in vain; that the nation shall under God have a new birth of freedom; and that the government of the people, by the people, and
for the people, shall not perish from the earth."

And while imagination shall last, while memory shall retain for man a lively and accurate knowledge of man's noblest deeds for the state and the people, and while the human mind shall serve to estimate and value in just and cordial appreciation such deeds, the heroism and courage, the brave and magnanimous conduct, the grand and magnificent achievements of Grant in military and civil life, will compel mankind to give him conspicuous, equal place with these other great men, as the one to whom the sword of the Confederacy was surrendered by Lee, and whose title of Savior of the Republic was justly won.

In the midst of the hallowed memories of this occasion Illinois will be pardoned should her heart swell with pride at mention of the names, with allusion however slight to the deeds of her noble sons, Lincoln and Grant. They were the sons of this great commonwealth. They are now the children of the nation. The old mother of Presidents, as Virginia was called once, can no longer claim Washington as hers. Content to keep and guard well the ashes of this great son of the nation, she unites in the general common applause this day offered by all the grateful children of the republic to his wise and patriotic life, which grows brighter and more luminous as the years of the republic multiply. So, too, history has placed in her highest and most honorable niches, as the sacred heritage of the nation to the latest day, the characters of Lincoln and Grant.

Forever shall the beautiful classic Potomac, upon whose banks slumber his remains, in the music of its gentle, joyous waves, chant the immortal praises of Washington. The breathing winds, musical in every tone, of the boundless prairie land in whose bosom his tomb is held consecrated in peace and glory, shall hymn forever the undying honor and applause of Lincoln; while the dashing billows of the Atlantic, near whose waters in the proud metropolis of our nation the people of all lands pay their constant delighted respects at the grave of Grant, shall perpetuate in everlasting strains of lofty exaltation the excellence and glory of his name. But the music of the river, the song of the prairie winds, the refrain of the ocean—God's own voice in sweetest, matchless harmony—shall be but accompaniment and support of nature in the living psalm poured out forever from the great swelling heart of the people in commendation and gratitude of their noble sons whose resplendent names shall shine to all the ages as veritable suns in the skies of our national life.

"ULYSSES S. GRANT."

BY THE HON. JOHN M. THURSTON.

The last toast of the evening was " Ulysses S. Grant." It was responded to by the Hon. John M. Thurston of Nebraska, who spoke as follows:

At the shrine of the nation's hero, Ulysses S. Grant, I bow an humble worshiper.

No eloquence of human tongue can add to the perfect measure of his greatness.

Yet, as an American citizen, I am glad of an opportunity to voice my reverent appreciation of his character as a man, his matchless achievements as a soldier, and his fidelity, patriotism and statesmanship as chief executive of the United States.

" He was great in council and great in war,
  Foremost captain of his time;
 Rich in saving common sense, and, as the greatest only are,
  In his simplicity sublime."

Grant came from good old Puritan stock. That strength of purpose which in him amounted almost to stubbornness was inherited from generations of Pilgrims, patriots and pioneers. His early years were passed in a community where man, woman and child were expected to share in the universal habits of industry and frugality. He accepted his daily task as a matter of course. He entered upon its performance with the same cheerful zeal and silent determination to succeed which so signally characterized him in those later days of mighty responsibilities and herculean undertakings. By birth and education he was of the people. He was taught to believe in the equality of men. His plain, simple, unconcerned demeanor in all the future time of power and glory was a continual protest against the slavish distinction of wealth and place. One of the most essential elements of his greatness and success was his thorough democracy of character. Every soldier of the army he led knew that the great commander held them all as men and brothers jointly engaged in the same great cause of preservation of their common country. This knowledge and belief hushed the voice of rivalry and envy and animated the whole Grand Army of the Republic with the irresistible vigor of an united purpose. In the presence of Grant the humblest citizen knew that he was held as an equal, and kings and princes felt themselves to be no more. Grant, although educated at West Point, had no love for a military life. His services with the army during the Mexican

War were valorous and honorable, but he could not endure the life of a soldier in time of peace. Nothing but the guns of a Sumter could have aroused him from the simple life of a humble citizen. The guns of Sumter—how they thundered through the land! Their echo awoke the loyal people of the North from their dreams of security and peace—awoke them to find that while the nation slept they of the South had stolen our forts, had stolen our arms, had stolen our arsenals, had stolen our munitions of war, had stolen from our beautiful flag one-third of its bright galaxy of stars and set them in a banner of their own. But the North once awakened, slept no more. Our boys in blue sprang to arms, retook the forts, retook the arsenals, retook the arms, retook the munitions of war, reset the stars in the azure of the flag, whence never again shall an enemy's hand dare pluck them out. Grant once more took up the sword at the command of country, but he never wielded it to advance his own ambition—only to protect our glory. He had none of the dash and fire of the ideal soldier. He had rather calm resolution, deliberate purpose and uncompromising tenacity. As a soldier, he accepted whatever duty was assigned to him, encountered whatever danger beset him. Always ready and anxious to fight, he never waited for a more favorable opportunity or delayed an attempt to accomplish present possibilities. His theory of war was to strike the enemy often and hard; to follow every victory with immediate pursuit; and never to give a defeated foe time to rally his forces or recover lost ground. His indomitable energy and courage communicated themselves to every soldier in his army and compelled victories where weaker men would have submitted to defeat. The simplicity of his greatness, both as a soldier and a patriot, is shown in his acceptance at the hands of President Lincoln of the commission of Lieutenant General of the armies of the United States. In assuming the exalted rank and tremendous responsibilities, he said: "Mr. President, I accept the commission with gratitude for the high honor conferred. With the aid of the noble armies that have fought in so many fields for our common country, it will be my earnest endeavor not to disappoint your expectations. I feel the full weight of the responsibilities now devolving on me, and I know if they are met it will be due to those armies, and, above all, to the favor of that Providence which leads both nations and men." Why spend time to trace the history of his successful victories? Donelson, Shiloh, Vicksburg, Chattanooga are monuments of his undying fame. Against the unbroken front of his splendid army the Confederate Government beat out its life. Lee surrendered, the Union was safe; the measure of Grant's fame was full. In the exaltation of final conquest his loyal, tender, generous heart went out in sympathy and sorrow to the prostrate foe. His terms of surrender to the heroic Lee were worthy of the greatness of the man. As he had subdued the hosts of the Confederacy by merciless war, he won their undying affection by his merciful love. What a splendid triumph to the great General when, the 23d and 24th of May, 1865, the war-worn, battle-scarred veterans marched in grand review through the streets of the capital of the nation their heroism had saved! The nation, saddened by the murder of our Lincoln, received them with profound, if solemn, joy. A million heroes wearing the laurels of countless victories were welcomed back, and received the priceless recompense of a people's blessing. In the supreme exultation of the hour, that other army of heroic dead holding their eternal bivouac where they fell, sleeping in unknown graves, were not forgotten in the welcome of their surviving comrades. There were cheers for the living, tears for the dead. Grant was the central figure of the war—the one great leader whose military genius and success dwarfs the mighty accomplishments of all others into complete insignificance. He never lost a battle or found it necessary to take a backward step. His final plans, executed by true and devoted subordinates who found their greatest honor in serving under him, drew the iron coils of the Union army closer and closer around the Confederate hosts and crushed them into unconditional surrender. He commanded the greatest army ever assembled on earth since the invention of firearms. In four years of unceasing battle this army participated in more than two thousand actual engagements. It subsisted all this time in the open field on a continual advance over the fortified territory of a brave, powerful and successful enemy. It was compelled to accept for its battle-fields those places selected by the foe and carefully prepared to resist attack. Added to this, it kept up an almost unbroken line of battle more than fifteen hundred miles in length, and a spectacle of war is presented of so great and wonderful a kind that it stands by itself without a parallel in history or tradition. The military fame of the hero whose undimmed skill and courage led this wonderful army by a series of unbroken victories to final triumph, is beyond the reach of criticism or the assault of envy.

But Grant's services to his country did not end at Appomattox. For eight years, as chief executive, he served his people faithfully and well. In that exalted position he remained the same unassuming, honest and loyal man. His administration was firm, just, wise and patriotic. During its continuation this nation greatly advanced its power abroad and its prosperity at home. Under it the rights and privileges of American citizens were respected and enforced. While he did not escape the passing shafts of political calumny, the deliberate judgment of the universal public opinion has left his fame untarnished.

The last year of his life was inexpressibly sad. At the time he knew himself to be filled with incurable disease, his whole property was swept away by the dishonesty of a trusted friend and he went down to his grave a poor man. But never did the grandeur of his courage shine out so clearly as in the presence of misfortune and expected death. The spectacle of that silent man on Mount McGregor, holding death at bay while he finished the memoirs whose sale was to preserve a home to his family, is the most wonderful ever presented for the admiration of the human race. His great work done, meekly and resignedly he awaited the end, reverently prepared to meet that Father whose overruling guidance and providence he had always believed in and enjoyed. May 8, 1885, God's angel spake to him the same sweet words he had spoken to the Union: "Let us have peace."

"Unbended courage and compassion joined,
Tempering each other in the victor's mind:
Alternately proclaimed him good and great."

When his great funeral cortege passed through the streets of the metropolis of the nation, following it with solemn step and sorrowing heart came Federal and Confederate side by side; and of the sincerest mourners at the bier of the great were the officers and soldiers of that heroic army his military genius had subdued.

He died as he lived, in the simplicity of his faith. The greatest citizen and soldier of the earth, beloved by friend and foe alike, who vie with each other in testifying to the high honor in which they held him living and the sincerity of their grief that he is dead.

His deeds speak for him better than can tongue or pen; the glory of his name will never die, and "I was with Grant" will be an open sesame to American hearts and homes so long as a single survivor of the Grand Army of the Republic blesses the earth.

Men and governments pass away, but the glory of valorous deeds lives on forever. Rome, that sat on her seven hills and from her throne of beauty ruled the world, has crumbled into ruin and decay. Her fleets, her conquering legions, her temples, palaces and triumphal arches, sleep almost forgotten in the dust of the ages; her power is gone, her nationality vanished, her language dead and unspoken of mankind; but the name of her Cæsar is as great to-day as when Rome was at the zenith of her power, when her fleets sailed into every sea, and her triumphant legions sought in vain new fields for conquest.

Napoleon, whose military genius dominated all Europe, who created for himself and family the greatest Empire of modern times, whose name made and unmade thrones and kings, whose victorious legions bore the eagles of France in triumph from Madrid to Moscow, died in enforced exile on a lonely island of the ocean. His Empire is obliterated from the map of nations; the sceptre of power has been wrested from the Napoleonic race. The last Empress of France, robbed of her country, her crown, and her king, lives on, deserted and desolate, in the land of the ancient enemies of her name. But the glorious achievements of the Little Corporal, side by side with those of imperial Cæsar, will fire the hearts of the youth of every land to deeds of valor in generations yet to come.

It has been said that as Cæsar was to Rome and Napoleon to France, so was Grant to the United States. He was this, but he was more; for Cæsar at the height of his military power turned his victorious legions against the liberty of his country. Napoleon dominated all Europe that he might place on his imperious brow the crown of despotic power. Grant won his battles for liberty, humanity and country; won them that an enslaved race might be free; won them that forever and forever, from the Atlantic to the Pacific, there should be an imperishable Union of states sacred to the brotherhood of man.

And Grant will live in the hearts of the people whose battles he won so long as the cause of liberty is dear to human hearts.

> "Then, soldier, rest, thy warfare o'er,
>   Dream of fighting fields no more;
>   Sleep the sleep that knoweth not breaking,
>   Morn of toil nor night of waking."

Yes, rest in peace, O mighty dead, rest in peace! the cause for which you fought can never be assailed again.

Sleep in peace, the race whose freedom you achieved will bless you to the end of time. Rest in peace, the Union you preserved remains forever, and liberty, equal rights and justice is the heritage of your descendants until the Judgment Day. Ulysses S. Grant is "one of the few immortal names that were not born to die."

VI

THE PYROTECHNICAL DISPLAY

THE PYROTECHNICAL DISPLAY

A notable feature of the celebration was the exhibition of fire-works in the evening on the Lake Front, at Lincoln Park and in the grounds of the West Side Driving Park Association.

The three displays were exactly alike and of simultaneous occurrence. Long before the darkness made it possible to open proceedings immense crowds began to gather at each of the appointed places. At the Driving Park there were at least one hundred thousand people, while the throng at Lincoln Park was even larger. The size of the crowd that jammed together on the lake front can only be approximately estimated. There were probably two hundred thousand people in the space between Michigan avenue and the lake, but these were only a part of the throng which filled Michigan avenue as far as the eye could see and extended its ramifications into all the intersecting streets for blocks. In view of the size of the crowd and the comparatively small space into which it was squeezed, it is remarkable that there were not more serious mishaps than there were. The one regrettable incident in the day's proceedings—the accidental crushing of a number of people during the Lake Front display—was trifling when the opportunities which the occasion afforded for similar disasters are considered.

The pyrotechnics were magnificent—probably no finer have ever been seen in America. Every known device of the pyrotechnist's art; every ingenious expedient of American or Japanese workers in powder and flame was used. Roman candles and sky-rockets in endless variety and profusion bombarded the heavens from 7:30 to nearly 11 o'clock. The set pieces were works of art—veritable paintings in flame. One of the best of them was a representation of the Capitol at Washington.   As the fac-simile of the nation's great law-factory came into view, with its dome a scintillating ball of white flame and its noble porticoes stretching away in splendors of polished marble, the huge audi- ence drew a deep, unconscious sigh of satisfaction and broke into spontaneous applause.

Another remarkable piece was simply the word "America" cut like an intaglio of flame out of the black sky.   The word sprang lurid from its dusky background, grew to a glistening white, dulled to orange, to deep red, leapt up in a last sapphire flame— and was gone.

Dozens of other pieces, wonderful in their art and in their beauty, were displayed.   Rockets swished into space on trails of fire and, bursting, let fall showers of golden rain.   Roman candles threw out starry constellations and golden misty nebulæ.   Pict- ures of Jefferson, of the White House, of the national flag and of the administering of the first presidential oath were given. Other rockets swung upward on their serpentine path and broke, emitting little clouds of white smoke, which formed themselves high in air into cameo busts of Washington, Jefferson and Adams. A bust of Martha Washington was succeeded by outbursts of cheers and another flight of rockets.   An American flag, lambent and glowing, loomed up before the multitude, to be followed by another burst of cheers and another rush of sky-rockets.

A bust of Washington, a magic piece of sculpture in pure white flame, appeared.   For several minutes it glowed undimmed, while the crowd shouted its cheers.   Then it paled and passed away as 1,000 rockets, all at once and all sputtering and swishing, tore up the violet sky, glimmered, glittered, burst—succumbed to the darkness.

VII

THE LOAN EXHIBITION

THE LOAN EXHIBITION

The Loan Exhibition, held in the Art Rooms of the Exposition Building, was one of the most interesting features of the Centennial celebration. It consisted of a collection of thousands of relics from the Revolutionary period, autograph letters, rare historical documents, portraits, firearms, newspapers, books, currency, garments of civil and military fashion, household utensils, etc.

In many cases the contributors were the descendants of the fathers of our country. Large contributions were also made by public-spirited collectors, and the exhibit was remarkable, both for its extent and for its highly historical character and worth.

The exhibition, which continued several days, was largely attended. Only a small selection from the many thousands of interesting items can be mentioned in the following catalogue:

1. Oil portrait of George Washington, by Gilbert Stuart. Loaned by Judge Tuley.

2. Oil painting of Washington, by Daniel McLeod, a young artist of Virginia, in whom Washington took great interest. Loaned by Mrs. Peter Daggy.

3. Oil portrait of Washington, by Stuart. Loaned by Mr. Eastman.

4. Tapestry portrait of Washington, made and loaned by Mrs. M. Malone.

5. Oil portrait of President Benjamin Harrison, by W. C. Knoeke of Chicago. Property of Mr. J. M. Huston, United States Treasurer.

6. Lyre, owned by George Washington. Presented to his niece, by Mrs. Jane Washington, by her to Mrs. John O. Wright of Chicago. Loaned by Mr. Chester B. Wright.

7. Oil portrait of Washington. Copy of Jo Trumbull's celebrated equestrian picture. Loaned by the Union League Club.

8. Oil portrait of Washington by Stuart. Loaned by Mr. C. F. Gunther.

9. Gen. Green's wedding vest. Loaned by Mrs. H. S. Peck.

10. Mrs. Gen. Green's wedding dress. Loaned by Mrs. H. S. Peck.

11. A silver porringer, made by Paul Revere. Loaned by Mr. Joseph Ward.

12. Brace of beautifully ornamented pistols, presented by Washington to Gen. Ward. Loaned by Mr. Joseph Ward.

13. Sword presented by the President of the United States to Ensign Joseph Duncan for services in the War of 1812, voted for the defense of Saunders, Ky. Loaned by Mr. Joseph Duncan.

14. Chair once used by George Washington. Loaned by Mr McCulloch.

15. Columbian album, 1816. Loaned by Mr. C. B. Wright.

16. Sword of Gen. George Reid, who commanded the New Hampshire troops at Bunker Hill. Loaned by Mr. Edgerton Adams.

17. Copper ale tankard, 176 years old. Loaned by Mr. George S. Knox.

18. Medallion of George Washington, made in Paris. Loaned by Mr. S. P. Bradley.

19. Mrs. Gen. Green's watch and silk muff. Loaned by Mrs. H. S. Peck.

20. Six tea spoons used by Washington. Loaned by Miss Angelina Wann.

21. Two silver chafing dishes, presented by Martha Washington to John S. Wright. Loaned by Mr. C. D. Wright.

22. Four dollar continental bill, paid to Stephen Walker for his service in the Revolutionary War. Loaned by Mr. John Kile.

23. Set of linen staves worn by Mrs. Capt. Henny, 1757. Loaned by Mrs. S. A. Cary.

24. A piece of satin sash worn at the Inauguration of Washington. Loaned by Mr. A. H. Stringe.

25. A badge in yellow ribbon, with Washington medallion, worn at the Inauguration of Washington. Loaned by Mr. A. H. Stringe.

26. Pistol, 1760. Loaned by Dr. C. W. Evans.

27. Snuff box, 1760. Loaned by Dr. C. W. Evans.

28. Razor, 1760. Loaned by Dr. C. W. Evans.

29. Five almanacs, 1797 to 1807. Loaned by Mr. James M. Grey.

30. Powder horn made by Indians in western New York. Loaned by Mr. W. A. Stahl.

31. Postoffice order, dated April 8, 1799. Loaned by Mr. B. A. Brenan.

32. Blunderbuses taken from the boat from which the tea was thrown overboard in Boston Harbor. Loaned by Mr. George S. Knapp.

33. Indian war club. Loaned by Mr. B. A. Brenan.

34. Powder horn used by J. I. Elliot in 1783. Loaned by Mr. P. A. Lovell.

35. Washington's account book. (F. S.) Loaned by Mrs. M. A. Patterson.

36. A painting formerly the property of Benedict Arnold. Loaned by Mrs. James Kent Pumpelly.

37. A towel woven by Mary Dalton Morris. Used by Gen. Washington on a visit to Lewis Morris on the return from his journey of inspection to Otsego Lake.

38. Silver bowl. This bowl was used at a breakfast at which the Marquis de Lafayette, Lewis Morris, Gov. Morris and Judge William Cooper, the founder of Cooperstown, were present. Loaned by Mrs. James Kent Pumpelly.

39. Photograph of a Lieutenant's commission granted to Richard Pixley, dated May 19, 1875. Loaned by Mrs. James Kent Pumpelly.

40. Pink satin petticoat worn by Mary Dalton Morris, wife of Lewis Morris, one of the signers of the Declaration of Independence, at the first ball ever given in Harrisburg, Pa. Mrs. Morris opened the ball with Gen. Washington; they danced the Minuet together. The garment is now the property of Miss Mary Elizabeth Fenimore Cone, a little girl ten years of age, thus having descended to the fifth generation of Maries. Loaned by Mrs. James Kent Pumpelly.

41. A picture of two friends, 1759. Loaned by Mr. S. B. Williams.

42. A soldier's discharge of a member of the Sixth Massachusetts Regiment, signed by George Washington. Loaned by Mr. Lafland.

43. Life of Washington. Loaned by Mrs. Shehan.

44. Powder horn of 1767. Loaned by Mr. Evans.

45. Ulster County *Gazette*, containing an account of the funeral of Washington. Loaned by Mr. M. Laflin.

46. Lantern with horn windows, used by Washington's body-guard. Loaned by Mr. George S. Knapp.

47. Iron candle stick, 1741. Loaned by Mr. Gecrge S. Knapp.

48. Brass tea pot, 150 years old. Loaned by Mr. George S. Knapp.

49. Warming pan, 1741. Loaned by Mr. George S. Knapp.

50. Coffee pot, 150 years old. Loaned by Mr. George S. Knapp.

51. Plate formerly the property of Simeon Crandall. Loaned by Mr. George S. Knapp.

52. Razor of Simeon Crandall. Loaned by Mr. George S. Knapp.

53. A piece of the Charter Oak, Hartford, Conn. Loaned by Mr. J. A. Welch.

54. New York *Morning Post,* Nov. 7, 1783, containing Washington's farewell address. Loaned by Mrs. L. Murphy.

55. Sword used by Capt. Simeon Crandall at Bunker Hill. Loaned by Mr. George S. Knapp.

56. Powder horn made at Mt. Independent, Nov. 14, 1776. Loaned by Mr. F. Hathaway.

57. Silhoutte of Simeon Crandall. Loaned by Mr. George S. Knapp.

58. Snuff tray. Loaned by Mr. George S. Knapp.

59. Old sword used in the Revolution. Loaned by Mr. E. W. Case.

60. Photograph of house 150 years old. Loaned by Mr. E. W. Case.

61. Cullender bowl over one hundred and fifty years old. Loaned by Hannah L. Wescott.

62. Tinder box, 1784. Loaned by Mr. George L. Knapp.

63. Snuff box made from the wood of the tree under which Jennie McCrea was murdered, 1777. Loaned by Hannah L. Wescott.

64. A pin made from the wood of the Charter Oak. Loaned by Hannah L. Wescott.

65. Indian work-box over one hundred years old. Loaned by Mrs. R. W. Campion.

66. Earthen tea pot used by Mrs. Starkweather of New York City, at a tea given to Gen. Washington. Loaned by Mrs. R. W. Campion.

67. Sash worn by Gen. J. B. Warren in the War of 1812, also two British buttons. Loaned by Mrs. R. W. Campion.

68. Tablecloth, woven in 1780 by Elizabeth Mathews. Loaned by Mr. C. H. Bradford.

69. Ivory miniature of Capt. William Coit Williams. Painted by Elkannah Tisdall. Loaned by Mr. Simeon B. Williams.

70. Two samples made by Lydia Perkins. Loaned by Mr. Simeon B. Williams.

71. Sermon in "The Duties" of a conjugal state. Loaned by Mr. Simeon B. Williams.

72. One dollar Continental currency, 1775. Loaned by Mr. R. Smith.

73. Letter from a boy, thirteen years of age, giving a description of the bombardment of Stonington. Loaned by Mr. Simeon B. Williams.

74. Valentine, 1786, sent to Lydia Perkins. Loaned by Mr. Simeon B. Williams.

75. Commission of Justice of Peace, issued to Rufus Ritman, Esq., April 29, 1787, and the eleventh year of the independence of the United States of America. Loaned by Mr. J. H. Buckingham.

76. Biographical memoirs of Gen. Washington. Loaned by Mr. William Cowan.

77. Passport to Chester Atwater, signed by Timothy Pickering, April 24, 1800. Loaned by Mr. G. Graham.

78. Account book for 1692 to 1708. Loaned by Mr. H. H. Tebbets.

79. A letter written by Agar Thompson, a soldier of the Revolution, April 10, 1773. Loaned by Mr. G. Graham.

80. Powder-horn used by members of the Tebbets family at the battle on the Heights of Abraham and at Bunker Hill. Loaned by Mr. H. H. Tebbets.

81. *Ulster County Gazette,* Jan. 4, 1800. Loaned by Mr. W. J. Scott.

82. Pair of steelyards and weights, hand-made, 1786. Loaned by Mr. George S. Knapp.

83. Portrait of Gen. Lewis, from the original portrait by Peale. Loaned by Mrs. C. U. Wann.

84. Picture of a house built at Wattapoisett, Mass., by Lieut. John Hammond, about 1700. Loaned by Mr. N. A. Partridge.

85. Blunderbus used at Valley Forge. Loaned by Mr. Mark Mitchell.

86. Sword used in the War of 1812. Loaned by Mr. J. M. Adams.

87. Columbia *Mirror* and Alexandria *Gazette,* Saturday, Aug. 25, 1798. Loaned by Mr. C. W. Miller.

88. Lace cap worn by the great-grandmother of Silas Adams, about two hundred years old. Loaned by Mr. William C. Vaughn.

89. A part of a child's apron, came down through the Adams' family from 1720. Loaned by Mr. William C. Vaughn.

90. Letter from George Washington to Gen. George Reid, Commander at Albany. Loaned by Mr. J. McGregor Adams.

91. A portrait of Gen. George Washington, painted by a soldier at Valley Forge. Loaned by Mr. Richard Barlow.

92. A portrait of Martha Washington. Loaned by Mr. Richard Barlow.

93. A copy of the Albany *Gazette*, Friday, Jan. 13, 1797. Loaned by Col. M. Sweeny.

94. Two letters of Bushrod Washington, 1735, 1760. Loaned by Mr. C. W. Miller.

95. Seven pieces of old crockery over one hundred years old. Loaned by Mrs. H. L. Nescott.

96. Yale diploma granted to John Willard, Sept. 11, 1782. Loaned by Dr. Samuel Willard.

97. Copper cent, 1787. Loaned by Mr. H. R. Rook.

98. Washington medal, 1781. Loaned by Gen. Thomas Wilson.

99. Centennial button, 1775. Loaned by Mr. F. Hagden.

100. Ohiman razor, and a sermon dedicated to Gen. Washington, 1783. Loaned by Mrs. Sheehan.

101. Pistol presented to Gen. Burgoyne by William R. Briggs. Loaned by Mrs. M. H. Andrews.

102. Diary kept by Samuel Benjamin. Loaned by Mr. George S. Knapp.

103. Pair of scales used by Deacon Moses Fitch, grandfather of Deacon Moses Fitch of Union Park Congregational Church, Chicago. Loaned by Mr. C. H. Marchant.

104. A water-color painting of the mill on Chester Creek, N. Y., where the corn was ground for Washington's army when encamped at White Plains. Loaned by Lucy Durham.

105. A piece of shingle from White Plains mill. Loaned by Lucy Durham.

106. Boston *Gazette* (fac-simile), March 12, 1776. Loaned by Mr. Alexander McDonald.

107. A printed calico picture, 1776. Loaned by Mrs. D. Kuhn.

108. Two old chairs used in the Continental Congress. Loaned by Mrs. Niscott.

109. Looking glass over one hundred and fifty years old. Loaned by Mr. J. F. Hughson.

110. Ulster County *Gazette.* Loaned by Mr. B. Gubirt.

111. Geography of the United States, 1796. Loaned by Mr. Harry Manning.

112. Picture over one hundred years old, claimed as a lost art. Loaned by Hannah L. Wescott.

113. The American flag and Washington coat of arms. Loaned by Mr. Isaac H. Taylor.

114. Tobacco box made and used by Capt. Josiah Woodruff. Loaned by Mr. P. G. Monroe.

115. The sword and pistols of Gen. Amasa Davis of the Continental Army. Loaned by Mr. P. G. and S. K. Monroe.

116. Powder horn, 1777. Loaned by Mr. L. Pifer.

117. Portrait and dress sword of Gen. Roger Nelson. Loaned by Mrs. Harry Manning.

118. A badge of the centennial birthday of Gen. Washington. Loaned by Mr. Thomas H. Watts.

119. A copy of the Boston *Gazette*, March 12, 1770. Loaned by Mr. George S. Knapp.

120. Muff, formerly the property of the grandmother of Gen. H. W. Halleck. Loaned by Mr. Frank Brust.

121. Knife, fork and spoon, 175 years old. Loaned by Mr. Frank Brust.

122. Rolling-pin, formerly the property of the grandmother of Gen. H. W. Halleck. Loaned by Mr. Frank Brust.

123. Portrait of Maj. Jabez Halleck, grandfather of Gen. H. W. Halleck. Loaned by Mr. Frank Brust.

124. A Masonic dimit of Washington's lodge, 1794. Loaned by Mr. George S. Knapp.

125. A Washington penny, 1791. Loaned by Mr. J. H. Gray.

126. Two belt buckles and two knee buckles, came over on the Mayflower, 1620. Loaned by Mr. George S. Knapp.

127. Three pieces of Continental money, 1767, 1776, 1780. Loaned by Mr. George S. Knapp.

128. A certificate of a volunteer fireman, city of New York, 1787. Loaned by Mr. George S. Knapp.

AUTOGRAPH LETTERS, DOCUMENTS, ETC., LOANED BY MR. C. F. GUNTHER.

129. Letter of Gen. Washington to Charles Pettit, dated headquarters, 9th Sept., 1778.

130. Letter from Washington in regard to the Wyoming settlements.

131. A letter from Washington to Gov. Clinton, dated headquarters, White Plains, July 23, 1778.

132.   Original daily order book of Washington's army at the siege of Yorktown.

133.   A letter of Maj. Andre, Jan. 4, 1786.

134.   A survey of lands on the Ohio River by W. H. Crawford, surveyor, May, 1771, patented in the name of George Washington and endorsed by him.

135.   Drawing of the plan of the residence of Washington while at Philadelphia.   Made by himself.

136.   The Philadelphia *Gazette*, dated May 26, 1802, announcing the death of Martha Washington.

137.   Will of Daniel Park Grant, father of Daniel Park Custis, 1679.

138.   Original survey and plat of land of the Ohio and Great Kanawha Rivers, made by George Washington, Mount Vernon, Dec. 25, 1787.

139.   Original account book of Washington of his Ohio and Kanawha River land expenses.

140.   A proclamation of Gov. Dinwiddie, given in Williamsburg, Feb. 19, 1754.

141.   A rare portrait of Washington, engraved by Savage, 1783.

142.   A resolution of Congress, Aug. 4, 1789, signed by Washington, to George Walton.

143.   A letter from Valley Forge, April 12, 1778, by George Washington.

144.   A list of lands belonging to Washington in Virginia, and Ohio, in Washington's autograph.

145.   A survey or sketch of lands owned by Mr D. Litchs, made by Washington.

146.   List of lands belonging to Washington, west of the Allegheny Mountains and in the great Dismal Swamp in Virginia, May 25, 1794.   Written by Washington.

147.   Letter from Washington, June 1, 1793, in regard to sending an Agent to the Chicasaws and Choctaws.

148.   A letter written by Betty Lewis, sister of George Washington, May 18, 1790.

149.   Original will of Mr. John Custis.

150.   A receipt in the handwriting of Washington from the teacher of Miss Custis, John Stadler, for one year's music.

151.   Original will of Lawrence Washington, deeding his property to the Washington family, and the Fairfax estates to George Washington.

152. A leaf of Washington's account book, April, 1786. Washington's message to the Senate and House of Representatives, dated United States, December 13, 1791, in regard to letting out the Capitol at Washington.

153. The probated record of the will of George Washington, January, 1800. Signed by George Steptoe Washington, Samuel Washington, Lawrence Lewis and others.

154. A letter of Washington, 13th July, 1798, accepting appointment as Lieutenant-General, to take command in the then threatening war with the French.

155. A letter of Martha Washington, Mount Vernon, Sept. 6, 1786.

156. A book, "View of the Internal Evidence of Christian Religion," presented by Martha Washington to her daughter, with autograph of Martha Washington.

157. Virgil's Æneid, "presented by Martha Washington to her beloved daughter, Elenor Park Custis, 1794."

158. Old engraving of the surrender of Lord Cornwallis.

159. A sermon delivered Dec. 29, 1779, on the death of Washington, by Mr. Samuel Miller.

160. Fine collections of many hundreds of early engravings of scenes and portraits.

161. Original resolutions of Congress, on the death of John Quincy Adams, written on parchment.

162. Ancient French colonial musket, the "Long Tom," captured by Kendrick Martin at the siege of Louisville, 1745.

163. A very rare original engraving of the Washington family, by Savage, 1796.

164. A sixteenth century student lamp.

165. Desk used by Gen. Lafayette during the Revolution.

166. An order that a day of thanksgiving be set aside, in handwriting of John Hancock, Oct. 27, 1774.

167. A proclamation for a general fast, 1766.

168. Order of exercises of the commencement of Harvard University, July 18, 1798.

169. Oil portrait of Washington, by Polk and Charles Wilson Peale, 1779.

170. A proclamation by John Hancock for a day of fasting, humiliation and prayer, March 4, 1793.

171. Order of a procession in honor of the establishment of the Constitution of the United States. Printed by Hall & Sellers.

172. First copy of the Declaration of Independence owned by Thomas Jefferson.

173. Print of an attack of the rebels on Fort Penobscott, 1785.

174. "Washington." An old steel engraving, "Patrae Pater," proof; original painted by Rembrandt Peale.

175. Old flint-lock muskets.

176. Oil portrait of Lafayette, painted by Rembrandt Peale, on the patriot's second visit to America, 1724.

177. Spurs worn by Gen. Stark of the Revolution.

178. Lock and key from Bemis Heights.

179. Four-shot flint-lock pistol.

180. Revolutionary canteen, 1776.

181. Continental currency.

182. Officer's uniform, used in the Revolution.

183. Chair belonging to Gov. Bradford of the Revolution.

184. A sword carried by Capt. John Boyd in the Revolution.

185. Chair brought from England, 1720.

186. Spinning-wheel of the last century.

187. Chair of New England, from the Ben Perley Poore colleclection, 1665.

188. Letter from Samuel Huntington to Gov. Clinton, dated Norwich, Jan. 31, 1793.

189. Letter from Brig.-Gen. James Clinton, relating to the exchange of prisoners, dated Dec. 23, 1778.

190. "Siege of Quebec," a sonata, composed by W. B. Knift, and dedicated to the officers engaged; Sept. 10, 1759.

191. A circular issued by John Hague, relating to the manufacture of carding and spinning wheels and carding and spinning machines.

192. An order from Guy Carleton, dated Jan. 8, 1778.

193. Letter from Israel Putnam, dated Headquarters, Peck's Mills, July 12, 1777.

194. A piece of the battle-flag of the New York regiment, siege of Yorktown.

195. An account of Thomas Payne, for services rendered to the Commonwealth of Pennsylvania, 1781.

196. A piece of the battle-flag of a New York regiment at the siege of Yorktown.

197. Chair used in the Continental Congress while at Lancaster, Penn.

198. Colonial bedstead upon which Washington slept many times, once the property of Col. Burwel Bassett, brother-in-law of Washington, New Kent County, Va.

199. A letter from Thomas Jefferson in regard to the construction of the University of Virginia, Monticello, Va., May 20, 1824.

200. A copy of the *American Herald of Liberty*, Exeter, N. H., Wednesday, 23d, 1795.

201. An "extra" of the London *Evening Post*, May 29, 1775, containing the first printed account in London of the Battle of Lexington.

202. Twenty-seven portraits of the British officers of the Revolution.

203. Etched portraits of the members of the Continental Congress.

204. A collection of newspapers, consisting of the following: *New England Weekly Journal*, April 8, 1728; *Dunlap's Pennsylvania Packet or General Advertisers*, July 17, 1775; *American Magazines* for May, 1744, November, 1743; *Essex Gazette*, April 19, 1774; *Independent Chronicle and Universal Advertiser*, Oct. 21, 1784; *Thomase's Massachusetts Sun*, Thursday, Jan. 27, 1785; *Pennsylvania Gazette*, April 5, 1750; *Columbian Sentinel*, July 14, 1798; *Western Star*, Stockbridge, Mass., Nov. 13, 1792; *The Star and North Carolina State Gazette*, Raleigh, N. C., Nov. 10, 1820; *Boston News Letter*, No. 507; *Salem Gazette*, Tuesday, Feb. 24, 1795; *Extra Boston News Letter*, containing an account of the King of Prussia's success, March 2, 1762; *Pennsylvania Gazette*, April 7, 1773; *New England Weekly Journal*, April 8, 1728; *The Boston Gazette and Country Journal*, Monday, Jan. 28, 1771; an extra of the *Register* office of Salem, containing the President's message, Dec. 25, 1802; *The Providence Gazette and Country Journal*, Saturday, July 20, 1776; *Maryland Journal and Baltimore Advertiser*, May 29, 1776; *New England Courant*, Monday, Feb. 4, to Monday, Feb. 11, 1775; the first newspaper printed by Benjamin Franklin, the New York *Morning Post*, Friday, Nov. 7, 1783.

205. A collection of flints, showing the process of making flints for muskets in the time of the Revolution.

206. A sermon preached by John Cotton at Boston, Feb. 8, 1728.

207. A letter from John Hancock, dated Philadelphia, June 14, 1776.

208. A letter from Anthony Wayne, dated Headquarters, Hobson's Choice, May 14, 1793.

209. Orderly book for the garrison at West Point for the Army of the Revolution, 1781.

210. Nine powder horns of the Revolution.

211. Colonial shoes, 1776.

212. Slippers worn by Margaret Carter, one of Washington's household.

213. Cartridge box used in the Revolution, 1776.

214. Pair of plated candle-sticks and snuffers used by Gen. Artemus Ward of the Revolution.

215. Silver plated snuffer tray, period George II., from John Hancock's house, Boston.

216. Copper cup owned by Paul Revere.

217. A bullet fired by the British at Bunker Hill.

218. Benjamin Franklin's ink stand.

219. John Hancock's watch, fob chain and seal.

220. An ancient tinder box used before matches were invented.

221. Powder horn, once the property of Gen. Sullivan, 1771.

222. Knife and fork from the camp chest of Lord Cornwallis at Yorktown, 1771.

223. Wine cup made of horn, used by Gen. Poor of the Revolution.

224. Gen. Israel Putnam's watch.

225. Curious snuff box, formerly the property of Gen. Artemus Ward of the Revolution.

226. Flute owned and used by a band man in Cornwallis' army at the siege of Yorktown, was carried back to London and again brought to America by George Waderin in 1841. Purchased by a descendant in 1889.

227. Two buttons from Franklin's coat.

228. Brass bullet mold used by the Rhode Island Minute Men in the Revolution.

229. Pocket tinder box, carried by a soldier in the Revolution.

230. Indian Wampum found with two skeletons under the Old William Penn Treaty Tree in Colonial times.

231. Blunderbus of 1750.

232. Glasses worn in 1687, when Sir Edmond D. Andros was Governor of the Colony of Massachusetts Bay.

233. A collection of New England Primers, 1637, 1756, 1773, 1777, 1761, 1801, 1818 and others.

234. The first Mother Goose, 1794.

235. Pamphlet containing account of a patent fire-place, printed by Franklin in 1774.

236. A Code of 1650, of the General Court of the Commonwealth, commonly called The Blue Laws.

237. A Thanksgiving discourse preached in Boston, May 23, 1776, by Jonathan Mayhew, D. D., occasioned by the repeal of the Stamp Act.

238. A German book, the first printed by Franklin, in 1742.

239. An account of the late revolution in New England, together with a declaration of the general commerce of Boston and country adjacent, April 18, 1689, written by Nathaniel Beifield, a merchant of Bristol, New England, to his friends in London.

240. The first book published in English by Franklin, entitled "A Treaty Held with Indians of the Six Nations, July, 1742, at Philadelphia."

241. The first printed Constitution of the United States.

242. A pocket almanac belonging to Thomas Jefferson, in which is recorded Chief Logan's speech.

243. "New England's First Fruits," book of the progress of learning in the College of Cambridge, Mass., published in London, 1745.

244. French Bible, printed in New York, 1815.

245. Sermon in manuscript by Cotton Mather.

246. The first Massachusetts Bible, Worcester, 1793.

247. The charters for the Province of Pennsylvania and the City of Philadelphia, printed by Benjamin Franklin in 1742.

248. The first arithmetic giving money problems in dollars and cents, 1793.

249. The first Episcopal prayer-book printed in the United States, 1803.

250. The Martyr Book, the largest book printed in the Colonies up to 1748.

251. A book containing the autograph of Martha Washington, 1800.

252. Record book of Maj.-Gen. William Heath, continental army.

253. Original order book of Ticonderoga.

254. Orderly book, Headquarters, Crown Point, July, 1776.

255. Record book, containing the manuscript copy of Gen. Jackson's farewell to his army in the handwriting of an orderly. The map of the march of the Second Massachusetts Brigade, September, 1785, to the disbandment of the army.

256. A collection of old almanacs, 1751, 1757, 1758, 1759, 1773, 1774, 1776, 1779, 1797, 1802, 1803, 1804, 1806, 1812, 1813, 1815, 1818, 1823.

257. A letter addressed to Gen. Washington by Gen. B. Lincoln, giving a detailed account of the origin of Shay's Rebellion and military measures resorted to for its suppression, dated Hingham, Dec. 4, 1786.

258. A record of the Council of War called to consider the evacuation of Fort Moultrie, and its investment by the garrison at Charleston, March 27, 1780.

259. An abstract statement from the Treasury Books of Expenditures for the United States, in support of the households of their respective Presidents, commencing November, 1781, and ending November, 1788.

260. A letter from Mrs. Janette Montgomery, wife of Richard Montgomery, asking Mr. Chew for a legal opinion.

261. Diary of Maj.-Gen. Lincoln, of his journey from New York to Charleston, to assume command of the Southern Department, Oct. 17, 1778.

262. Journal of Maj.-Gen. Lincoln.

263. Original manuscript of the order of the procession at Boston, on Friday, Feb. 10, 1788, for the ratification of the New Constitution, which was adopted the day before.

264. A steel engraving of Robert Fulton, and letter written by him, dated New York, Dec. 3, 1814.

265. Thomas Jefferson's speech, delivered at his installation, March 4, 1801. This speech is printed on silk.

266. A letter from Gov. Shirley to Gov. Thomas, May 20, 1744.

267. Thomas Jefferson's letter recalling Robert R. Livingston from France; James Madison, Secretary of State.

268. Letter of John Adams to Dr. Waterhouse, July 25, 1813.

269. Original manuscript for the first proposition to celebrate the 4th of July with fireworks, to the Supreme Executive Council of the Commonwealth of Pennsylvania.

270. Original cipher letter of Benjamin Franklin, August 16, 1781.

271. Original manuscript of General Warren, who fell at Bunker Hill.

272. Proclamation of Sir Henry Clinton to American rebels to lay down their arms, March 1, 1780.

273. Original manuscript of John Adams, on throwing tea overboard in Boston Harbor.

274. Letter of Robert Orme, Aid-de-Camp to General Braddock, giving the particulars of his defeat, of Braddock's death and of the gallantry of Col. Washington.

275. A letter from George Washington Lafayette, son of Lafayette.

276. Silk sash worn by the ladies of New York at the reception of Lafayette.

277. Order of Gen. Joseph Sullivan, army of the Revolution, July 26, 1777, pardoning Daniel Brown and John Murphy, sentenced to be shot for house-breaking.

278. Medal given for the capture of Lewisburg, 1758.

279. A collection of medals given to the Indians of Canada for their aid in the Revolution by George III.

280. Sword of Lafitte, the pirate of the gulf.

281. Compass and chain used in laying out the city of Philadelphia by John Ladd, who came there with William Penn.

282. A corset of the colonial period.

283. A letter from Sarah Henry, mother of Patrick Henry, dated June 5, 1777.

284. A letter from Martha Washington, Nov. 2, 1778.

285. A letter from Abigail Adams, wife of President Adams, dated Jan. 7, 1801.

286. A letter from Elizabeth Schuyler, wife of Alexander Hamilton, May, 1819.

287. A letter from Paul Jones.

288. The naval dagger of Paul Jones.

289. Abstract containing the encouragement offered by Continental Congress for such as should enlist in the Continental Army.

290. Original printed articles of agreement between George III. and the Penns, and also Lord Baltimore, giving lands in America.

291. Extra of the London *Gazette*, announcing the capture of Philadelphia by the British, in England.

292. Paper containing the account of the marriage of John Hancock, who was in Lexington on the evening before the battle to see his sweetheart.

293. Original order of George the III. to Lord Carmathen to have the American Minister, John Adams, present his credentials.

294. The original resolution, sent by Charles Thomson, Secretary of Congress, urging the different states to take the most effectual measures for the suppression of theatrical entertainments, horse-racing, gaming and such other diversions as are productive of idleness, dissipation and general depravity of principles and manners, and that all officers in the army are strictly enjoined to see that good and wholesome rules be provided for the preservation of the morals among the soldiers.

295. Order issued by Gen. Cornwallis, dated Dec. 11, 1776.

296. A letter from E. Rutledge, concerning the Declaration of Independence.

297.   A letter from Brig.-Gen. John St. Clair, with Braddock in the French and Indian War, dated about July 14, 1776.

298.   Letter of Baron Steuben, dated Yorktown, Jan. 19, 1778.

299.   Original manuscript of Benedict Arnold, apology to America for his treason.

300.   The patent issued to Robert Fulton's steamship.

301.   Minutes of a treaty held at Easton, Pa., October, 1758.

302.   A copy of the certificate for membership in the American Philosophical Society, dated Jan. 20, 1786, signed by Benjamin Franklin, President; John Ewing, William White, James Vaughan, Vice-Presidents.

303.   Thomas Jefferson's book of astronomical observances.

304.   Pottery, representing the landing of Lafayette on his second visit, 1804.

305.   A beaker, formerly the property of Paul Revere.

306.   Medallion of Benjamin Franklin, on wood.

307.   Very rare Benjamin Franklin plates, illustrating the residence of Gen. Lafayette.

308.   American independence pottery: Landing of Gen. Lafayette at Castle Garden, 1824; McDonohue's factory, Lake Champlain; confederation of the thirteen states; cup and saucer, landing of Lafayette, New York.

309.   Silver lustre cream pitcher, used by N. Appleton, Boston, Mass., April, 1776.

310.   Cups and saucers, owned by Gen. Lee of the Revolution.

311.   Fruit dish and stand from Washington's headquarters, Salem, Mass.

312.   Sugar bowl from the Green Dragon Inn, 1776.

313.   Plate used by Gen. Washington when in New Bridgeport, Mass.

314.   Six plates, once owned by Dr. Joseph Warren.

315.   Ginger jar, once owned by Paul Revere.

316.   Whale oil lamp, once owned by Joseph Warren

317.   Pitcher, once owned by Washington's mother.

318.   Letter of Gen. Putnam, Jan. 17, 1777.

319.   Almanac, "Poor Richard Improved," by Benj. Franklin, 1762.

320.   Letter of Brig. Gen. Richard Montgomery, Princeton, Nov. 16, 1777.

321.   Proclamation by Robert Munckton, Captain General and Governor in Chief, Province of New York.

322.   Letter of Patrick Henry, Williamsburg, Sept. 8, 1777.

323. Oath of office of Robert Yates, Justice of the United States, 1790.

324. Pamphlet, "Ode on the Bones of the Immortal Thomas Paine," literary transport from America to England, by the no less Immortal William Cobbett, printed in London, 1819.

325. Circular by a German minister and his flock to Germany to induce immigration to New England, printed 1750.

326. Original report of the President for the formation of the Society of the Cincinnati, organized by Baron Steuben in the Cantonment of the American Army of the Hudson River, May 10, 1783.

327. Letter of Silas Deane to the Rev. Benj. Trumball in reference to early colonial government of Connecticut, 1774.

328. Autograph document of Isaac Winston and Daniel Boone, Kentucky's first settlers.

329. Commission made by Marquis Duquesne, 1754, appointing a Sac chief over a portion of territory.

330. Letter of Cornwallis to Lafayette in regard to exchange of prisoners.

331. Letter of Nathan Dane, 1788, member of old Congress, author of the Ordinance of 1787, regulating slavery in the North-west territory.

332. Letter by Baron Steuben, Nov. 22, 1780.

333. Letter by Abigail Adams, wife of President John Adams, 1800.

334. Autograph resolutions of J. Q. Adams, which resulted in the War of 1812 with England.

335. Proposal of Alexander French, to bring flax workmen to America, to a Committee of his Majesty's Council, 1680.

336. Letter of James Smith, signer of the Declaration of Independence, dated April 26, 1771.

337. Pass for Indians and their victuals from Biddeford, Maine, to Cape Ann, by Gen. Elwell, 1754.

338. Document of Lord Culpepper, Governor of Colony of Virginia, 1682.

339. Letter of Jethro Sumner, a general in the Revolution, to Gen. Washington, April 18, 1784.

340. Log book of the frigate Constitution's cruise in 1812.

341. Advertisement of line of stages between York, Lancaster and Philadelphia, 1815.

342. Letter of Sally Lee, wife of Gen. Lee, April 14, 1788.

343. Conveyance of land by Thomas Lee, in the name of the Hon. Cath. Lady Fairfax, sole proprietor of the Northern Neck of Virginia, 1716.

344. List of invalid pensioners belonging to the State of New York, March, 1796.

345. List of invalid pensioners belonging to the State of Connecticut, September, 1795.

346. Letter by widow of Gen. R. Montgomery.

347. Inventory and appraisement of negroes, 1732.

348. Instructions to Maj. Merriweather by Maj. Gen. Lord Sterling, 1779.

349. Returns of a company of militia, County of Essex, Second Regiment of Massachusetts, 1776.

350. Letter of Ira Allen, Vermont Council of Safety, written at Bennington, 1777.

351. Original manuscript speech of John Randolph of Roanoke, in Congress, 1820.

352. Leaf from manuscript copy of Baron Steuben's military treaty.

353. Letter of Francis Asbury, first Methodist bishop in America, Jan. 8, 1787.

354. Letter by Edward Shippen to Gov. John Penn of Pennsylvania, Lancaster, Dec. 14, 1763.

355. Bill against Province of Massachusetts for mending utensils and locks on guns for troops under command of Capt. Williams, certified to by Ebenezer Pomroy, 1749.

356. Constitution of the New Jersey Society for the promoting of abolition of slavery, printed by Isaac Neale, 1793.

357. Notice of meeting of the Maryland Abolition Society, signed by Joseph Townsend, Secretary, July 2, 1793.

358. Letter of Samuel Johnson, D. D., first convert to Episcopacy in the Colony of Connecticut, afterward president of King's College, Jan. 2, 1747.

359. Pass by Gen. Howe, signed by Rall of the Hessian Army,

360. Autograph letter of the Rev. James Murray, father of Universalists, July 7, 1784.

361. Order by Brig. Gen. Enoch Poor to keep a soldier in gaol April 9, 1779.

362. Letter by George Wythe, signer of the Declaration of Independence, June 11, 1774.

363. Certificate of Paul Revere, Lt.-Col., Castle Island, Dec. 31, 1751.

364. Order signed by Gen. Moultrie, Charleston, Dec. 21, 1785.

365. Commission by Gov. George Clinton, 1783.

366. Assurance policy, 1795.

367. Bill for services, by Gen. John Sullivan, 1785.

368. Letter of Gen. Thomas Gage, Jan. 13, 1766.

369. Check on bank, signed by Baron Steuben, Aug. 6, 1791.

370. Order of Lord Sterling, 1778.

371. Bill of purchases for the Continental army, June 5, 1782.

372. Commission by John Hancock to Adam Ott, First Lieut., March 24, 1777.

373. Order for goods, signed by Thomas Jefferson, Sept. 13, 1780.

374. Letter of William Bradford, May 25, 1779.

375. Autograph document signed by John Winthrop, second governor of Massachusetts Colony.

376. Autograph document signed by R. Wolcott, Governor of Connecticut, May 17, 1718.

377. Autograph document signed by John Endecott, Governor of Massachusetts, 1655 (Mayflower).

378. Document signed by Gov. Edward Winslow, Plymouth Colony, 1643.

379. Document signed by William Pomfrett, Massachusetts, 1657.

380. Document of Cecil Calvert, first Lord Baltimore, proprietor of Maryland, 1649.

381. Document of Massachusetts Bay Colony, signed F. Breeden and Edward Rawson, 1662.

382. Letter of Benedict Arnold, Sr., Newport, 1673.

383. Letter of Isaac Allerton, one of the Mayflower Pilgrims and signer of the compact, 1653.

384. Letter of Roger Williams, first settler of Rhode Island, 1658.

385. Pay and muster roll of field and staff officers commanded by Col. Jacob Gerrish, Dec. 2, 1778.

386. Muster roll of a detachment of militia commanded by Capt. Nathaniel Sage, army of Gen. Burgoyne, April 2, 1778.

387. Manuscript sermon of the Rev. Mr. Bean, Wentham, Mass., 1766.

388. King George's instructions to E. and R. Penn, 1753.

389. Official document signed by Gayoso, Spanish Governor of Louisiana, at Natchez, Feb. 8, 1797.

390. Official document signed by Walpole, 1777, for transporting criminals to America.

391. Letter, Horatio Gates, Jan. 31, 1777.

392. Resolutions of Continental Congress in autograph and signed by Charles Thompson, Sept. 4, 1777.

393. Original music, written by Gen. Wolfe.

394. Resolutions of House of Representatives of Massachusetts Bay, signed by Joseph Warren, March 17, 1777.

395. Resolutions of Congress, Feb. 20, 1781, in regard to composition of the Southern Army, signed by Geo. Bind, department secretary.

396. Original MSS. speech by John Randolph.

397. Letter of Benjamin Franklin from Passy, France, November 30, 1780.

398. Original poem on death of Joseph Schemmel, who fell at capture of Yorktown.

399. Original report of killed and wounded on the field of battle of To-ho-peka, army of Andrew Jackson, March 27, 1814.

400. Document signed by Cæsar Rodney, Dover, N. H., April 17, 1778, signer Declaration of Independence.

401. Square metal plate representing the signing of the Declaration of Independence.

402. Original water color portrait of Washington.

403. Certificate of admission to society of the Cincinnati, signed by Washington.

404. Music performed (original program) on death of Washington, at St. Paul's Church, New York, Dec. 31, 1799.

405. Original autograph and portrait of French artist, Houdon, who made sketch of Washington.

406. Original letter of William Short, first man who received a commission from United States by Washington.

407. Letter of Col. Innes, giving details of battle of Great Meadow, Winchester, July 12, 1754.

408 Inspection return of music in the army under Gen. Washington, West Point, 1782.

409. Letter of Mary L. Custis, 1827.

410. Letter of Lord Fairfax, April 25, 1772.

411. Letter of Eliza Fairfax, wife of Lord Fairfax.

412. Letter of Eliza Tillman, with whom Washington boarded in Valley Forge, dated April 21, 1757.

413. Letter of Martha Washington, July 1, 1792.

414. Letter of Betty Lewis, Washington's sister, April 19, 1792.

415. Original returns, capitulation of Hessians at battle of Trenton, dated Philadelphia, Jan. 6, 1777.

416. Letter of Daniel Park Custis, first husband of Martha Washington, Jan. 16, 1756.

417. Original account current by Washington to George W. Fairfax, March 14, 1775, to March 17, 1786.

418. Survey of land by Washington, April 8, 1751.

419. Letter of Fielding Lewis, brother-in-law of Washington.

420. Letter of Washington, Middlebrook, Dec. 17, 1778.

421. Order of discharge of John Cogden, signed by George Washington, June 8, 1783.

422. Letter of Washington, headquarters Valley Forge, March 20, 1778.

423. Order, dated Valley Forge, March 9, 1778, signed by Washington as Commander in Chief.

424. Piece of Washington's copy book, when twelve years old.

425. Letter of Mary Washington, mother of George Washington.

426. Manuscript of Augustine Washington, father of George Washington.

427. Letter of George Washington, Williamsburg, Nov. 20 1772.

428. Letter of George Washington, Middlebrook, May 13, 1779.

429. Original manuscript book belonging to John Custis, father of Daniel Park Custis.

430. Letter of Daniel Park Custis, giving his son, D. P. Custis, permission to marry.

431. Miniature portrait of George Washington.

432. Letter of Martha Washington, Dec. 18, 1761.

433. Autograph of Washington's ancestor in England, in an old book.

434. Directory of Philadelphia, 1796, giving Washington's occupation as President of the United States, and his address.

435. Lock of George Washington's hair in a gold locket.

436. First engraved portrait of George Washington.

437. Letter of Valley Forge, March 7, 1778.

438. Letter of George Washington to Mary Stockton, thanking her for recipe for colic for Mary Washington.

439. Receipt of Martha Washington for her annuity.

440. Original returns of British prisoners at Yorktown.

441. First patent issued by the government of the United States, signed by George Washington.

442. First Thanksgiving proclamation by George Washington.

443. Letters of George Washington, Mt. Vernon, Aug. 5, 1798; Philadelphia, March 1, 1796, and Valley Forge Headquarters, April 6, 1778.

444. Ulster County *Gazette* in mourning on account of the death of George Washington, published Boston, Jan. 6, 1800, with order of funeral procession.

445. Letters of George Washington: Mt. Vernon, June 25, 1786, March 26, 1778; Philadelphia, Nov. 1, 1795; Mt. Vernon, Dec. 2, 1799, Sept. 28, 1795, Oct. 22, 1798.

446. Original order to establish the first mint in the United States, signed by Charles Thomson, Secretary Continental Congress.

447. Desk made for Washington, 1779.

448. Oil portrait of Gen. Jackson, from life.

449. Chair from the Hall of Independence.

450. Pewter plates from Washington's estate at Mount Vernon.

451. Letter of the famous Polish Count Pulaski, who fell at Savannah, dated May, 1778.

452. Letter of William Pepperell, July 21, 1743.

453. Proclamation of Horatio Sharp, Esq., Governor and Commander-in-Chief in and over the Province of Maryland, April, 6, 1760.

454. Order of Gen. Fitzbourne, division order on the Hudson, just before Arnold's treachery, dated New Bridge, July 21, 1780.

455. Pitchfork of Gen. Putnam.

456. Warming bed pan of Gov. Shirley.

457. Three colonial umbrellas.

458. Continental uniforms.

459. Pewter plates once owned by Gen. Burgoyne.

460. Sword of Col. Prescott.

461. Cannon balls from Bunker Hill.

LOANED BY MR. CHARLES SPEATH.

462. Framed collection of 150 miniature portraits of Gen. Washington and Mrs. Martha Washington, engraved during the Revolutionary period and since.

463. Framed portraits of President Washington and Mrs. Martha Washington, in original frames, 1789.

464. Military order bearing Washington's signature, dated New York, July 21, 1776.

465. Lottery ticket signed by George Washington.

466. Washington buttons worn by citizens at time of inauguration, 1789.

467. Uncut copy of the oration delivered on the death of Washington, by Gen. Lee, year 1800.

468. Copy of Washington's Funeral Ode, 1 and 2, sung at Old South Church, Boston, Mass., Feb. 8, 1800.

469. Washington medals, made by Eccleston, Westwood and other artists of one hundred years ago.

470. Silk badges worn in 1832, at centennial of Washington's birthday.

471. Silk badges of Washington, worn at different periods.

472. Collection of Continental money.

473. Colony tax stamps of 1765.

474. Collection of English and German almanacs, embracing dates from 1760 to the year 1800.

475. Commission to Jonathan Trumbull, Jr., signed by John Hancock, with very rare old portrait of Hancock, 1775.

476. Old newspapers: Pennsylvania *Chronicle*, July 13, 1767; Massachusetts *Spy*, May 20, 1773; Norwich *Packet*, Aug. 25, 1774; *Columbian Sentinel*, June 17, 1799.

477. Scarce copy of the Pennsylvania *Intelligencer and Advertiser*, of Sept. 19, 1787, containing first publication of the Constitution of the United States as framed by committee of which Gen. Washington was chairman.

478. A document signed by Benjamin Franklin, Philadelphia, Sept. 29, 1778, with portrait.

479. Dinner invitation, signed by Thomas Jefferson.

480. Receipt for gunpowder, by Josiah Bartlett (signer of Declaration), May 17, 1777.

481. Power of attorney, signed by Robert Morris, Feb. 7, 1793.

482. Letter of Gen. Drake, Aug. 3, 1779, to Gov. Clinton, relative to seizing stock of those who joined the enemy.

483. Letter of Col. Shaw, author of the Order of Cincinnati, relative to bearskins presented by Mr. Rensselaer of Albany to army officers, Nov. 21, 1779.

484. Business letter of Peter Stuyvesant, Feb. 23, 1790.

485. Letter of Alexander Hamilton to Gen. Lee, dated Sept. 13, 1770, relative to promotion.

486. Letter of Aaron Burr, dated Dec. 6, 1796.

487. Army order, by Gen. Green to Maj. Harry Lee, July 12, 1780.

488. Letter of Edmund Randolph to Charles Lee, Germantown, Aug. 28, 1793, relative to yellow fever epidemic at his home in Virginia.

489. German letter by Rev. John Christ, Gobbrecht, March 1, 1765, to his son Johannes, in Germantown, Pa.

490. Pass from the Continental Congress, signed by Samuel Huntington, president, for Mrs. John Hunt, dated April 7, 1780.

491. Case of drawing instruments, used in Germantown, Pa., over one hundred years ago.

492. Small sun-dial, set in a cube of wood, from Germantown, Pa., 150 years old.

493. Pocket-books made and used in 1783.

494. Cash-boxes, from Holland, brought to this country by Van Schaack over 200 years ago.

495. Horn spoon, from Boston, used by Miss McClutch (spinster), 1786.

496. Photograph home of Washington's ancestors, in England.

497. Pair of old scissors from Virginia, 1783.

498. Virginia army blanket-pin, Revolutionary War, 1776.

499. Virginia trinket-box, 1783.

500. Grape-shot balls, from old Fort Williams, New York, plowed up in 1790.

501. Embossed medal, obverse portraits of all the signers of the Declaration of Independence; reverse, Declaration in full.

502. Medallion locket, containing very small portraits of the signers of the Declaration.

503. Washington medal, smallest specimen ever made.

504. Thomas Jefferson's last letter, printed on silk.

505. Medicine pouches, of Blackfoot Indians, made in 1777.

LOANED BY THE REV. FRANK M. BRISTOL, D. D.

506. Autograph letter of Martha Washington announcing the death of Mrs. Tobias Lear.

507. Autograph letter of Tobias Lear mentioning the President.

508. Deed of Virginia land, signed by Thos. Lord Fairfax, 1754.

509. Autograph letter of Miss Francis Bassett.

510. Gossips about the Washingtons and Custises at Mount Vernon.

511. Book, Cicero's "Cato Major," printed by Benjamin Franklin, Philadelphia, 1744.

512. Book from the library of George III.

513. Original manuscript from Irving's "Life of Washington," framed with portrait.

514. Warrant of arrest for trespass in Fairfax County, Va., time of George II.

515. Autograph letter of Charles James Fox.

516. Autograph letter of Richard Brinsley Sheridan.

517. Document signed by William Pitt and George III. 1789.

518. Book, "the Code of 1650," Blue Laws, 1822.

519. Page from old account book, with account of Abraham Lincoln of Pa., for "tody, etc.," 1789.

520. Autograph note of President Thomas Jefferson calling a Cabinet meeting, 1808; framed.

521. Account of Dr. John Knowles with George A. Washington, mentions Gen. Washington, 1789.

522. Autograph letter of Gen. Arthur St. Clair, with portrait framed.

523. Several long petitions to Gov. Mifflin from the alarmed inhabitants of the frontier of Pennsylvania, after the defeat of St. Clair by the Indians, 1792.

524. Order to pay money and guns to Indians, signed by William Allen, Thomas Willing, Hugh Crawford and many Indians, 1767; framed.

525. Autograph letters of the Quaker preacher, Nicholas Waln.

526. Autograph letter of Phineas Pemberton, an early Quaker; came with William Penn, 1697.

527. Autograph letter of Israel Pemberton, when a boy, 1697.

528. Draft on William Penn, by William East, 1682.

529. Autograph letter of David Lloyd, signed also by Isaac Norris, 1701.

530. Book presented to John Dickinson by Bishop Asbury, with autograph of Dickinson.

531. Certificate written by L. Weiss, government interpreter, 1763.

532. Autograph letter of Robert Edward Tell, agent for the Penns.

533. Letter of the Rev. Richard Peters, announcing his ascerting the new Governor of Pennsylvania, Denny, to Philadelphia, 1744.

534. Very rare old English manuscript collection of poems, written about 1660, containing an "Elegie on the death of Mr. Washington, page to Pr. Charles, who died in Spayne."

535. Collection of Continental money; framed.

536. Poem, "Gen. Washington, with some remarks on Jeffersonian Policy," 1801; framed with six portraits of Washington.

537. Document signed by George III.; portrait framed.

538. Circular letter signed by James Madison, 1807.

539. Autograph letter of Gen. John Armstrong, signer of the Constitution, 1788.

540. Document signed by Charles Thomson, who, as secretary, carried to Washington the announcement of his election to the Presidency.

541. Letter signed by Robert Morris, signer of the Declaration of Independence, 1776.

542. Document signed by Arthur St. Clair before the Revolution.

543.   Autograph letter of Gen. Henry Lee ("Light Horse Harry").

544.   Autograph letter of Gen. William Eaton, 1800.

545.   Autograph letter of Gen. Henry Dearborn, 1800.

546.   Document signed by Gen. Elias Dayton.

547.   Document signed by Gen. James Troine.

548.   Letter of Timothy Pickering, 1796.

549.   Money order from Fort Charters and Kaskaskia, signed by Thomas Hutchins and others, 1769.

550.   Book of Dr. Richard Price, "Observations on the Impor tance of the American Revolution," 1785.

551.   Book of a German almanac with engravings of scenes in the Revolution, 1784.

552.   Indenture, with several signatures and red seals, Philadelphia, 1750.

APPENDIX

THE COMMITTEES

APPENDIX

THE COMMITTEES

GENERAL EXECUTIVE COMMITTEE.

S. W. Allerton, Chairman,
E. F. Cragin, Secretary,
A. C. Bartlett,
J. Y. Scammon,
H. N. Higginbotham,
J. W. Ellsworth,
R. S. Tuthill,
G. Schneider,
J. McGregor Adams,
E. G. Keith,
R. E. Jenkins,
C. L. Hutchinson,
H. S. Boutell,
F. H. Head,
John A. Roche,
J. S. Grinnell,
William Vocke,
P. A. Sundelius,
J. Rosenthal,
J. Anderson,
C. R. Matson,
H. L. Hertz,
W. B. Sullivan,
John Ginocchio,
A. Mastrovalerio,
S. Costikyan,
T. Schintz,
J. J. Schobinger,

L. G. Wheeler,
T. W. Henderson,
E. G. Hirsch,
A. Kirkland,
F. A. Brokoski,
W. Kasper,
A. Kraus,
Griffith Griffiths,
George Birkhoff, Jr.,
J. H. Barrows,
W. H. Busbey,
George Driggs,
H. B. Hurd,
Joseph Medill,
J. A. Sexton,
Graeme Stewart,
A. G. Lane,
Milward Adams,
Herman Raster,
Richard Michaelis,
J. F. Ballantyne,
W. K. Sullivan,
M. J. Russell,
J. R. Walsh,
H. F. Boynton,
Robert Clark,
G. F. Bissell,
W. H. Hubbard,

GENERAL EXECUTIVE COMMITTEE—CONTINUED.

W. H. Wood,
Peter Kiolbassa,
P. S. Peterson,
C. F. Goss,
D. F. Bremner,
W. A. Angell,
W. P. Henneberry,
W. L. B. Jenney,
J. Frank Aldrich,
H. N. Hubbard,
E. F. Chapin,
W. Miles,
S. D. Kimbark,
J. M. Larimer,
J. W. Scott,
E. C. Delano,
Victor F. Lawson,
Clarence I. Peck,

T. B. Bryan,
I. P. Rumsey,
E. F. Getchel,
William Saunders,
Frederick Ullman,
Joseph Chalifoux,
Richard Prendergast,
Andrew Wallace,
R. C. Givens,
H. M. Kingman,
A. H. Revell,
C. F. Gunther,
A. G. Spalding,
C. B. Whitney,
J. H. Johnson,
Murry Nelson,
A. Peterson,
S. Walton.

FINANCE COMMITTEE.

S. W. Allerton, Chairman,
J. B. Drake,
F. W. Peck,
J. Irving Pearce,
O. W. Potter,
J. G. McCullen,
Louis Wampold,
P. H. Armour,
George Schneider,
Nelson Morris,
Byron L. Smith,
C. R. Cummings,
E. S. Dryer,
H. H. Kohlsaat,
H. A. Haugan,
Potter Palmer,
J. L. Woodward,
William Stewart,
Jesse Spaulding,

Andrew Cummings,
P. Studebaker,
W. A. Fuller,
F. C. Kimball,
T. D. Randall,
G. H. Webster,
H. M. Kinsley,
J. J. Parkhurst,
F. Madlener,
J. Ginocchio,
A. N. Reece,
Edson Keith,
J. McG. Adams,
George Miller,
P. J. Hennessy,
J. A. Kirk,
Joseph G. Peters,
Charles Schwab,
C. H. Cutter,

FINANCE COMMITTEE—CONTINUED.

M. T. Green,
D. A. Kohn,
A. C. McClurg,
John Black,
Robert Law,
C. E. Maxwell,
W. H. Kellogg,
G. T. Burroughs,
W. P. Rend,
A. Peterson,
R. A. Keyes,
W. C. Seipp,
C. H. Wacker,
J. H. McAvoy,
E. S. Pike,
Leopold Bloom,
Marvin Hughitt,
E. A. Cummings,
M. C. Eames,
C. J. Singer,
N. B. Ream,
W. D. Kerfoot,
C. W. Drew,
C. B. Holmes,
O. W. Barrett,

F. H. Winston,
Marshall Field,
R. R. Cable,
R. Scott,
H. H. Porter,
Albert Hayden,
Sidney Kent,
B. F. Gardner,
C. M. Henderson,
J. W. Nye,
H. J. McFarland,
J. H. Bradley,
George M. Pullman,
L. Wolf,
F. G. Logan,
M. E. Page,
J. C. Neemes,
William Deering,
John C. Black,
M. C. Hickey,
R. B. Wardmell,
E. B. Gould,
W. S. Gilbert,
C. O. Francis,
Seymour Walton.

FINANCE SUB-COMMITTEES.

COAL DEALERS—Robert Law, W. P. Rend.

WHOLESALE GROCERS—Franklin MacVeagh, J. W. Doane, R. A. Keyes.

MILLINERY—Edson Keith, D. B. Fisk.

CLOTHING—D. Cohn, C. L. Willoughby, L. Wampold, Charles P. Kellogg.

THEATRES—J. A. Hamlin, W. J. Davis, R. M. Hooley.

INSURANCE—F. S. James, R. A. Waller, R. S. Critchell.

ARCHITECTS—Dankmar Adler.

BAKERS (wholesale)—W. W. Shaw, D. F. Bremner, Henry Evans.

CORNICE MANUFACTURERS—James A. Miller.

CARRIAGE MANUFACTURERS—Peter Studebaker, F. C. Kimball.

CHINA AND GLASSWARE—Pitkin & Brooks.

FINANCE SUB-COMMITTEES—CONTINUED.

CANDY MAKERS (retail)—C. F. Gunther.

CANDY MAKERS (wholesale)—M. E. Page.

CAPITALISTS—H. S. Vail.

DRY GOODS (retail)—E. J. Lehman.

FLORISTS—J. C. Vaughn.

FURNITURE—Andrew F. Johnson, J. S. Ford, Francis B. Tobey.

IRON FOUNDERS—J. M. Larimer.

JEWELERS—J. B. Mayo, Elmer Rich.

BANKS AND BANKERS—George Schneider, E. S. Dreyer.

BOARD OF TRADE—C. J. Singer, F. G. Logan.

LUMBER DEALERS—Jesse Spaulding, A. G. Van Schaack.

HOTELS—J. Irving Pearce, H. H. Kohlsaat, Andrew Cummings, Warren F. Leland.

COMMISSION MERCHANTS—T. D. Randall, J. H. Barnett, George C. Scales, A. M. Thacker, R. A. Burnett.

DRY GOODS—J. K. Harmon.

REAL ESTATE—W. D. Kerfoot, E. A. Cummings.

HARDWARE—A. F. Seeberger, D. Kelly.

MANUFACTURERS—L. Wolf.

PLANING MILLS—Frost Manufacturing Company.

RAILWAY SUPPLIES—George M. Sargent, William J. Watson, Mr. Ettinger, William Wilson.

PAINTS AND OILS—C. H. Cutler.

UNDERTAKERS—C. H. Jordan, J. J. Healy.

NATIONAL OFFICES—W. C. Newberry.

COUNTY OFFICES—C. R. Matson, H. L. Hertz.

CITY OFFICES—Arthur Dixon, John Summerfield, E. F. Cullerton.

SEEDSMEN—Albert Dickinson.

STREET RAILWAYS—F. S. Winston.

PATRIOTIC ORDER SONS AMERICA—A. Dickerson.

LAUNDRIES—G. M. Munger & Co.

LAWYERS—William E. Page, Frank Collier, William B. Sullivan.

MERCHANT TAILORS—R. J. Walsh, Henry Turner.

MEAT MARKETS—John Ford, Easland & Duddleston.

MUSICAL INSTRUMENTS—A. C. Camp, G. W. Lyon.

PRINTERS—F. P. Elliott, J. M. W. Jones, W. P. Henneberry, Charles J. Stromberg, John Morris.

ROOFING—M. W. Powell.

FINANCE SUB-COMMITTEES—CONTINUED.

RUBBER—W. D. Allen.

STATIONERY—E. E. Maxwell, A. C. McClurg.

GROCERS (retail)—C. Jevne, C. H. Slack, Fred D. Rockwood, C. H. Tebbets.

BOOTS AND SHOES—John J. Harkins, J. M. Jessen, J. C. Graham, Robert Neely, A. Donant, M. S. Varley, A. M. Nelson, George Welhaus, J. M. Johnson, Smythe Crooks, A. J. Weeks, R. B. Haaker, Henry Brandt, S. Johnson, S. Youngquist. C. E. Wiswall, D. L. Streeter, H. C. Smith, F. T. Chiniquy, N. Loeb, N. Bermerle, I. L. Klein, George S. Bullock.

COMMITTEE ON AUDIENCE.

D. F. Bremner,
William B. Sullivan,
H. N. Higginbotham,
R. A. Keyes,
J. A. Sexton,
W. S. Brackett,
E. B. Knox,
L. G. Wheeler,
Charles Fitzsimmons,
E. P. Jones,
Victor Gerardin,
D. H. Williams,
J. Chalifoux,
L. Hesselroth,
John Ginocchio,
F. Khout,
C. F. Korsell,
M. J. Russell,
E. Nelson Blake,
G. B. Swift,
H. P. Thompson,
Max Stern,
H. L. Hertz,
P. S. Peterson,
W. P. Rend,
I. A. Enander,
C. J. Sundell,
S. W. Ingraham.

COMMITTEE ON ORGANIZATION.

E. G. Keith,
W. C. Newberry,
C. R. Matson,
John Anderson,
E. G. Hirsch,
Willard Woodard,
Frank H. Collier,
Victor Lassagne,
L. G. Wheeler,
William Kaspar,
Peter Kiolbassa,
H. T. Weeks,
W. C. Seipp,
R. W. Patterson,
John R. Walsh,
W. Penn Nixon,
R. Michaelis,
Victor F. Lawson,
W. K. Sullivan,
F. B. Wilkie,
P. O. Stensland,
F. B. Zdrubek,

COMMITTEE ON ORGANIZATION—CONTINUED.

T. V. Matejka,
Washington Hesing,
A. Mastrovalerio,
David Swing,
T. N. Morrison,
H. W. Bolton,
J. Lloyd Jones,
Slason Thompson,
C. G. Lindborg,

H. W. Thomas,
G. C. Lorimer,
S. J. McPherson,
F. A. Noble,
F. A. Lindstrand,
J. H. Burke,
W. P. Henneberry,
H. A. Wheeler.

COMMITTEE ON HALLS.

J. W. Ellsworth,
W. V. Jacobs,
J. H. Dole,
J. Irving Pearce,
R. M. Hooley,

David Henderson,
Milward Adams,
J. H. McVicker,
J. V. Farwell, Jr.,
T. W. Harvey.

COMMITTEE ON SCHOOL CELEBRATION.

Graeme Stewart,
Louis Nettlehorst,
Ferd W. Peck,
J. W. Fernald,
Mrs. E. Mitchell,
Mrs. E. F. Young,
Miss Lizzie L. Hartney,
Frank Mitchell,
J. R. Doolittle,
D. F. Bremner,
W. G. Beale,
M. B. Hereley,
C. Kozminski,
E. C. Delano,
John McLaren,
T. Brenan,
C. J. Sundell,
F. Wenter,
A. G. Lane,

W. J. Onahan,
E. F. Dunne,
J. W. Goudy,
F. E. Halligan,
J. C. Burroughs,
A. R. Sabin,
George Driggs,
Norman Williams,
C. B. Holmes,
George Howland,
Fred W. Forch, Jr.,
F. W. Parker,
U. S. Baker,
Leslie Lewis,
W. H. Ray,
H. L. Boltwood,
O. T. Bright,
M. W. Robinson.

CENTENNIAL SOUVENIR FOR CHILDREN.

Victor F. Lawson,
Victor Lassagne,

C. I. Peck.

COMMITTEE ON SUSPENSION OF BUSINESS.

S. D. Kimbark,
J. W. Larimer,
H. J. McFarland,
G. F. R. Dodge,
Peter Van Schaack,
John A. King,
Ezra J. Warner,
W. Moseback,
Levi Bane,
C. L. Willoughby,
J. G. Williams,
J. H. Walker,
John Alling,
J. W. Nye,
E. L. Maxwell,
J. B. Mayo,
Paul Morton,
J. C. McMullen,
W. H. Wetherell,
C. F. Shaw,
P. L. Underwood,
John Cudahy,

J. H. Hamline,
M. C. Bullock,
W. H. Fuller,
Edson Keith,
J. Harley Bradley,
O. H. Horton,
J. H. Harmon,
J. H. McAvoy,
Arthur Dixon,
J. G. McWilliams,
E. F. Cullerton,
Joseph Ernst,
C. H. Tebbets,
C. Jevne,
G. M. Porter,
E. F. Heywood,
G. M. Grannis,
F P. Roach,
M. J. Helm,
Stephen Mann,
Thomas Collins,
Fred Rockford.

COMMITTEE ON MUSIC.

J. J. Schobinger,
T. W. Henderson,
William Vocke,
W. L. Tomlins,
S. D. Pratt,
F. W. Root,
Franz Amberg,
Hans Balatka,
J. Vilim,
G. F. Root,
W. Miles,

J. Wegman,
J. L. Swenson,
J. W. Coberg,
J. Nettlehorst,
T. Elberg,
E. DeCamp,
R. C. Halle,
P. A. Otis,
G. C. Lorimer,
E. G. Newell.

COMMITTEE ON DECORATIONS, MOTTOES, ETC.

W. L. P. Jenney,
Joseph Stockton,
George Mason,
C. F. Gunther,

W. Best,
G. B. Carpenter,
A. L. Coe,
A. H. Revell,

COMMITTEE ON DECORATIONS, MOTTOES, ETC.—CONTINUED.

I. K. Boyeson,
W. F. Poole,
F. M. Bristol,
F. W. Gunsaulus,
W. E. Stockton,
T. S. Cunningham,
C. D. Roys,
L. S. Blackwelder,

John A. Jamieson,
Thomas A. Banning,
J. York,
Thomas Robinson,
P. S. Peterson,
J. A. Pettigrew,
C. McArthur,
M. W. White.

COMMITTEE ON OUTSIDE DECORATIONS.

A. G. Spalding,
C. B. Whitney,
E. J. Lehman & Co.,

Marshall Field & Co.,
Willoughby, Hill & Co.

COMMITTEE ON PYROTECHNICS.

George M. Pullman,
Richard Waterman,
C. K. Billings,
E. W. Brooks,
C. C. Lake,
I. P. Rumsey,
E. A. Hamill,

H. M. Bacon,
E. F. Getchell,
C. W. Drew,
E. F. Bayley,
Joseph Stockton,
Charles Fitzsimmons,
W. J. Wilson.

COMMITTEE ON LOAN EXHIBITION.

C. F. Gunther,
F. M. Bristol,
J. B. Jeffery,
I. N. Camp,
George C. Prussing,

J. B. Smith,
Potter Palmer,
Solomon Thatcher, Jr.,
Sydney C. Eastman,
C. R. Vandercook.

COMMITTEE ON OBSERVANCE OF THE DAY THROUGHOUT THE NORTHWEST.

Thomas B. Bryan,
E. B. Sherman,
A. H. Terry,
Lyman Trumbull,
L. L. Bond,
J. P. Runnels,
J. B. Bradwell,
Julius White,
A. C. Ducat,

W. C. Newberry,
Gwynn Garnett,
Jesse Spaulding,
Moses Wentworth,
I. N. Stiles,
Henry C. Prevost,
Curtis H. Remy,
Charles T. Trego,
Moses D. Wells,

COMMITTEE ON OBSERVANCE OF THE DAY THROUGHOUT THE
NORTHWEST—CONTINUED.

W. A. Douglass,
J. H. Hobbs,
D. W. Irwin,
Charles E. Judson,
O. R. Keith,
E. F. Getchell,
J. B. Kirk,
George S. Lord,
O. W. Meysenburg,
J. J. Mitchell,
P. S. Montgomery,
Henry Field,
William A. Fuller,
Amos Grannis,
William E. Hale,
Charles D. Hamill,
David G. Hamilton,
Charles Counselman,
N. K. Fairbank,
Marcus A. Farwell,

John V. Farwell,
Charles H. Fargo,
O. W. Barrett,
Chauncey I. Blair,
John T. Chumasero,
Silas M. Moore,
W. K. Nixon,
Edward A. Packard,
C. H. Case,
J. S. Gadsden,
William Warren
R. J. Smith,
S. S. Gregory,
W. J. Onahan,
D. C. Osman,
Thomas Templeton,
Alexander Sullivan,
Hempstead Washburne,
Frank A. Riddle,
George P. Smith.

COMMITTEE ON SOUVENIR VOLUME.

John F. Ballantyne,
Lloyd G. Wheeler
S. W. Allerton,
E. F. Cragin,

F. M. Bristol,
J. H. Barrows,
William Vocke,
Thomas B. Bryan.

CPSIA information can be obtained
at www.ICGtesting.com
Printed in the USA
BVHW090918060219
539622BV00035B/2011/P